'19

BAR FLIES

BAR FLIES

TRUE STORIES FROM THE EARLY YEARS

EDITED BY AMY SILVERMAN AND KATIE BRAVO

PHOENIX, ARIZONA

Bar Flies: True Stories from the Early Years
Edited by Amy Silverman and Katie Bravo

Typeset in Arno Pro, Century Gothic Pro, and Coluna Condensed
Book Design by Jake Friedman / JSF Literary
Cover Art and Design by Kyle Dehn

Printed in the United States of America by JC Printing
10 9 8 7 6 5 4 3 2 1

ISBN 978-0-578-59121-6

To Phoenix

CONTENTS

LOVE

MUSIC

FAMILY

BELIEF

ADVENTURE

SELF

HOLIDAYS

GOODBYE

INTRO

TRUE STORIES.
AND DRINKS.

THAT'S ALL WE PROMISED when we started Bar Flies on a hot Phoenix night in June 2015. Lucky for us, it was enough to get people through the doors of a basement bar and into the seats of our very first show.

Hundreds of essays and countless cocktails later, we present the Bar Flies anthology, featuring 60 of our favorites from our first four seasons.

Cheers.

LOVE

ANCIENT MAGIC OF THE HIGHEST ORDER

REBEKAH BAGGS

I WAS SIPPING BEERS WITH MY FRIEND LARISSA on a summer afternoon at a pub in London when I first signed up for Tinder and Bumble. Mostly for kicks, to compare user interface designs—*for work research, okay!* We laughed over the multitude of gym selfies and made bets over how long it would take for me to get a dick pic. But secretly, I was hoping to meet someone special.

It'd been two and a half years since I'd split with my ex and ended our eight-year marriage. Two and a half years of self-imposed celibacy, and self-exploration, and self-care. Time alone was what I needed to heal and understand my part in our failed relationship. But turns out going that long without any form of intimate, romantic relationships was really, really hard.

It was worth it. I emerged stronger, kinder, refreshed, and more sure of myself than ever.

And I was ready to ease back into things. But this time around I would be smarter, and wiser, and I promised myself not to get involved in casual flings with anyone I couldn't imagine myself really falling in love with. People are little universes, you never know what you'll get sucked into.

Now, if this seems like a tall order for the likes of dating apps—it was. So far, things hadn't gone any further than going on a couple dates with anyone. Sometimes it was fun. I met a few weirdo creeps. Mostly it was just awkward and time-consuming. I was growing tired of the phone-lit nights swiping left and swiping right, endless small talk via messaging back and forth, perpetually high on the possibility of "what if" and low on battery life.

I was nearly ready to put down my phone and just embrace joyful singlehood and acceptance of whatever life organically brought my way.

And then WE matched. His name was Matt. His profile read "Looking for someone to share beauty in the smallest things. No Trump supporters. Sorry." Um, yes!

He looked warm and mysterious and intelligent and my kind of devastatingly handsome. The stuff Bumble dreams are made of.

Our texting conversations were ear-to-ear-grin inducing, too. He was philosophical and well-read. He liked nature and exploring the outdoors, fed the homeless on Sundays, and we both had the same sort of weird relationship with church and unconventional ideas about Jesus. Turned out he had spent every summer of his childhood visiting his grandparents and rambling around the small town of Palatka, Florida—where I'm originally from, too! His grandpa was actually my family's dentist. Just wild.

My friends cautioned me that it was probably too good to be true. He was either a stalker, a narcissist, married, or the owner of a very small penis. But I wasn't hearing any of it. We chatted for a few weeks and finally decided to meet up in person. I can't remember a time I'd been more excited for a first date.

We met at Valley Bar a little before the Bar Flies reading that night. He sat there, patiently waiting at a booth tucked into the corner. I was running late, 15 minutes late, but he still greeted me with the warmest smile. Real life Matt looked exactly like he did in his profile pics, only kinder, and sweeter, and maybe a bit worldly wise.

My heart was racing from all the nerves, I steadied my breath and slid into the booth across the table from him. Matt radiated calm and easygoing nonchalance. I was so nervous I don't remember much of what we talked about before the reading began. But I do remember there was a moment where my eyes met his and I felt it throughout my entire person. And as we sat side by side during the storytelling that night, I couldn't help but notice how oddly familiar he felt. Like I'd known him my whole life.

One date turned into two, two into four. We spent the first few weeks getting to know one another gradually—he'd been sober for six years, he was divorced and had become a father when he was just 18. Matt had three kids. His oldest was just about to start college and his youngest was nearly in high school. (So his wise demeanor was hard-earned).

We explored art, and music, and Downtown Phoenix, and each other. Staying up all night talking, trading each other puzzle pieces from our past, and hopes and dreams for the future. We went away on a trip to Seattle together and everything seemed like a dream. It was exhilarating and exciting. I'd never felt so brand new.

And then Matt wrote me the most beautiful poem. The opening line read, "Baby, we are dolphins in flight with fins for wings and saltwater mist against freshwater eyes." I just melted.

This wasn't just easing back into the dating scene. This was more like…ancient magic of the highest order.

Four months into it and we were trading weekends at his place and mine. Making Saturday breakfast together and reading on the patio with coffee on Sunday afternoons. It felt like everything was falling into place.

And that's about the time I started getting hungry. More like HANGRY. I was so hungry I felt like I could eat three breakfasts before lunch. Even Chris, my best bud and business partner, commented on my ferocious appetite.

The mysterious hunger went on like this for a few weeks. I thought it was a fluke or due to the change in my workout routine. One weekend I *casually* mentioned this to Matt and he *casually* suggested that I should take a pregnancy test. This possibility had not occurred to me before. I was on birth control. I was always careful. I had managed to be a 35-year-old divorced woman without a single unplanned pregnancy or baby child to my name. I had it on lock.

But we bought the tests anyway. Just to be certain. The first test read…two lines. The second…two lines. THE THIRD: Two lines. I felt numb. Suddenly everything I'd hoped for felt like it was crumbling around me.

I scheduled an ultrasound to confirm the pregnancy. And that day would become the first day I ever laid eyes on *her*. She was teeny tiny, and only eight weeks along. But her heartbeat was loud and strong and true. I was expecting to feel despair or revulsion or fear, but all I felt was overwhelming love for this little human. And I knew, in spite of my fear, *I knew in my bones* that no matter what happened, she and I, we were meant to be.

So there I was, four months into a new relationship and *two* months pregnant. It seemed impossible. I wasn't in any position to have a baby, I'd just quit my job to start a business a little over a year ago. I was starting over. Matt certainly wasn't excited over the idea of raising another child with a woman his kids hadn't even met yet. And he was done with the whole baby thing, his kids were nearly grown.

I was still processing all of this and making sense of things when out of nowhere one day, I looked down and my jeans were soaked in blood that ran nearly to my knees. I wasn't prepared for how viscerally devastating this would feel. Without a second thought, I reached into the toilet and grabbed at the lump of bloody mass that had escaped from between my legs, looking for any sign of something that resembled my little embryo of a baby. Later at the hospital they said that I was still pregnant, but likely having a miscarriage. It was too early for them to do anything. I should go home and wait it out and rest.

That miscarriage never happened. But I did have a serious internal hemorrhage that landed me in the "high risk" pregnancy category. Despite two trips to the ER, and being on bedrest for a month, she persisted. Meanwhile, my relationship with Matt felt like it was unraveling. And for the next few months things between us were strained, to say the least. Instead of "how can I possibly sleep when this amazing person is lying next to me," it was "how can I show you this ultrasound pic without us resenting each other."

We had some of the hardest conversations of my life. Gut wrenching. Like when Matt said, "I'll always be there as a father for our child, but I don't see how we'll make it as a couple. Maybe if this had happened after a year, and we had met each other's families we'd have more of a chance…." And that was all valid, but that wasn't the way life happened. I spent a lot of the time feeling angry and confused and just heartbroken.

Somehow, in spite of everything, spending time together still felt like the best medicine. And so we held on, waiting for her arrival.

I do not have words to tell you the all-consuming joy that was meeting our daughter. I could try to explain to you how looking into her eyes for the first time felt like warm healing light for everything hurt inside me, but I would fail miserably. One thing that comes close is a poem by Nayyirah Waheed. It reads:

> "she asked 'you are in love, what does love look like' to which i replied 'like everything i've ever lost come back to me."

One sun dappled afternoon, in those first few weeks home with our new baby, Matt and I were celebrating our one year anniversary and remembering those early conversations on Bumble. We both realized we'd never actually deleted our dating profiles. And so we logged in and decided to do it together. I looked over the list of all my old matches, there was Matt. The handsome stranger who had somehow turned into the father of my child and best friend. I decided to send him one last message before closing my profile down.

"Hi, Matt. You're cute. Would you like to go out with me sometime? We could listen to some live storytelling and then maybe… make a baby?"

"That sounds good. Actually, all I want is to make a baby. Can she be perfect? We could name her Virginia Rose."

"Deal! See you Thursday night. You can be the handsome fellow in the corner booth and I'll be the girl that's 15 minutes late."

REBEKAH BAGGS is a mother, content strategist, and speaker based in Phoenix. Follow her on instagram @rebekah.baggs and find her online at rebekahbaggs.com.

KISSSSSSSSSS ME

LAURIE NOTARO

SERIOUSLY. Who doesn't want almost free food? And not only was it almost free, it was delivered to me, the meals of my choosing. I didn't have to stand in line at a food bank, I didn't have to plead my case to the local Department of Economic Security, and things on the menu included steak, fried chicken, and korma!

All I had to do was buy a Groupon, and I'd get a week of HelloFresh meals for 39 dollars, and if that meant that I didn't have to go to Safeway for a week, count me in.

Any excuse not to enter that vortex of mayhem otherwise known as Safeway is one that I will adopt, so I bought the Groupon and immediately signed up. The next week, on Wednesday, UPS would deliver an enormous package with each meal brilliantly organized in its own box with hipster ingredients (the tiniest jars of Sir Kensington's mustard and ketchup, organic herbs in their own miniature clamshells, and spice mixes in adorable paper bags with cute labels) and instructions.

As I unpacked the contents, my husband picked up the recipes and started looking them over.

"Do you know what I think would be awesome?" he said after a moment.

I looked up and shrugged.

"If we cooked *together*," he said. "I think it might be fun, and we could increase our couple coordination that way."

"You want to be a team?" I asked reluctantly. "You want us to be more coordinated?"

"Yes," my husband answered. "Don't you think that would be fun?"

"No," I said blankly. "I do not. I already know how to cook, and you are a six-foot, two-inch man, and this is a very small kitchen. We have like three square feet here. And you take up four."

Aside from his André the Giant stature, my husband is a master at Man Cooking, which is just basically throwing together two or three ingredients within his field of vision. For example, he lays claim to the fact that he invented "Salsa Spaghetti," which entails boiling some pasta and christening it with Taco Bell sauce. Another favorite is a sleeve of saltine crackers smashed in a glass of milk and stirred, otherwise known in the civilized world as "spackle," and once, for a special treat on his birthday, he asked me to make him toast with canned vegetable soup poured over it.

"We have very different cooking styles," I replied. "I like to make things I enjoy eating, and you make things like you're living by the river and cooking in a can heated by a Bic lighter."

"Well, maybe if we could work on our partnership skills, we wouldn't have been such a—" he started, then suddenly stopped.

"Ooooooooooh," I said, shaking my pointer finger. "I get it. I get it. This is all about the Kiss Kam, isn't it?"

My husband waited for a moment.

"I'm just saying that if we had better timing together, we would have been more in sync and maybe that wouldn't have happened," he finally said.

"I know you want to blame me for the Kiss Kam, but it was not my fault," I stated without question. "That was not my fault."

My husband opened his mouth.

"NOTMYFAULT," I said loudly, and pointed my finger at him.

We had been married 20 years, happily, enjoyably, and satisfactorily. We were proud of our accomplishment, we were pretty much good with our life and the choices we had made. We drank wine in the evenings, we made each other laugh on a daily basis, and sometimes to the point of urination, which I found particularly impressive until that same thing started happening when I was simply trying to get out of bed in the morning. In any case, things were good. We were married. We felt that we had married the right people. There were no regrets, there were no shadows of doubt.

Until the Kiss Kam.

We recently got season tickets to Eugene's farm league baseball team, mainly because my husband discovered he likes baseball and I have always liked the dollar hot dogs and the 12-dollar nachos. He bought us both baseball caps with the team logo on them. It's a great reason to get out in the beautiful Oregon summer weather, the mascot is Bigfoot, and there's always a chance an asshole is going to get hit in the head with a baseball. So far, that has come very close to happening, and the asshole was me.

But apparently, there's a lot of downtime in baseball and, thus, the reason for audience participation during those recesses. The corporations need their time (there is a Taco Race sponsored by Taco Bell, and a cheeseburger building race by Carl's Jr.); then there's the ring toss, in which little kids get a chance to win a free ice cream, and a tug-of-war that is usually hilarious, with a fat kid and a skinny kid on each end of the rope.

And then there's the Kiss Kam, which scans the stands for unsuspecting victims, looking for people who look like couples—which is a very dangerous proposition if you ask me, rife with the potential for a lawsuit. The camera then stays on the couple until they kiss.

Usually, this is the cue for either one of us to get nachos, but before I could even reach down and grab my wallet, my husband gasped.

"What's wrong?" I asked. "Kiss Kam," he hissed between closed teeth. "I know," I said. "I'm going to get nachos now." "Tooooooo late," he hissed again, and motioned his eyes toward the baseball jumbotron screen to see my largest nightmare come to life. There I was, reaching down in between my legs for my purse, my eyes wide as saucers and my husband frozen as if he had just had a stroke or Darth Vader had turned him into carbonite.

"Holy shit," I saw my mouth say.

"You're going to have to kiss me," my husband struggled to emit.

"Act like brother and sister," I hissed back, the camera still on us.

Apparently, patting someone's leg indicated a sibling relationship in my husband's family, because that's exactly what he did. The cameraperson who steadied his camera on us, however, saw that as a symbol of commitment and kept the lens exactly where it was.

"It's not working," my husband slurred. "You're going to have to kiss me."

"Oh god," I said. "Kissssssss me," my husband insisted. I was mortified. Despite my past, I am a bit of a Victorian who would really prefer to abstain from public displays of affection if at all possible. I felt my face get super hot, and I tried to figure out what to do.

"Kissssssss me," my husband hissed again.

The pressure was enormous. I felt like I was getting sucked into a black hole and as the seconds ticked away endlessly, my husband finally turned toward me and I had no choice.

In hindsight, I remember the incident frame by frame. The slow approach of my husband's face coming toward me, the furrowing of my brow, the implication of reluctance, his lips reaching out toward mine, my lips puckering up toward his, coming together, closer, closer, closer until—

BAM!

The brim of his baseball hat hit me in the forehead, and the brim of mine hit his, and thus, reaching for one another but solidly stuck four inches apart, our puckery lips tried to reach the other side but only moved like little fishes in a bowl.

And we stayed like that for moments, trapped in an accident of physics or something of that order that simple minds fueled by one-dollar hot dogs and 12-dollar nachos cannot easily comprehend. Governments have fallen and people have died dramatic, notable deaths in less time. When my husband realized our blockage and finally took off his hat and we successfully made contact, 2,000 spectators and several baseball players from Costa Rica had witnessed the gold standard in Kiss Kam failure, so horrible that people didn't even laugh and simply grew silent, probably believing that they had, indeed, just watched a brother and sister kiss.

I never got my nachos that day. We just left. We honestly had no choice. It was either that or wait for the Kiss Kam to return at any time, and we already both had developed cramps.

"That was worse than when I tried to run the mile in seventh grade, thought I was having a heart attack, and demanded that the even slower girls behind me go back for help, and they did," I said as we trudged to the car.

"I have never been so horrified in my life," my husband said.

"No, no, no," I pooh-poohed him. "What about the time a drop of my face lotion got on the seat of the toilet and you wanted to go to the emergency room because you thought it was going to burn a hole through your ass?"

"Yeah? Well your face lotion had salicylic acid, which sears off warts," he countered. "My whole left side was on fire. To this day, I know you're lying about there not being a scar on that side. Someday, someone will tell me the truth."

The wound of the Kiss Kam Katastrophe sat on our marriage for the rest of the day, my husband analyzing every second of the play to see how we could have averted such disaster.

"I just can't believe we failed the Kiss Kam," he said repeatedly, until I couldn't take it anymore.

"The fact that we collapsed in the face of a public challenge is not our fault!" I asserted. "It's the manufacturers of the baseball hats that are to blame. They need to be retractable, so that when an intern with the baseball team homes in on you like the Death Star, you have some recourse. We had no warning, we never had a chance. Plus, you weren't the one who had her head in between her legs while wearing a dress on a hundred-foot screen."

"No, but I was the man who couldn't figure out how to kiss his wife!" he replied, and suddenly turned toward me. "Kiss me!"

"Fine," I sighed, and obliged.

We each leaned in, and it took less than a second for us to halt four inches apart, exactly as we had before.

"Take the damn hat off!" I cried.

"*No*," my husband said emphatically. "We need to practice. We need to prove that we can do it."

So for the next 10 minutes, we had to practice kissing with our hats on, from one side to the other, taking turns from every angle and every direction. Then he made us try a stop, turn, and kiss maneuver to use if we ever got caught on the Kiss Kam again to stun everyone who had watched our disaster.

While the wound eventually healed, the scar of doubt remained as puckered and red as our searching lips on that awful day.

So when this new opportunity presented itself in the box of HelloFresh dinners, my husband wanted—no, demanded—that we use it to prove our in-tandem couple skills.

"We do plenty of things in tandem," I complained. "We watch TV together, we go to the movies together, we eat dinner together every night."

"But we can't eat popcorn out of the same bowl," he mentioned. "And that is a tandem activity."

"That's because you hover," I said. "And your hand is the size of a baseball glove. In fact, I've never seen you put popcorn into your mouth. Your hand is always just there, right above the bowl like it was a Magic Eight Ball. If I wanted to go as you for Halloween, all I would need is a bowl of some salty snack and my hand just hanging over it."

"Then that's proof that we need to work on our couple coordination," he said. "Let's just try it and see how it goes. Let's make a deal that we will cook these three meals together, and if it's another failure in our relationship spectrum, then we'll stop. I won't bug you again. I promise."

"What do I get for my trouble if all I get is aggravation?" I said. "What's in it for me if it doesn't work?"

He thought for a minute.

"I give you my permission as your partner, in the future, to have an individual popcorn bowl," he said, luring me in. "All to yourself."

"Fine," I said, giving in.

"Let's make one tonight!" he said, and I agreed, if only to hurry up and get this thing over with.

At 6 o'clock, he pulled out the box that held the seared steak dinner and put it on the kitchen counter.

"You ready?" he asked. "Yep," I answered. "Okay," he said, holding the recipe card. "There are four elements to this dish. How about we split it half and half? There's couscous, roasted cauliflower, romesco sauce, and the steak. Which portions of the dish do you want?"

I thought I would be kind. A baby could make couscous if it didn't require boiling water, and chopping some caulifower seemed easy enough. "I'll take the steak and the romesco sauce," I said.

He winced. "I would really like to give the romesco sauce a shot. It looks like it has an interesting taste profile, and there's a lot of chopping. I'd like to work on my knife skills," he said.

I shrugged and tried not to laugh. This is the man who, when I'm out of town, eats Fritos and beans mixed together as if it's a French delicacy. "Okay, then... I'll take the cauliflower?"

"Sure," he said, tossing me the head as he went over to the knife block. Here we go, I thought to myself. We're going to argue over the best knife. This should be awesome.

Knife fight 10 seconds in.

But he passed over my favorite knife, dawdled over my second favorite, then went to the top of the knife block, pulled out a cleaver, and went back to the cutting board with it.

"Really?" I said when he pulled out the red pepper. "You're going to start with the 'Friday the 13th' knife? Let's calm down, cowboy, and take a run with a paring knife first."

He shook his head. "I like this one. Feels solid."

"You know," I said slowly, "if you took the pepper out to the driveway and ran over it with the car, it's the same amount of overkill as your ax there."

"Worry about yourself," he cautioned. "I'm not concerning myself with your choice of knife."

"No problem," I said. "But when you realize you only have four fingers on one hand, use one of them to call 911. Because I'm worrying about myself, you know."

"Thanks," he said. "The oven needs to be preheated to 400 degrees."

"I already did that," I replied.

He put his sickle down and walked over to the oven, next to where I was cutting the cauliflower with the right-sized knife. "You only got it to 375," he said, as he turned the knob an increment. "Wait. STOP. STOP cutting the cauliflower. STOP. Please."

I stared at him and waited for him to say, "Watch out for that wilted piece," or "Oh my god, there's a worm!" but, instead, he picked up the instruction card and read aloud, "Cut the cauliflower into bite-sized florets."

Then he looked up at me. "Yeah?" I replied. "I think maybe you're taking the easy way out," he said earnestly. "You're a half inch over bite-sized there. Shouldn't bite-sized mean I should be able to pop it in my mouth? I couldn't do that with most of those."

I just stared at him.

"That one, right there, like, who has a mouth that big? Like Steven Tyler could eat that bite, Mick Jagger, sure. But to anyone else with an average-sized mouth, you're just going to run into trouble there," he continued. "You're promising something you can't deliver."

I paused.

"Considering that I'm sharing this meal with the person who has the biggest mouth on the planet, I'm not too worried," I said, and started chopping the cauliflower into egg-sized chunks.

"I'm just following directions," my husband said, and went back to his red pepper slaughter.

"Yeah, well, the recipe didn't call for a sword, but that did not deter you at all," I replied.

"I am comfortable with my food preparation decisions," he said, turning away from me.

"As am I," I retorted, leaving half of the cauliflower head intact as I shoved it into the oven.

I had the cauliflower roasting and was seasoning the steak when my husband posed a question.

"What exactly is a pinch?" he asked. "Does it matter which fingers I use? Because if I pinch with my pinky and thumb, that is considerably less than pinching with my thumb and fore finger. The water for the couscous requires a pinch of salt, but is that just a rhetorical reference?"

I stopped seasoning the steak.

"Would you do me a favor?" I asked. "Would you run upstairs and get that piece of paper that says you have a Ph.D. on it? The one with the gold sticker? I want to make sure you didn't get it from the University of Phoenix or the place where you draw the turtle and pirate."

"That's so funny, because I don't see a pinch of sarcasm anywhere in the ingredient list," he said. "Careful it doesn't leave a bitter taste in your mouth and ruin the dish."

"How about I show you what a pinch feels like?" I asked.

He put down his scythe and turned toward me.

"I thought we were supposed to be a team doing this together," he said. "But when it comes down to the execution, I am not taking the blame for your mistakes."

"Are you saying you'd throw me under the bus?" I asked.

My husband just shrugged. "I'm just saying I'm not going down because of your attitude."

I gasped.

"You have four minutes until my steak is done," I said harshly. "And then it's hands up. *Partner.*"

I tossed my steaks into the sizzling pan, crushed the garlic, removed the cauliflower from the oven, and drizzled it with olive oil and some Parmesan cheese that was *not in the recipe*. I was taking matters into my own hands, creating the profile I knew would work, and with 30 seconds left and counting, I flung the last tablespoon of butter into the pan and let the steaks rest in the foam as it sizzled.

"Who turned my burner off?" my husband screamed as he tended to his couscous. "My burner's off!"

"...three, two, one," I said, slapping my steak tongs down on the kitchen counter. "Hands up!"

My husband sighed and put his hands up.

"I didn't get to plate," he said bitterly, shaking his head. "Sabotage."

"I didn't touch your burner," I said. "Let's just eat," he suggested. And, as we sat down at the coffee table where we eat because we are savages, my first bite of steak was awesome, and because I took all of the bite-sized pieces of cauliflower, our meal rocked. My husband's couscous, despite the irresponsible approach to salt, was delightful, with raisins and pistachios in it. The romesco sauce was the perfect pairing for the steak, and three bites in, we complimented ourselves on a job well done.

"I like the Parmesan," he said. "Worth the risk."

He turned his head from me, stopped, then he whipped it around, yelling, "Kiss Kam!" and came at me, all puckered up.

LAURIE NOTARO's marketing budget for her last book was cut and then reallocated to the marketing budget for Amy Schumer's book. Laurie is quite bitter.

HAPPY HOUR / FISH FRY / DANCING

MICHAEL GRADY

I HAD THE MOST AWKWARD CONVERSATION a few years ago. A coworker I barely knew asked me out for coffee. We sat in this tiny café while I held up both sides of the discussion and he studied me like a bug. Uncomfortable silences kept falling. I'd say anything—stupid things— to bat them away. And when I did, he'd tilt his head the way golden retrievers do when you make a balloon animal.

Finally, I asked: "What am I doing here?"

"I thought we might see each other socially," he said, "with an eye toward developing a friendship."

"Is this how it's done now? 'Cause I was hoping for a process that was a little less like passing a kidney stone."

"Is that sarcasm?" he asked. "That's funny."

He really wasn't a bad guy—though he may have been voice-activated software— but it made me yearn for the days when making friends wasn't such a stiff, self-conscious dance.

* * *

I met Sapo at a late night poker game 30 years ago. It was at a North Tucson construction site—the type of place normally reserved for ransom drops. We walked in and he was already shuffling: leather fedora and a dangling cigarette. The cards rattled like small arms fire in his hands. "You ready?" he asked.

I thought: 'I am losing money to this man.'

And so I did.

But at the end of the evening he was kind enough to let me walk my money to his car. "I appreciate you not … gloating."

"No," he assured me. "I hate gloaters. Your cash is really enough."

"Is there anything I can do to make myself better?"

"As a person?"

"As a card player."

He took a long, thoughtful drag on his cigarette. "…I think almost anything you would do would make you better as a card player. The best advice I could give you—and I say this honestly, 'cause it'll probably cost me money—is to maybe step back from the card table until…"

"Until what?"

"Until, you know… your death."

* * *

We were thrown together by proximity and hardship. Sapo and I were both professional actors, then. In the glitzy showbiz vortex that is Tucson, that means you're unemployed about 99.4 percent of the time. When we worked, we often worked together. We played small roles in big theatres, doing characters with adjective names: "3rd citizen," "angry townsmen," "sad waiter." You'd come in at 7, costume and makeup, sit in the greenroom. At 9:10, you say, "Monsieur does not like the veal?" and you're done.

"Did you make them see the veal?" I'd ask, when he came offstage.

"I said 'veal,'" Sapo'd reply. "But I made those bastards see themselves."

And we played big roles in small theatres. We did Michael Frayn's "Benefactors" in a theatre that had one bathroom, but you had to share it with the audience. If having an actor break the fourth wall to talk to you makes you uncomfortable, imagine Iago pacing outside your restroom stall waiting for you to flush. So, Sapo and I would rush out during intermission, to urinate in an alley a block away. That's what we were doing the night a pair of headlights bore down on us.

"This isn't good." I said.

"He'll turn."

"He sees us."

"He'll turn!"

"I think it's a squad car."

They say men can't multi-task. But if you've ever fled law enforcement, while urinating, in full costume and pancake makeup, you know otherwise.

These are the circumstances that bond friends.

* * *

I think friendship is aspirational, too. You see qualities in the other person you wish you had yourself. While I angst-ed my way through rejection letters and girlfriends, Sapo was very Zen. "Your twenties are hard," he advised me, after a breakup. "It's like you're running full steam into brick walls, over and over."

I looked up from my beer. "And that changes in your thirties?"

"No. But, by then, you're so damaged from the wall, you start running into it slower."

He had this uncanny ability to accept life on its own terms. Once, on tour, they put us up near a nameless strip mall bar with "Happy Hour/Fish Fry/Dancing" painted on the window. We opened the door to a silent, empty establishment. "Happy Hour/Fish Fry/Dancing's" only occupant was a mountainous angry woman tending bar.

"We're here for Happy Hour."

"THAT'S NOT TODAY."

"Okay," he said. "How's the fish fry?"

"...FRYER'S BROKEN!"

Sapo nodded, and glanced at the sign. "Wanna dance?"

* * *

He also had patience—which I did not have. In my late twenties, with a little local success, I yearned for fame and fortune. I confided to Sapo that I wanted to be a household word.

"Like spoon?" he asked. "You shake your head, but go anywhere in the world, and say, 'spoon'? People will know what you're talking about."

I wanted to be a spoon. So, I cut my ties with Sapo and everyone and left Tucson for Chicago. Then San Diego. Then Phoenix and Chicago again—a quest that, I was sure, would end on an opening credits montage or an awards podium.

Truth was, I had to run into the wall a few more times.

* * *

"Hey Sapo, it's me."

I made the call—a call I'd been dreading—from Chicago.

"Hey, champ!" And he just rolled into some quirky little Tucson story like we hadn't been out of touch for two whole years. There were pauses, and I wasn't filling them. "...how're you?"

"Ohhh, not good. I, uh, kinda… had a nervous breakdown, out here."

This is the stop where a lot of friends change trains. You can hear the cars uncoupling in the silences that follow. If you're the funny guy in a group? You're expected to bring the funny. If people ask where you've been, or why you're quiet, and you say, "I had a nervous breakdown," they always *think* you're being funny. So they respond with "P-b-b-b-b-bb-blt!" or "Kill anybody?" or "How'd you dial from the straight-jacket?"

It forces you to say something like, "No, really. I was diagnosed with depression. It took some doctors and a whole lot of pills, and… I'm tryin' to get back on the horse again."

Then they realize: You're serious, and they've dug themselves a hole. At this point, most people decide it's just easier to find a new funny guy.

"Listen," I just kept talking. "I have this speaking engagement in Flagstaff. I booked it before… all this. But I always thought, 'If I can make this gig, it'll mean I'm getting my life back.' Now, I know this is a lot to ask, because Flagstaff is five hours away and you haven't heard 'boo' from me in two years. But I don't know anyone in Flagstaff, and—"

"When and where?" he said. "Hold on, I'll get a pen…"

* * *

The great thing about guy friendships is that you can neglect them for years. Then pick them up one day—and it's like you never skipped a beat. I moved back here. Fell in love. Got married. Sapo was my best man. I left acting—acting and I were both relieved—but Sapo didn't. Even though we had different careers in different cities, we shared each other's success.

One day, at my paper, I get a call.

"I'm in Kansas City."

"Still understudying 'To Kill a Mockingbird?'"

"No," he said. "The bastard playing Atticus got sick. I gotta go on tomorrow and be Atticus in the matinee."

I'd never heard him that nervous before.

"Well, I wish I was there," I said. "Because you're going to be awesome. You'll go out there, the lights'll hit you and you'll have fun. And we both know how good you are onstage when you're having fun."

If there is something better than saying the right thing, at the right time, for someone you love? I do not know it.

The bad thing about guy friendships is this: because you can neglect them, for years at a time, you often do.

* * *

Sapo's wife, Kathy, is one of those strong-willed people with a positive outlook on every-thing. I didn't take that into account last month when I opened her Facebook message titled: "Good news."

Cancer. They found a spot on his lung, and had to go in. The "good news" was that they only had to take a third of his right lung.

Suddenly, after years of "we should get together" and months of "I should call him," I had to hear my friend's voice right away. But I couldn't. I spent the next 24 hours think-ing of all the people I've lost, and the things I didn't say. I wrote them into eulogies, and obituaries. But no matter how well you write those things, you're never going to reach the person you're aiming for.

"Hey champ…" I said it overly casual. Stupid casual. Trying too hard.

"Hey champ…" So many things to say. Heartfelt. Honest. Supportive things you could say. And, of all of them, I said: "You sound like Darth Vader, breathing through a humidifier."

And he laughed, which, in that context, was like stabbing him with a steak knife and jiggling him like a piñata.

"Could you…" he wheezed "…not be funny for… awhile?"

"Yes," I said. "I've been not-funny for long whiles…"

"I know…"

"The '80s, for example—"

"I know."

It was another awkward conversation. Long pauses. Short answers. Cryptic medical talk and gurgling.

I had to hold up both sides of the discussion again. And was never so grateful for the chance.

MICHAEL GRADY is a playwright/freelance writer and columnist, whose plays include Past History, The Harmony Codes, Lights and White Picket Fence. He lives in Prescott.

GOODNIGHT NOISES

MELISSA EDDY CAMPANA

IT'S 9 P.M. ....

And I'm crawling into bed, humming the theme song to "Full House." My husband and I have been trying to put our twin daughters—each one-and-a-half years old—to sleep since 7 o'clock tonight. When we exhausted our repertoire of lullabies we switched to TV theme songs, and feel-good family sitcoms from the early '90s appeared to be their kryptonite. By the time we were wondering whatever happened to predictability, the babies were out.

Richie and I actually have three girls: A three-year-old and the aforementioned twins. The nightly routine is straightforward enough—bath, bottles, bed—but tonight looked a little less "Goodnight Moon," and a little more "Miley Cyrus music video." My three-year-old is going through a "pajama party" phase, which, as any parent will tell you, is when a preschooler pulls down her unicorn costume from Halloween and prances around the house singing "Shake It Off" at the top of her lungs. The twins—who believe their older sister to be the reincarnation of Jesus—marched loyally behind her throughout the performance, their tiny fists pumping in the air like miniature backup dancers for Beyoncé.

Now, though I'm pretty positive my three-year-old is still awake in her bed, the house is finally, blissfully, quiet. I'm a stay-at-home mom, so by 9 o'clock I don't care what the fuck they're doing as long as they're doing it quietly and in their own rooms. If anyone asks, it's a Montessori method.

I wish my husband goodnight and good luck, and fall into a fitful sleep, where my dreams involve Mr. Feeney sending Kimmy Gibbler and me to detention for talking in class.

* * *

It's 11 p.m. …

…And a baby is crying.

I nudge my husband.

—Rich. Rich. Richie. RICHARD.
—Hmmph? What?
—Can you get the baby? Do you mind? She probably just needs a new diaper.
—What? Yeah. No. Okay. Sure. I'm on it.

I watch his silhouette in the moonlight as he stumbles out of our room. He looks good. I have to remember to tell him that when he gets back. We've been married for eight years and we have three kids under the age of four, so we don't really say those things out loud to each other anymore. Actually, the only things I say out loud to him these days are "Did you call the pediatrician back?" and "We need to go to Costco again." And "Lady Mary is a bitch but she sure can manage the hell out of an estate."

—Was it her diaper? I ask when he gets back.
—Yeah, he replies. She pooped.
—Aww, poor little thing. Thanks, Rich.
—Of course. Goodnight, Melissa.
—Goodnight. I love you.
—I love you too.
—Richie?
—Mmm?
—We have the best kids, don't we?
—Yeah, we really do.

I smile. Parenthood is a funny thing. Earlier tonight, I was ready to wring the kids' necks, and now it's all I can do not to grab my phone and scroll through recent pictures of them, because I already kind of miss the little buggers. It's hard to believe that just three and a half years ago, none of the tiny people down the hall even existed.

Richie and I met in our early twenties, and we only dated for about a year and a half before getting engaged. We were the first of our friends to get married, but it never felt "too soon." From the start, his laid-back Italian style seemed to be the perfect match to my stubborn Irish nature. We both came from tight families, loved to travel, and wanted to have lots of kids. But the twin thing was a pretty big surprise, which is kind of like saying Russia is a "pretty big place," and the past year and a half has definitely been a challenge.

I'm lucky, though. Most of the moms at my daughter's preschool talk about their husbands like they are helpless idiots. To be fair, they're not all wrong. But Richie is the opposite: He's fantastic with the kids, he takes equal responsibility around the house, and he always lifts me up when he can tell it's been a rough day at home.

I look over at him and suddenly I'm overwhelmed with the urge to tell him how much I love him. That I feel so lucky to do this whole "life" thing with him, and that I couldn't ask for a better partner to raise a family with. But he is already fast asleep and looks so peaceful that I can't bear to wake him. I kiss his shoulder and roll over, glancing at the clock on the nightstand.

11:30.

If I fall asleep right now, I can still get seven hours in before the kids wake up.

* * *

It's 1 a.m. . . .

. . . And a baby is crying. It's the other baby this time, which makes it harder to be annoyed, though not impossible. It's not her fault her sister has already kept us up half the night, but I'm so tired, and so jealous of how sound asleep the man beside me seems to be.

—Rich. Rich. Richie.

I shake him.

—RICHIE.

I kick him in the shins, only slightly harder than one might kick a field goal, but to no avail. By the time I get to the babies' room, the first twin's sobs have woken the second twin. I rock one—while the other cries—then switch. Where are Joey and Jesse when you need them, right? Do you think Danny Tanner was really a widow, or did his wife leave because three daughters is a fucking nightmare and he's just too embarrassed to talk about it? By the time I get back to bed, my adrenaline is pumping too hard to fall asleep right away. I debate waking Richie up to tell him how crappy the last hour of my life was, but I know that would be unfair. So, I pick up my phone…which is basically volunteering for another hour of being awake. I play Bubble Mania. I check to see if Kimmy Gibbler has an Instagram account. I scroll through Facebook until I hate everyone. I go to sleep.

* * *

It's 3 a.m. …

…And one of my stupid kids lets out a stupid yelp in her stupid sleep. This wakes up one of my other stupid kids, and now two out of three kids are crying loudly, threatening to wake up the third.

I look over at Richie. Nothing.

As I begin the long walk down the hallway again, I wonder: what my prospects might look like as a 30-year-old divorcee. Wait, am I 30? No, shit, I'm 31. Well, anyway, I'm essentially still in my prime. I mean, sure, I'm starting to get gray hairs and my yoga mat has seen more action as a changing pad lately than anything else, but I'm still basically attractive, right? My bottom teeth have shifted since getting my braces off in high school. I run my tongue over them as I change a baby's diaper. A lot of people with bad teeth have plenty of sex appeal, though. Look at Keira Knightley. I put Baby A down and go to Baby B's crib. Divorce is probably a lot of paperwork, though. I hold her arms at her sides and use my knee to pin down her legs so I can change her diaper. After all, it took me the better part of a year to change all my credit cards to my married name, for godssake. I don't know if I could deal with that again.

Fuck it, I think as I walk back down the hall to our room. I look at my husband, now deep in a REM cycle and snoring loudly.

Asshole.

* * *

It's 3:30 a.m. …

…And I am woken by the sound of my three-year-old calling out for me. That is, if you can call it being woken up when you've been asleep for 30 seconds.

—Mom? Mooo-oooom? Mom! Mommy!
—Richie, will you PLEASE go get your daughter?

It's no use. He's comatose. Before I know it, my three-year-old has found her way to our room and is tugging on my pillow. She has had a dream about a scary tiger and the snow monster from the Nana movie and is it okay if she sleeps with me?

—Of course, sweetheart, I say as I pull her into bed next to me. It's probably our last night all under one roof together anyway as your father and I will almost certainly divorce tomorrow. Unless the sleep terrorists down the hall wake up first, in which case I'm getting straight into my car and driving to Mexico.

—What's a divorce? she asks sleepily.

—When two people love each other very much, I reply, but one of those people is a douche bag, sometimes they get a divorce.

—What's a douche bag?

—That, I'll explain when you're older.

—Like when I'm six?

—Like when you're six.

—My birthday is August 10th, she reminds me.

—I know, I say.

—Can I have a divorce for my birthday?

—We'll see.

I kiss her on the forehead and take a mental inventory of the furniture I will take with me to Mexico, and fall asleep practicing my Spanish.

* * *

It's 11 a.m. . . .

. . . And I wake up with a start. Something is not right. The light peeking through the curtain is all wrong, and the house is entirely too quiet. I fling my arm across the bed but feel only the indentations where my husband's body and my daughter's tiny one used to be. What the hell? I sit up and grope blindly for my glasses. Where is everyone? What time is it? I reach for my phone on the nightstand but my hand finds a plate of cold eggs and a mug of tea that has been there a while. There is also a note:

Meliss,

Everywhere you look, everywhere you look, there's a heart, a hand to hold onto. Everywhere you look, everywhere you look, there's a place of somebody who needs you.

When you're lost out there and you're all alone, a light is waiting to carry you home. Everywhere you look.

Love,
Richie

PS Took the girls to the park so you could get some sleep.
PPS Thank you for our daughters.

That asshole.

MELISSA EDDY CAMPANA is a Phoenix native living in Ireland, where she writes, raises three kids, and misses Mexican food terribly. Find her at melissaecampana.com.

OPERATION: REVENGE DATE

GENEVIEVE RICE

IT ALL BEGAN WITH TRAGEDY. When I was 17, Bryce, my high school boyfriend of four months, broke up with me, on Halloween no less. If you've never been broken up with while wearing a Miss America Halloween costume, I would not recommend it. But I will admit that crying did help me look spooky and more in line with the holiday. We both worked together at the same Sears, I in intimate apparel and Bryce in sporting goods. That Sears in late '90s suburban Oklahoma City was the beginning and end of my social universe, a very sad thing for me to admit. And to make things worse, Bryce immediately took up with another girl, who was described as having "a dancer's body." My life was truly in tatters.

So naturally, I had to pick up the pieces, and first order of business was to find a man, any man, to make Bryce jealous. And one day I found that special any man, in a place where people often are sold things they do not actually want: a mall kiosk. Specifically, it was a Sunglass Hut kiosk in a prime location, right between a Wet Seal and an Auntie Anne's Pretzels. It's truly the tenderloin of the mall.

I may have been lured into his kiosk by an affordable selection of sunglasses, but nothing could shield my eyes from his glittering charms. He noticed me, too, and soon I was flirting hardcore with a man who looked like a Disney Prince who just happened to sell discount sunglasses at the mall. His name was Lance. He was 19, new to the city and wanted to take me out. So, we made a date for the next week. He would pick me up at work on a day my ex just happened to be working. Operation: Revenge Date was in full effect.

So, the plan for the date was simple. First, Lance would pick me up at my register at work, sweeping me off my feet in front of my envious but supportive coworkers. Then, he would walk me past my ex-boyfriend's register in such a way that would remind my ex of what he had truly given up. And with that fire reignited with Bryce, Lance would whisk me away to the most romantic place in the world to a sheltered 17-year-old teen, the Olive Garden, where enchantment and pasta bowls are both never ending.

But, alas, my elegant plan did not go as arranged. Lance showed up 20 minutes late, which means I also had to hang around work awkwardly an extra 20 minutes. When he showed up, he was not quite the shining Adonis I remembered. He was shorter, scrawnier and less suave than memory served. It was like the other day I had seen the oil painting and today I was seeing the rough sketch. Instead of envy, my coworkers had concern dancing in their eyes. But I was in too deep to turn back now.

So, we commenced with walking past my ex's workstation, his empty workstation. Where was Bryce? Who was there to ring up dumbbells, or to fall back in love with me? No one, apparently. I racked my brain for a way I could make this work. Could I somehow hang around sporting goods until Bryce came back? Was there a way to walk by again? I came to the soul-crushing conclusion that none of these things would work. I had failed to recapture lost love, and now I was going to Olive Garden with a perfect stranger. Or was I?

Olive Garden was closed. So we went to IHOP, which is the most opposite chain restaurant of Olive Garden. Olive Garden's lighting is dark and soft, whereas IHOP's lighting is bright and sobering. IHOP is where people go after making bad decisions. No one celebrates anything at IHOP. It's a place for reconciling your life. If Olive Garden is espresso sipped by two paramours, IHOP is hot brown coffee poured down your throat by a cop in the drunk tank. But they serve a mean pancake.

So we're at IHOP. My plans to pick up the pieces of my shattered life were dashed, but I was still determined to have a good time. Here I was out on a date on a non-school night with I man I had, at least for a few minutes, found charming. Perhaps we could recapture the magic we once felt in the stallspace of the Sunglass Hut kiosk. So, I ask him questions about his life. He starts a talkin' and he doesn't stop. And he's mumbly. At first, I ask him to repeat himself. But after a while, I give up and just use context clues to help gauge whether I think he's telling me something sad or funny, all the while masking my deep regret for going on a date with the teacher from Charlie Brown.

Dinner is done, and I have probably not politely giggled at his grandmother's death. So, I drive him back to his car (that's right, I drove). I'm hoping for a polite businesslike exit to this date. But the only business he had on his mind was monkey business. He grabbed me and shoved his tongue down my throat. And his tongue was...sharp. And heavy. Maybe I even heard it clank? I was so young, I thought, are some tongues just like this? Maybe this was why he was so hard to understand? He finally withdrew and sheathed his tongue. As he exited my car, he turned to me and said something that sounded like "I love you." And I responded with, "Well, goodnight."

I returned to work the next day, hoping the previous night was a silly folly left largely in a mall parking lot. But this proved to be foolish. As I approached my workstation, my co-worker Lana greeted me excitedly: "Somebody's got a boyfriend!" And then she pointed to a Bath & Body Works gift basket. Attached was a handwritten note tag that said "Geneva [not my name], I love you [no you don't], Lance." What's worse it was a Juniper Breeze gift basket, arguably the worst scent (unless you like smelling like a gin and tonic left in the forest). Fuck. I was going to either quit my job or break up with him.

Ultimately, Sears won out, so I headed down to his Sunglass Hut kiosk, Bath & Body gift basket in tow, to do the dirty deed. At first, he was happy to see me, but that quickly faded as I quickly explained why this wouldn't work. I think I even said something about "needing to concentrate on school." Before I left, he asked me for one last hug. As we hugged, he whispered something I didn't quite catch, but I like to think he said, "We'll always have the Sunglass Hut kiosk."

Back at Sears, my co-workers rallied around me. Jessica from costume jewelry served as a stealth Lance lookout, letting me know when it was safe to go back to Wet Seal. Nicole from juniors introduced me to several eligible boys who I'm happy to report did not have heavy tongues. And Lana kept tabs on Bryce and dancer's body, presenting me with weekly detailed reports on why she thought they were on the outs, an impressive feat in the pre-Facebook era. And eventually, we all even made it to the Olive Garden.

GENEVIEVE RICE is definitely not several raccoons in a trench coat. She lives in Phoenix with her husband, daughter, and a lifetime of regret.

LITROS. KILOS. METROS.

VALERIA FERNÁNDEZ

SARA TREMBLED, her eyes closed. Her small, 18-year-old figure was there in the passenger seat of my car, but her mind was locked behind a closed door. She grabbed her head. A vein in her forehead was swelling; it was as if her thoughts were exploding.

I was there in response to a desperate call. She said she was alone and afraid. Deeply afraid. She said she needed someone to talk to. It was 10 at night; I drove across town and picked her up.

I didn't know what to do next.

Sara is from El Salvador, but her story is familiar. Sara (that is not her real name) is the face of hundreds of thousands of unaccompanied minors who have come to the United States from Central America. She left behind a childhood of abuse, bringing along the wounds of trauma. Once she arrived in this country, the mental health services she needed were not always readily available.

That night with her immigration status in limbo and no health insurance, I had concerns about what inadvertent doors I would open if I took her to the emergency room.

Would they keep her for the night? How would she afford it? Would they refer her to immigration authorities?

It was also awkward for me to be there, because I'm a journalist. You don't typically get involved helping someone that you might write about. Back then I thought Sara needed rescue, and I acted on it. Only time would show me we both needed something else.

It's been four years since I've known Sara.

I met her by chance in the waiting room of an immigration attorney's office in Phoenix. I was there working on a story about another kid. The 2014 World Football Cup was underway, and I made a joke about my country's soccer team, Uruguay.

I said: "I'm from Uruguay, but I don't bite." We had a player that bit someone in the middle of a game.

She laughed.

I remember her dark black hair neatly pulled back and her square glasses that looked just a bit like mine.

Impulsively, she blurted, "What kind of literature do you read?"

She told me she really liked a book called "Mandingo." It is the story of an African slave in the southern United States who falls in love with his captor.

At that point, all I knew was that she had come to the U.S. alone. I suggested we keep in touch via Facebook, which seemed less personal than a phone number, since I was intrigued by her love for books and felt she might have a story to tell.

A few days later, her name popped up on my Facebook chat feed. She was curious about me. I explained I was a reporter doing research on unaccompanied youth coming from Central America. I told her I had to get back to my writing.

Another day, she was back in the chat box talking about soccer, but quickly changed the subject—big time.

"Can I ask you a question? Do you believe in God?" she asked in Spanish.

"Yes," I said.

"Is it true that if you feel empty God can fill that emptiness?" she asked.

"It's a question that could take me hours to answer," I said. "But I'm going to tell you what I humbly believe…"

She interrupted.

"I don't know if that's not true or if it's me that doesn't feel it."

Then she went on.

"I don't have anything or anyone," she said. "I feel desperate for someone to listen to me."

And that was the day I decided I had to be her friend.

Sara and I went to bookstores together, and the public library. I loaned her books in Spanish. We went for Salvadoran food and talked about literature.

She was unemployed and lived with the family of a shelter staffer who had helped her.

She often had flashbacks of her past. She had strong headaches and would withdraw from conversation. She agreed with me that she needed help from a mental health specialist but wouldn't dare to ask her immigration attorney, so I did it for her.

They looked for help, but it wasn't easy. Sara didn't have an immigration status yet; that means no health insurance, which meant she couldn't have access to affordable mental health services. Two months went by. Every night, I would receive messages Sara sent from her cell phone telling me about losing hope, or emoticons with tears pouring from their eyes.

I gave her a number for a suicide hotline. There were nights I was on the verge of calling it for her.

Finally, through her attorney's connections, the International Rescue Committee started offering her services. The IRC helped pay for six months of her rent; they also got her a job at a hotel as a maid. Still—with no health insurance she couldn't get mental health services.

"It's great to have your basic needs, but you can't succeed just with the apartment, the refugee card and a job," she said. "You can't keep that up if you're not doing well emotionally."

As time went by, I came to learn more about Sara's past.

Her mother left for the U.S. when Sara was three, eventually settling with Sara's grandmother and an uncle in California. She never met her father.

As a young child, Sara had lots of tiny curls, as she does now. In El Salvador, they call that type of hair *colocho*. She spoke fast and a lot, she recalls, because she felt adults didn't listen. So when she got a chance to speak she tried to get to say as much as she could.

Sara says that for a long time, she believed her world was perfect. Until, she realized it wasn't. She was sexually abused since she was eight.

"It wasn't one time or one person, it was several," she told me.

I'm not going to talk about those details now. Sara had to share all of these with many other adults at different points in her life. And when she came to the U.S. in front of an immigration judge. That was nerve-racking because it would send her to a place where she didn't have control anymore. It will trigger her.

Still she did it and won her asylum case.

But things didn't get better for her.

Around May 2015, I got a call. I was on my way to the airport for a work trip. She was in the hospital. Her voice sounded small.

"Don't be mad," she said in Spanish. "I'm all right now."

She told me later that she had taken every single painkiller and allergy pill she could find at home to try to shut down what she saw.

"With my history, I already had so many problems with people taking me seriously, I didn't want to say anything," she told me.

Sara had been working in a hotel for several months, cleaning 15 rooms a day; she was doing well, even won employee of the month. She lived alone in a small apartment with a blue couch and her own set of plates and cups. She still didn't speak much English. Life felt lonely, and senseless.

After many ups and downs, Sara started to take medication to help her deal with anxiety. A psychologist she had met when she was at a shelter for children started giving her regular therapy *pro bono*.

She got on her feet again. As she always has.

Sara has friends who are missing, living on the streets somewhere in Phoenix. They came here as unaccompanied children and while they have documents, the past still haunts them.

She worries about them. She once told me: "They all have the same type of confusion I had, the same reasons why I stopped eating and sleeping, all of those things that caused me not to have a normal life or will to live. They have the same thing in different words."

"They're trying to tell the world, 'I need mental health, my mind is driving me crazy.' It's not that they're crazy, simply, imagine that all your life you were taught to destroy, to use drugs, to see that as normal and all of a sudden you see reality."

She spoke again about emptiness, but this time it wasn't a question, it was her answer.

"I understand what that emptiness is, it's not that they lost something. It's not that they lost their mom or dad, what they lost is themselves," she says.

"They've reached a point, they don't know who they are."

As the years have gone by, my friend Sara has continued to write her own story.

I drove her quickly to the hair salon at the last minute for her wedding. We've walked together silently along Tempe Town Lake. I have shared with her the wonders of Gabriel Garcia Marquez's magic realism, and she took from my hands "Steppenwolf" from Herman Hesse. A book that broke my brain, and I cautioned her… you may not be the same after this book.

She's raised her voice politically about the treatment of youth that come to this country like her, she's put her soul into paintings, and she's challenged her own beliefs.

She has challenged me with her street smarts to look at the world from her lenses, she has shown me the powerful voice she has on her own.

She's made me ask myself: How can I help without causing more hurt?

I believe in reparations. That while we can't erase or ignore the past, and we can't heal for others, we can work towards unconditional love now. It is a lifetime of work, and Sara has showed me how it can be done.

I often joke about how we both came together, a Uruguayan journalist, a Salvadoran lover of literature, and we chose to be family for each other.

One day, not long after we become friends, Sara sent me a text message and she signed it: LKM.

Not knowing what it meant, I joked in Spanish: "Litros. Kilos. Metros." The measurements in Latin America for liquids, weight and distances.

We often say goodbye that way: Litros. Kilos. Metros.

What it really means is: I love you.

VALERIA FERNÁNDEZ is an independent journalist in Phoenix. She writes about the intersection of mental health and immigration. Follow her @valfernandez.

MUSIC

WHAT REMAINS IS FUTURE

SARAH VENTRE

THE ICONIC PUNK CLUB CBGBS closed on my 21st birthday. It was that last part of old New York—the gritty, raw, manic part where anything is possible and rules are nothing more than vague suggestions. The venue was known for incubating acts that were, at one time, the forefront of being loud and unconventional, bands like the Ramones and Talking Heads and Blondie. The final night, Patti Smith was set to play an epic, no-holds-barred set with a handful of secret special guests. So as an almost-adult who had, to that point, spent pretty much her whole life in Tempe and was dying to do something exciting and meaningful and maybe even a little bit dangerous... I had to go.

The *minor* obstacle was that I was a broke college student 2,400 miles away with no ticket to the show.

I scraped together enough money for a red-eye flight and hoped for the best. I also convinced a friend of mine to come along, and another friend who lived in Philly to take the train up to meet us. I figured we had a will, so there must be a way.

Once we were in New York we checked into a hostel in Upper Manhattan and made a plan. It seemed foolproof—mostly because we hadn't factored in that we were the fools. We would steal some pillows and blankets from the hostel, take them to the Lower East Side on two different trains, and camp out the night before the closing so that we'd be first in line when the venue opened the next night. Then I'd take the remaining $45 from my bank account and bribe the doorguys to let me in. Done.

After quickly realizing the plan had some holes in it, we spent the night hanging out at CB's sister bar—a club next door known as "the gallery" that had smaller shows. I got drunk and started carding people at the door.

It was a memorable experience, but it didn't help much with figuring out how to get in for the Patti Smith show.

The next day after recovering from my first legal binge, I threw on some red lipstick and hoop earrings and prepared to brave the cold October evening with one goal only: get into that show by any means necessary.

My friends came with me and we started standing in line sometime around 3 in the afternoon. A door guy from the club came out periodically to make an announcement to the line that stretched around the block.

"If you don't have a ticket, leave now. NO ONE is getting in without a ticket."

I looked from side to side and planted my feet a little firmer. If I had learned anything from my records back in Tempe, it was that punk rock was not about following the rules.

After almost three hours of standing in this line, my friends had had it. They had come along for the ride, and they would have loved to see the show, but they hadn't really planned for all this. "Sarah…we're not getting in. And we're starving. We're going to go get some food—wanna come?"

"I can't," I said. "I have to stay here. If I leave then there's really no way we're getting in. But bring me back some food?"

After they left I continued my mental calculations about how much money it would take to bribe each door guy to get in, and I started worrying that the $45 might not be enough.

At the same time, I noticed another woman who was by herself walking up and down the line. There weren't a lot of women by themselves, so I looked up and smiled at her.

"Do you have an extra ticket?" she asked.

"No. I don't even have one for myself. But I've been waiting here for a few hours and I'm not leaving until they make me."

She told me her name was Lucia, and she was stunningly beautiful. She was Italian and had long brown hair and huge brown eyes. I watched as men quickly fell in love with her. Not in lust—but in love. And while I wasn't in love with her, I did feel a certain kinship.

We linked arms and dug in together. We were sisters in rock.

Pretty soon my friends came back with some leftover pizza. "You owe us $15," they said.

"Sorry, I'm gonna have to get you back later. I need that money to bribe the doorguys."

I was really convinced that $45 could work, and that the $15 would make all the difference.

They explained to me that they too were broke, and needed the money for train fare.

I reluctantly paid them. They wished me luck on my impossible dream and headed home for the night. I grabbed a piece of pizza and offered Lucia a slice. We needed to fortify. It was getting dark and close to the time doors were opening. We had no idea what we were up against.

Then I heard someone yell from behind me. "Hey—you selling pizza?"

Without thinking I screamed, "No! I'm giving it away."

"What??" He couldn't hear me.

"Yeah!" I screamed.

I felt a little bad. Punk rock wasn't about capitalism, but these were desperate times.

"How much?" he asked.

"Two dollars a slice."

"What???"

"Three dollars a slice!"

Within 45 seconds all the pizza was sold and I was feeling a little better. My blood sugar was up, I had a rad woman by my side, and my pockets were padded with a little extra much-needed cash.

We kept waiting, and pretty soon the guy in front of us turned around and started chatting with us. Well, he started chatting with Lucia.

His name was Adam and his family owned a café at the foot of the Brooklyn Bridge. They were old New York too. He asked Lucia about the café she worked at on St. Marks, and what part of Italy she was from, and what shows she had seen. We asked him how he had gotten his ticket and he said that the venue owners knew his family because of the café. He was on the guestlist. He made an offhand comment about trying to get us in, but no promises.

The doors opened, and the line finally started to move. Hundreds of us who had waited for hours…bonded by a love not only of the music CBGBs gave us, but also of the electric feeling that comes from the experience you have with a group of strangers when you're part of something truly magnificent together. If you've ever been to one really amazing, really life-changing show, you know that feeling.

When Adam got to the front he told the door guy he was on the guestlist.

"Which one?" the doorguy asked.

Who knew there was more than one?? This was clearly not going to work. We were fucked.

"The house list," he said calmly.

The doorguy walked away and returned a minute later. He put a wristband on Adam and his +1. Then Adam looked this doorguy in the eye and said, "Actually I have a +3."

It was a boldfaced lie. I knew it. He knew it. Lucia knew it. The doorguy had to have known it.

Without hesitation he produced two more wristbands and placed them on Lucia and me.

WE WERE IN.

As soon as we got into that hallowed hall I grabbed Adam and kissed him and told him I was buying him and his friends drinks all night. Certainly it was another miscalculation of funds, even with the pizza money, but it was done in good spirit.

I ran to the front of the club and made it to within about seven rows of people from the front of the stage. Patti Smith stood in front of me and sang and danced and screamed and cried and spit and read poetry. She knew this thing she had been a part of—that she helped build and grow—she knew it was ending. And in that moment she challenged the audience to continue its legacy. She pleaded, "We created it! YOU take it over!" She handed out pins at the end of the night that said, "What Remains Is Future." She handed one to me. Her drummer tossed his sticks into the crowd. I caught one.

After the show I stayed and watched them cut down the iconic awning outside of the club. I went on a 3 a.m. walk through the Bowery with Lucia and our new friend Bobby who we met that night—he had been the drummer for Bad Religion.

I got back to the hostel and whispered to my friend, "I got in."

She gave me side eye that indicated a mixture of overtiredness and slight annoyance. She hadn't expected my plan, or lack thereof, to work, and I could tell she had some second thoughts about leaving. I was still so high on adrenaline I didn't even have the compassion to feel bad. I knew she couldn't have toughed it out like I did.

The whole long flight back home and the ensuing weeks of trying to finish out the semester seemed like a blur. I was constantly exhausted but I felt like I had a new direction in life. A mission. A responsibility given to me by none other than the punk rock priestess Patti Smith. "YOU take it over."

After that show *I* started working the door of a local venue. That same month I started writing about music. Almost 13 years later I still write about music and tell stories and talk to strangers in line. I still think about what Patti asked me to do. I still reach for moments of wild determination and unreasonable persistence because on that night, it was a virtue.

SARAH VENTRE makes podcasts and radio, produces The Moth Phoenix StorySLAM, and is a founder of Girls Rock! Phoenix. She loves chile relleno and red lipstick.

CALIFORNIA GIRL

BECKY BARTKOWSKI

"WHAT."

I croaked out the single syllable, my first of the morning, over pre-work coffee with my husband, unable to contain my groggy but intense rage at the latest TMZ headline: "Orlando Bloom & Selena Gomez All Over Each Other in Vegas."

Are you fucking kidding me, I thought. How could he do this to Katy?

Filled with pictures of the "Pirates of the Caribbean" actor cuddling the grown-up Disney star slash alleged subject of Justin Bieber's "Sorry" at a Vegas club, the story broke just a week after Orlando accompanied unlucky-in-love pop diva Katy Perry to the Met Ball. She bleached her eyebrows and paired leather with velvet. They sported matching Tamagotchis as accessories for the man-meets-machine gala. I deeply disliked the pairing then, but their very silly, yet on theme outfits had nothing to do with it.

Now, though? My girl was being made a fool not because she chose electric blue eyeliner administered à la raccoon, but by a duo who are no strangers to splashy tabloid journalism. Selena and Orlando's history is fairly well chronicled. To quickly debrief:

Selena Gomez has been romantically linked to squirrel-loving manchild Justin Bieber (whose stabs at becoming compelling have kind of succeeded in my opinion). The Biebz reportedly cheated on her, they were on-again, off-again. And during one of their many breaks, it just so happened that Orlando had also split from his wife, Victoria's Secret model Miranda Kerr. Justin bragged about hooking up with Miranda. Then Orlando and Selena were spotted chatting on a curb outside a club. The dramatics culminated with Bloom punching Bieber in his adorably stupid face when the two clashed at a party.

This all worked public-relations wonders for Orlando the time. This was before Bieber's alleged repenting, when we were all signing that petition to deport him back to Canada because he had been spending his time egging people's houses, peeing in janitorial buckets, and drag racing with his father. You know, how dads and sons do. The punch, greeted with cheers heard round the nation, forced us to take a closer look at this Orlando guy. And it seems that in the eyes of Katy Perry, it also marked him a worthy suitor.

The Vegas photos emerged, and Katy referred to them as, I quote, a "dumb conspiracy." But the same masterful pop star who brought Missy Elliott from the abyss to create the greatest Super Bowl halftime show of all time also has a long history of attaching herself to, and this is a technical term, dirtbags. She married Russell Brand, then did time with John Mayer (which is truly upsetting), and now finds herself with Orlando, whom she's been dating for, depending on your news source of favor, a year-ish. Though I am not the sort of diehard fan who wears any of KP's four perfumes, I am the kind of KatyCat who wants better for her, having spent innumerable hours getting acquainted with the artist formerly known as Kathryn Elizabeth Hudson during repeat listening to and loudly singing along with her gorgeously constructed pop masterpiece "Teenage Dream."

I graduated with a degree in journalism in May 2010, the same month Katy released the insta-hit single "California Gurls." I spent that summer first balking at the lyric "sun-kissed skin so hot we'll melt your popsicle," then coming around to its inescapability, and finally becoming a full convert, cranking it up each and every time I found it on the radio.

At the time, I was working at a Tempe, Arizona, record store called Hoodlums, helping customers choose the best Stooges record, deciding how many copies we should order of Sleigh Bells' eyeroll-worthy debut, and coveting used records by reggae-punk girl group The Slits while delving into the Montreal-folk catalog of the McGarrigle sisters. One of my personal triumphs as the only girl behind the counter was correcting a middle-aged white man's pronunciation of Mark Ribot's name, which he made more akin to the sound a frog makes. "Ribbot."

That's not how you say it.

However, I am a tried and true poptimist, someone who doesn't dismiss the value of something because the public at large also enjoys it—nor because one mode of an artist's expression involves shooting fireworks from her pointy bra. I found more music I liked than I could listen to—high art, low, middlebrow. But that summer, there was one sparkly single to rule them all—a song that ended up a weightier anthem for me than anyone might expect.

After months spent applying for jobs across the country in both the music industry and journalism and temporarily moving into my boyfriend's one-bedroom apartment while I attempted to figure out what I was supposed to do with my adult life, I landed an interview that actually went somewhere.

I was invited to spend a couple days exploring Palm Springs, California, while staying at a casino and discussing the possibility of working at the city's newspaper, a Gannett joint called The Desert Sun.

Because I knew I could not spend eternity alphabetizing albums, I decided to give their all-expenses-paid trip a shot. I packed a duffel bag with a few pencil skirts, my laptop, and a notebook—and started to wonder how different it might be trading the Sonoran Desert for, well, another part of the Sonoran Desert.

Hopping on Interstate 10, I was so full of nerves that I ran a red light leading to the freeway on-ramp. I put on the local NPR affiliate KJZZ in hopes that whatever news— good or bad—could distract me from my thoughts. I would pinch my leg and give my face the slightest slap to focus on the voices reading something about whatever, and as a reminder to breathe. But as the horizon expanded and the freeway shrank around mountains and sprawling creosotes, my radio options quickly ran out, lest I subject myself to a station nicknamed "river rat radio."

I've always been able to deep dive on a piece of media that I really like. As a kid, I'd reach the end of my Shania Twain tape, flip it back over and start it again. During my sophomore year of college, I put on "I Heart Huckabees" every night for two months and then did the same with "Sleeping Beauty." Which is why it wasn't so odd that, for my four-and-a-half hour journey to Palm Springs, I had just one CD in my brand new Toyota Yaris. I chose the 44-minute, 12-song "Teenage Dream," Katy Perry's third studio release, which would go on to be the first album by a woman to chart five number-one singles on Billboard.

I thought about what it meant, leaving behind my boyfriend, Arizona, and—if things went well with the interview—the music industry (where I'd worked and interned for three years, a virtual millennium to a millennial like myself). Speeding along, I also thought about a story my childhood friend Rachel told me. She said knew someone whose friend's family was decapitated by an 18-wheeler. I really did not want to lose my head.

So I drove, zipping past swaying semis with boulders on either side. And the CD looped back to the beginning, from Snoop Doggy Dogg on the stereo to the regrettable "Peacock-cock-cock" and "E.T.," a song about wanting to be taken away by aliens that is backed by a beat originally created for Three 6 Mafia. Which is not a joke. There's Daft Punk weaved into disco and sugary teenyboppery. I drove more, stopping only to pee at a McDonalds, buy gas at the neighboring Pilot, and check if the Quartzite mini-mart carried my favorite kind of sour Lifesavers gummies. They didn't.

As I approached the California state line, I began skipping tracks because I needed number three. If I was going to be a California Gurl with a "U," I needed to start practicing being fine, fresh, fierce, and getting "it" on lock.

Between the blasting saxophone solo of "Last Friday Night" and the glittery pat on the back that is "Firework," I heard what I needed to hear—a girl power mantra that's pretty and powerful and pink.

I did get that job. I moved to Palm Springs. I had a terrible time. But over the next year, I listened to "Teenage Dream" I honestly cannot estimate how many more times while road tripping between California and Arizona to visit my boyfriend (who's now my husband).

I like to think that I couldn't have done it without Katy. She had a direct line to me, and when I read about Orlando Bloom being a doofus and the latest bitchery in her spectacular feud with Taylor Swift, I wish I had one back to her, so I could express in pop platitudes something that might be of comfort to her when everything is changing and weird and stupid and unpredictable.

With some backing synthesizers and a dope beat, I'd want to say something like… You'll make mistakes, but there are no take-backs, baby. No matter how hard you try, the answer could be "maybe."

And also electric blue eyeliner never did anybody any favors.

BECKY BARTKOWSKI is the features director at The Arizona Republic. Follow her @beckybartkowski on Instagram and Twitter. Read more at beckybartkowski.com.

EMO SONGS HAVE UNNECESSARILY LONG TITLES AND THIS STORY DOES TOO

JESSICA E. HILL

MY PHONE BUZZED and I glanced at the screen. The notification bubble alerting me of a new text message listed a number, not a name, but I knew who it was. Despite deleting him from my phone a decade ago, he had stepped into my life in a time before every number was saved in a cell phone, and his is one of maybe five numbers I still know by heart.

"Hey there, since you're hip with it in the music biz, I wanted to see if you happened to have 2 tix to Warped Tour you're trying to get rid of," the text read.

The touring punk rock festival had been a summer staple in my late teen years, and it had been announced that the summer of 2018 would be its last full-country run.

I let him know that I didn't have any tickets and scrolled up in the text history. The last text I had sent him was three months prior, congratulating him on the birth of his baby girl, a weird message to compose to someone you once daydreamed with about what you'd name the children you'd have together someday. The chat thread was made up of occasional questions or hellos every three to six months, checking in on how life was going. My phone buzzed with his reply.

"Word. Figured I'd ask the only person I still know crushing it in the biz."

Nick and I had met in our church youth group in high school. He was a gregarious sophomore with pop punk style, seemingly always wearing a hat turned slightly to the side with the bill curved up, Dickies pants and skate shoes. I was a junior with a 4.0 GPA and a schedule packed with college-app worthy activities, hoping desperately that friendships built with the cool kids at my church would help me fit into their group at school. He was a drummer in a local band. I had maybe been to two concerts in my life. He was a flirt and a romantic, leaving notes with flowers picked from my neighbors' yards at my front door. I ate up his attention and fell for him hard.

He took me to shows and my circle of friends quickly became filled with musicians…and the girls who dated them. I learned how to set up his drum kit and often helped with load-in and load-out at his band's shows. Eager to help expose them to new fans, I used my place on the high school student council to create an event on campus and booked his band to play. I had found my spot among a completely different group of cool kids.

Our first kiss felt straight out of a movie. It was January, and we were at the church's annual retreat for high school parishioners, three days and two nights spent in dorm-style cabins in the pines of northern Arizona. He asked me to go on a walk with him one night, and as the distance between us and the main cabin grew, we veered off the path into the moonlit woods. He turned me towards him and pulled a pair of headphones out of his pocket. He gently slipped them over my ears and hit play on the CD Walkman tucked away in his jacket.

"Look at the stars. Look how they shine for you." Coldplay's "Yellow" played as Nick wrapped me in his jacket and we slow-danced under the stars, stars that felt like they really did shine for me in that moment. As the last notes of the song trailed off, he kissed me. He'd perfectly chosen the soundtrack for that moment, the opening song for the mixtape defining the biggest moments in our relationship.

He found a way to repeat the magic for our first I love yous. He'd introduced me to Dashboard Confessional, sure I would love the simple songs of acoustic guitar and vulnerable lyrics. I drove him home one night, and we sat in my '95 Honda Civic parked in front of his house, holding on to every minute we could before I'd have to leave to make it home by curfew.

The lyrics to "Screaming Infidelities" told the story of singer Chris Carrabba, pining after a girl who'd left him. Not exactly a love song, but it was a favorite of ours.

"Your hair is everywhere," he sang. Nick always sang that line the loudest to me, running his fingers through my long, thick hair. That night, as we listened to the song in my car, he pulled me close and held my face in his hands, waiting for the song's last guitar strums to whisper, "I love you." Butterflies filled every inch of my body, but I couldn't miss the moment. I whispered it back in that second of silence between songs.

Our penchant for emo bands was perfect for when we broke up the first time. He'd decided we should take a break, so I could truly experience college and be available to meet new people. He swore we would be together in the end, despite my insistence that I didn't want to date anyone new. A few months passed and when I did go out with someone else, I received a mix CD, filled with songs written by scorned lovers. The leading track was Taking Back Sunday's "Cute Without the 'E' (Cut From the Team)" and its opening line got his point across.

"Your lipstick, his collar. Don't bother, Angel. I know exactly what goes on."

After a year and a half, he asked me to be his girlfriend again. He and his bandmates each still lived at home, so my house became the go-to spot for parties and a crash pad for smaller, touring bands that came through town. Despite how much we loved each other and the fact that we'd always thought we'd get married, I couldn't ignore the feeling that we were moving towards our futures in different ways. I was going to school and working multiple jobs. He was chasing the dream of making it big and living a rockstar life. I was booking bands to play on campus, DJing at the college radio station and running the promotions team for the local alt-weekly. His band was going on occasional tours, hoping to get signed to a record label.

We'd broken up again the summer before my final year of college, with another promise that it was temporary. We were meant to be together after all. And when Nick left on tour that summer, he came through with another song to act as the score for my loneliness and my hope that it would all work out. Plain White T's had written a song seemingly straight out of our lives.

"Hey there, Delilah, don't you worry about the distance. I'm right there if you get lonely. Give this song another listen...Hey there, Delilah, I know times are getting hard, but just believe me, girl, someday I'll pay the bills with this guitar... Hey there, Delilah, you be good and don't you miss me. Two more years and you'll be done with school and I'll be making history like I do. You know it's all because of you."

Over the years, I'd find that practically every girl that dated a boy in a band around this time had been told that *this* song was *their* song. When he came home and we didn't get back together and months passed and we still didn't get back together, I decided I needed to move on. Four years of off-and-on had, as Chris Carrabba had put it years before, "taken its wear."

I graduated the following year and landed a gig producing parties and festivals that featured local food, art and music. It took a few years, but Nick eventually settled on studying respiratory therapy and ended up working in hospitals, helping kids who struggled with breathing, just as he always had. I had found love again with someone I spent the remainder of my twenties with. Nick got married and they had a daughter.

After 10 years at the same company, I was offered a position at a new music venue being built in downtown Phoenix, and it was too good to pass up. A week before we opened, my relationship that had lasted those same 10 years came to an end, and the heartbreak was overwhelming. I threw myself into work, happy to spend every night lost in a crowd of 2,000 people with music loud enough to drown out my thoughts. Working there was what got me through the hardest days after the break up.

The venue had been open nearly a year when Nick sent those texts about Warped Tour. Not long after, he reached out asking if he could come by to see the venue—his band occasionally reunited, and that visit would ultimately result in a reunion show with some other local bands they used to play with all those years ago. As I showed him the space that day, it seemed crazy to me that he had never been there and it was me who helped manage the place. The next day I texted him to thank him for making music a part of my life. It had colored some of my best and most vibrant memories. Finding my place in that world had brought me confidence, and while he didn't know it, in my toughest of times, it had gotten me through.

JESSICA E. HILL is the general manager of The Van Buren, a music venue in downtown Phoenix. She has produced food and music festivals in Arizona and California.

THANK YOU FOR THE MUSIC

MICHAEL ANDERSON

SPENDING THE FIRST 12 YEARS OF MY LIFE OVERSEAS meant that I had a lot of catching up to do when we moved to the States in 1978. Up to that point, my musical tastes were defined by the theme music of Korean cartoons and my dad's fanatical devotion to Pavarotti. Dad traveled overseas quite a bit and would always bring back something for my sister and me. For me, that meant bootleg tapes of the top hits of the late '70s. I was particularly fond of the ABBA and Peaches and Herb cassettes. I can envision my dad running into the airport gift shop in Malaysia and asking the clerk what the "kids" were listening to.

As I began high school, it was pretty apparent that my classmates did not share my love of disco. Wanting badly to fit in, I began to take note of the band names scribbled on the book covers of my fellow students. I figured if a band was good enough for a teenager to scrawl their name a hundred times, they're probably worth a listen. I used my book covers to keep track… the Clash, Sex Pistols, Black Flag, and X all made the cut, but there was one that stood out: the Ramones. Admittedly, there were other names that sounded more rock and roll (Sex Pistols?) but after listening to "Blitzkrieg Bop" I was hooked. I loved the frenetic pace of the music and crushing sound that came out of my tiny Radio Shack stereo. Make way, ABBA—punk rock is taking over.

I managed to make some great friends in high school, and we bonded over our love of music. More than one afternoon was spent in my buddy Dave's room listening to the newest record from bands we were sure made us cooler just by listening to them. When the record needle hit the song "Alex Chilton" on the Replacements' "Pleased to Meet Me" album, I knew I had to see the band live. The next day, we bought tickets for their show at the Living Room, and I spent that evening making a homemade concert t-shirt.

I had heard of the Living Room but hadn't been there yet. That part of downtown was "iffy." Driving into the parking lot for the show, I remember thinking that this was the coolest thing I had ever done. For those of you who haven't had the pleasure of attending a performance at the Living Room, imagine what a condemned building might look like and then add awesome. The club wasn't very big but instantly felt comfortable, like a living room. The floors sagged with years of beer, sweat and urine, and the place smelled of bleach. We shoehorned our way as close to the stage as we could get and waited. The Replacements took the stage and the crowd swelled forward like a tsunami of teen angst. We danced and sang along with the boys as they tore through their set, singing one anthem after another. Every so often, someone from the crowd would be launched into the air and was propelled toward the stage on the raised hands of the exuberant crowd. After the band played their encore, the house lights came up and we surveyed the scene. My once artfully drawn Replacements t-shirt was now soaked with sweat and the ink turned into a smeared black mess that bled onto my skin. I remember smiling. A lot. Dave and I knew that we had been part of something special. The Replacements played their hearts out, but there was something about the Living Room that made an indelible mark on me. This, I thought, was what made music real. It was then that I resolved to see as many shows at the Living Room as I could.

It seemed like I was at the Living Room every weekend seeing bands like the Pixies, Husker Du, Throwing Muses, and finally…the Ramones. Records are fine, but if you wanted to experience the Ramones, you had to go to a show. Ramones shows were involuntarily participatory. As the band peeled the paint off the walls with a nonstop barrage of sound, the crowd was enlisted as backup singers yelling the chorus of each song at the top of their lungs. If you were there on a special night, Zippy the Pinhead would make an appearance by running around onstage and would sometimes dive headfirst into the waiting crowd. Since the Room was part of the Ramones' standard East Coast tour stops, I managed to catch a few of their shows, and each time I left drenched in sweat with the biggest smile I could manage.

By the time 1988 rolled around, I felt like I knew what good music was. I mean, I listened to bands that no one had heard of, had a very punk rock leather jacket and was constantly going to shows. While reading the paper one day, I noticed a help wanted ad for a security guard. Not a particularly appealing job, but as I read further I saw the location: the Living Room. I think I may have broken all the speed limits on my way up to

Providence. I drove into the familiar parking lot and ran up the stairs that I had climbed many times as a spectator. As I waited to speak with the owner, Randy, I was struck by the gravity of the moment. Me? An employee of the greatest club in Rhode Island? For reasons that I don't understand to this day, I was hired.

Unless you were a bouncer with seniority, you never really knew what job you'd have for the night until you got there. The senior guys got to cherry pick the best shows and jobs, leaving noobs like me with the leftovers. You might be doing a load-in, which is when we'd help the band schlep in equipment from the van/trailer/truck into the club, or it might be as simple as working the door, checking IDs and collecting the cover charge. There was one thing you did know: who was playing that night. Who was booked dictated the kind of night you'd have. It didn't really matter to me what show it was, I was in. Being on the other side of the crowd was everything I hoped it would be. I met some of my music idols and saw the love they had for what they did. I gained an entirely new appreciation for what music gives people, especially me.

I was relaxing at home late Saturday morning when I got a call from Doggie, one of the bouncers from the Living Room. Dog asked me if I could cover his shift for him that night. I was kind of looking forward to a day off, but I was still fairly new and really wanted to impress the other bouncers. Before I committed, I asked, "Who's playing?" "Hang on," he said as he looked for his schedule, "…the Ramones." I'd forgotten that the boys were back in town. I couldn't get "yes" out of my mouth fast enough. After being a face in the crowd, I'd have an opportunity to meet the band that launched my love of rock. The shift was a load-in/show combo, which meant I'd be at the club pretty much all day. I hustled down in hopes of meeting the band but instead had the pleasure of moving 143 Marshall stacks.

After a long afternoon, I was sitting at the bar when I saw a tall, slender figure came through the front doors. Kind of looked like a mop turned upside down. It took a minute before I realized it was Joey Ramone. Joey. Fucking. Ramone. There were a few pinball games in the corner of the club that no one ever played. Joey locked on them and shuffled toward the one with the brightest lights. As he got closer, I said, "Hey Joey! Big fan. Looking forward to the show." Without altering his gaze, he replied "Mmmfrhfs." In his right hand, he held a clear Ziploc bag full of quarters. He plunked them on the glass of the pinball machine and started to play. I quickly realized that Joey was no pinball wizard, but he seemed to really enjoy playing. As Joey played, I continued to talk at him. I say "at him" as he didn't reply to anything I said. Well, not in English anyway. After what seemed like hours, Joey grabbed the bag and the few quarters he had left and shuffled back toward the green room. A few hours later, the Ramones took the stage and played one of the best shows I've ever seen. It seemed like Joey flipped a switch and became Joey Ramone, rock legend. The wall of sound that Joey, DeeDee, Marky, and Tommy produced was deafening in the best way possible. The three-second pause between songs was just enough for Joey to yell "One two three four!" I can't recall what I did as an employee that night, but I do remember shouting "Hey ho let's go!" about 50 times.

The Living Room is long gone but music continues to be an important part of my life. I still go to shows (but not every weekend), I still look for that new band that no one has heard of, and I still smile every time I hear "Dancing Queen."

MICHAEL ANDERSON is a music lover and community advocate in Phoenix.

THE HEALER

JESSE TEER

"I swear to fulfill, to the best of my ability and judgment, this covenant..."

THAT'S WHAT MY GRANDFATHER SAID at his med school graduation in the early 1950s. A lot of programs shied away from having their graduates recite traditional Hippocratic oaths by the time my mother became an M.D. in the '80s. In early memory I waited up for her to come home from working late rotations. It's hard work, honorable hard work, healing folks.

On summer days my brothers and I would run around her office. It must have always been a real hope that one of us would carry on her father's legacy. I remember "sitting in" on a prenatal ultrasound when I was about six. Hank, a giant, very hairy and loveable imaging tech, showed an expecting mother her baby while a strange six-year-old stood at her side.

But one day my father dusted off his old set of Zeppelin vinyl. I turned my cello (a promising tool for reeling in a college scholarship) onto its side on my lap and strummed it like it was a guitar. A *damned guitar*. The disappointment was clear when I told my folks I wanted rock and roll to be my career path.

So, I quit the Phoenix Youth Symphony and got a ride to some seedy west side spot where I sold the poor cello, which, at this point, must have been a little confused about its own orientation.

I walked down to ABC Music, a hole in the wall that housed a guitar teacher named Milo, and got myself a loaner electric guitar. It was a bright yellow Gretsch. It was so rock and roll. I'm so not rock and roll. But that guitar gave high school years a real purpose. I was hooked.

That guitar, being previously used and banged up, didn't even come with a case. I walked myself over to the music shop twice a week, sweating in the summer, holding the bright yellow Gretsch over my shoulder. Passing cars honked; whistles came in my direction. I was *never* cat-called before, and haven't been since. That guitar was a piece of crap, but it made me feel *so* cool.

So that's how I broke my mother's heart for the first time, and with it, I broke some promise of doctoring that she continued to hold me to through the years.

Now I realize how bad at songwriting I was at first, but it was addictive and I spent all my time on it. Not attending your classes at the University of Arizona gets you failing grades. So after one year in Tucson I just drove away. I fled the state for California as a college dropout with a handful of very poorly written songs and a cloud of disappointment hanging over my childhood home in the rearview.

* * *

Some failed "bands" later, and I was back in Phoenix. I lived in my '94 Honda Accord. Bridges were still scorched with my family. I came back, though, to the promise of a new act, new guys, very talented guys. We still sucked, in retrospect.

But I started listening to Cash—real Americana music. Real stories. And the first song I ever recorded was about that promise that I hadn't really set out to break:

(*Sung:*)

> *"Don't lose your way back home // the world's a bigger place now // don't lose your way back home now, boy."*

Music is good when it is honest. I knew that much. And I kept chasing it until I did eventually have to grow the hell up. I think I just got tired of being poor, living in my car, falling asleep standing upright during shifts on stockroom floors. So I decided to put the damned guitar away.

It really wasn't for a lack of effort that I failed to realize any scrap of success then. Maybe this was just my 40 years in the desert.

* * *

And a few years later, I graduated *summa cum laude* with a Microbiology B.S. from ASU. In that last year of college things were good again with my folks. Med school applications were in the works. I was about to head off to Africa to do HIV intervention work. But I couldn't go.

I hadn't played a guitar in years. When my brother came back from Memphis we started writing songs. I guess I just needed a partner in crime. So I lived a double life: writing a folk album with Adam while I got ready for medical school. When we had that album finished I gave all thoughts of Hippocratic oaths and white lab coats up, for good this time.

Again came a high degree of parental disappointment and disownment. I suppose that's how I broke my mother's heart a second and final time. But we were driving around the Southwest playing good music. And I met Lauren.

I wrote a song for her back then that might have been all about her and just as much about music. I didn't realize it at the time:

(Sung: 'Battle Hymns' verse and chorus:)

> *I have the same sweet dream // under a Cherry Tree // I lay down my axe and I kiss your lips // you send me reeling...*

> *... Love it won't let me be // I hear a symphony every morning // I wake to the same refrain // It's been you all along knocking at my door // I sang my battle hymns // you you're a sweeter song*

> *You were in white // dressed like my honest lies // you took my hand and ran down those steps // still don't know where it ends*

We first kissed on a stranger's front doorstep in San Diego. She came to see me play a show there. I fell in madly love with her that weekend.

After we married, Lauren asked me to make a different promise, one that I could not have expected and one that I cannot break. She asked me to swear that I'll never stop writing music. That I'll never ignore this burning feeling deep down in my gut to share music with you. And, to play my damned guitar.

Lauren is right. Folk music—all music—brings people together. It's me being honestly me. And it turns out that it is healing. Maybe my mother is more right than she realized. Maybe someday she'll come around to it.

I couldn't, like my grandfather did, swear to do no harm.

But I can promise that I'll keep on singing medicine.

And I'm the most proud that my little boy loves to sing and dance and strum the damned guitar.

JESSE TEER is a folk musician and songwriter, performing with Phoenix-based The Senators. Find him on instagram @senators_music and thesenatorsmusic.com.

BURNING MUSIC

RACHEL ESEOGHENE EGBORO

LIKE MOST PRETEENS, I hated getting up in the mornings. I'd set my clock radio 30 minutes early so I could press the snooze button every 10 minutes until I gradually awoke at 6:30, when I'd finally slide off my bed and into the bathroom.

One Monday morning, I was going for an extra snooze when instead of hitting the button I knew so well, I tuned the dial up from 90.3 FM—Phoenix's Christian station—to Power 92.3 and Missy Elliot was telling me how Supa Dupa Fly she was. I was intrigued. My head moved in a way it never had before. The DJ announced that I'd just stumbled upon Phoenix's hip hop station.

Next up was "What's So Different" by Ginuwine. By the bridge I was sold.

But I have a dilemma…because Ginuwine not only asked "what's so different," but "what the H-E-double hockey sticks is different." Secular music and a curse word!

It was too late to go back. I was already awakened to a new world.

As the eldest of two this was truly uncharted territory. Especially because our media intake was highly censored. Only the Christian and education stations were allowed. My dad had this uncanny ability to sniff out any missteps with his super papa powers. And our disobedience, such as sneaking out to go trick or treating, watching a soap opera or earning a grade lower than a B…these missteps were never worth the discipline (i.e., spankings) that they incurred.

My dad ran our house with the same strictness he experienced in Catholic boarding school—except he couldn't send us home when we stepped out of line.

So he sent us to church. A LOT. It was my second home. There was always something going on: youth group, play rehearsal, choir practice, Bible study. I participated in these activities…sometimes. Other times I'd skulk around the parking lot searching for God in the stars. I always made sure to return to my seat in the back before the end of service. My parents were delighted that I spent so much time with my church friends—because what could possibly go wrong?

In youth group, I rocked out to a song similar to "Smells Like Teen Spirit." Both songs were rallying cries for independence and rebellion—in their own ways. The song was "Jesus Freak" and it was written by a band called DC Talk. One of the lines from the song comes from the bridge and it goes:

"People say I'm strange. Does it make me a stranger, that my best friend was born in a manger?"

Cheesy, right?

Us *youthers* would head bang and mosh and air guitar like we were hardcore. We looked like any other group of teenagers who hated rules and occasionally our parents. Our dark clothes reflected our dark moods and we claimed the term "freak" with pride because…we were freaks…freaks for Jesus.

Once a year the church held a bonfire. Anything illicit, mainstream or secular was up for burning. Magazines. Books. Music. These items were highly discouraged because once you exposed yourself to them you were highly likely to backslide right into sin.

I remember watching my mix tapes curl and their jeweled cases melt in the flames. I'd say a little prayer and say goodbye to 112, the Fugees, B.I.G., Aaliyah, Jay-Z, Busta Rhymes…. After that mental inventory of everything I was losing in the fire, I vowed to never listen to secular music again. To read my Bible religiously. And to honor my parents like the commandment says.

I'd stay on track for a couple days. Maybe weeks. Then one of the college kids in the house behind ours would blast "Killing Me Softly" as they drove through the neighborhood. The car would be long gone by the time I realized that I had earworm. And the best remedy for earworm is to listen to the actual song that's stuck in your head. Fortunately, I'd held onto one favorite mixtape while the rest went up in flames during the bonfire. "Killing Me Softly" was the third track.

I crouched next to my boombox and played the song as softly as I could. My parents were in their room down the hall and this was before I had my own portable tape player. But soon my inner monologue overpowered even Lauryn Hill as I tried to reason with my guilt:

Is this a sin? Would God really mind if I listened to this one song? If I died tonight would I go to hell because of this one song?

I promised to repent as soon as the song is over. But it's never just one song. I listened to both sides of the tape before I remembered myself and my promise.

There was just something about secular music. The lyrics. The riffs. By the time the bridge comes along my heartbeat and the bass are one and I'm dancing like a freak in my own music video.

Music was my own private rebellion. The more hip hop I listened to the more R&B I discovered and vice versa. I began to express myself in dance and writing in ways that I never felt like I could before. It was like I'd found a new dictionary to accurately express my angst.

Christian music sounded more bland and cheesier than ever. The musicality went way down without the sex, money and drugs. These subjects provided a soul that my spiritual music lacked. I was being turned on to all these new sounds and Christian music wasn't cutting it for me anymore.

In junior high Brandy and Monica dropped "The Boy Is Mine." I identified most with Brandy. Obsessed. I even wrote a story called "In a Waxy Build Up" where we switch places after I touch Brandy's wax figure and I take her place in the middle of a concert. And of course, in the story, we both loved each other's lives and become best friends.

Her CD had a permanent place in my Sony Walkman and I knew all the words to the title track. One afternoon, I got sloppy and left the CD case out on the dining table. Brandy is artfully suggestive on the cover with the hint of a tube top arm piece thing. The rest of her body is left off the cover and up to the imagination.

I'm sitting at the computer checking Myspace and watch as my dad picks up the case and examines it.

He holds it up. "Is she Christian?" he asks.

"Yes," I say. "See?" I point to the last sentence on her list of thank yous. "She's thanking God on the album cover."

"What's this about?" he asks, pointing to a song on the list of tracks. "Who is He?" The song is called "He is" and I quickly say, "*He* is Jesus."

"Mmmmm," he says gazing at the list. "And this?" He points to the song titled "When You Touch Me."

"You know... like the Holy Spirit."

You get the picture. Convinced, my dad puts the case down and leaves me to it.

A week later my dad, enlightened by a friend who was more in touch with the mainstream, takes my Brandy CD and cracks it in half with his bare hands.

I apologized and played innocent. I told him one of my church friends gave it to me as a present. I tried my best to look aloof and focused on Myspace even though my musical rebellion had been outed. On the inside I was freaking out that he'd want to inventory the rest of my musical library.

He didn't. Thanks to Napster I replaced that CD with a burned copy and eventually stopped dealing with CDs all together once I got an iPod.

These days my dad has come to accept my taste in music—as long as he doesn't have to listen to it. I still go to church, albeit it's not my second home anymore. And Christian music has come a long way since the '90s. Now my Spotify is a mix of Christian, hip hop, indie-pop and anything else that's just good music. And I gotta say... I still love me some Ginuwine.

RACHEL ESEOGHENE EGBORO is the creator and story cultivator of The Whole Story, a live storytelling series that repaints Black narratives at Phoenix Art Museum.

FAMILY

FOOL ME ONCE

KATIE BRAVO

I'VE COME TO ACCEPT that there are certain things in life that I will never understand.

I will never understand the premise of purely decorative fruit trees.

I will never be able to reason with the existence of scented tampons.

And I will never ever wrap my head around why my dad thought it was a good idea to leave me on a roof 22 years ago.

My parents were divorced long before I could walk or talk—not that anything I could have said would have stopped them. Never have I known two such opposite people to willingly enter into a union together.

My mother is like Oprah. She's a good listener, a highly empathetic person, and, while they might not be hidden under your seat, she likes to surprise people with gifts.

My dad, on the other hand, is like the universe. He's dark, hard to reach, and utterly indifferent to your suffering.

While my mom is vehemently opposed to firearms, my dad believes that guns, much like scented candles, are easy go-to gifts for any holiday occasion.

He attempted to give me a pistol for my Sweet 16, a shotgun for Valentine's Day a few years back, and I can only assume what will be waiting for me in his pickup come Christmas.

My father is a character. And I don't mean that in a silly, two-dimensional Donald Duck sort of way—though they do both share an affinity for not wearing pants.

My dad looks like a Greek George Clooney, but with a slight lisp and a cowboy persona. He's wildcard, complex and unpredictable. And when I was kid, he had custody of me every other weekend.

It was anybody's guess what would go down in our 48-hour visits. Sometimes we would go camping, occasionally we would go out to his favorite fine dining establishment, Hometown Buffet, but most of the time, due to my father's lack of a stable job, our activities resided at home.

Technically it was my aunt's home. My dad lived there with her and her two boys. Their dad, my uncle, was in and out of prison for drugs most of our childhood. So, in exchange for his not contributing much in the way of utilities, my dad acted as a sort of interim father figure for his nephews, and incidentally me—when I would visit.

Going to my dad's every other weekend filled me with a mix of emotions. I imagine it's a lot like what climbers must feel as they're preparing to scale Mount Everest. You know you're going to walk away with a great story, but you also know that you might not walk away at all.

That's because my dad has his own obscure definition of fun; the type of humor that evokes both LOL and PTSD. He gets a laugh out of what other people might find traumatizing.

My earliest memory of my father and of his comedy happened when I was roughly three years old. It was monsoon season in Arizona, and the cacophony of rain and thunder was scaring the shit out of me. As I started to cry, my father put on his most comforting demeanor and assured me that everything was going to be okay. He convinced me to put my little hand in his and follow him outside so I could see for myself that the storm really wasn't that bad.

Spoiler alert: It was that bad.

As soon as we stepped foot on the front lawn, he let go of my hand, grabbed me by the waist, thrust me up to the sky, and yelled, "Take her! She's ready! Take her!"

I screamed and writhed in his arms, waiting for the lightning to strike. He laughed and brought me back inside. As my eyes opened and my body unfroze, my fear slowly faded and new sentiments began to wash over me. I felt shocked. I felt angry. I felt... straight up betrayed.

While I didn't have the necessary verbal skills to express it at the time, this moment set in motion what would eventually become my lifelong mantra: Fool me once, motherfucker.

And so it went, every other weekend for years I would wonder, what godawful prank did my dad have in store for me and my cousins? What fun exercise did he have to remind us of our own crippling mortality?

His usual antics included letting go of the steering wheel when he drove, so that I, out of sheer instinctual panic, would take over from the passenger seat, or catching my cousins and me off guard around the home so he could indulge in what seemed to be his favorite hobby: pulling out our arguably loose baby teeth.

But the peak of my father's pranks, the pièce de ré·sis·tance of really sticking it to us, happened not on the ground but on the roof.

My dad was watching his one true love, televised football, when the reception started to get fuzzy. As he headed outside to fix the antenna on the roof, he invited my cousins and me to join him.

Naturally, we jumped at the chance. I mean, what other eight year olds did I know that had been up on the *roof* of their *house*? As we followed him outside, I imagined the spectacular views that came from being on top of the house. I figured there were probably hidden treasures up there, relics from previous residents and maybe a skeleton....

In reality, it was mostly just pine needles and bird poop. And since we lived in a one-story ranch home off 19th Avenue and Northern, the view was nothing you'd put on a postcard. It was also a fairly steep pitched roof so any chance of active exploration was inhibited by the fact that we had to side step in any direction to maintain our balance.

Once my dad finished adjusting the antenna, he climbed back down to the front of the house. My cousins and I lined up along the rain gutter and extended our arms toward him in the classic help-me-down gesture, but rather than reach out to grab us, my father smiled and took a few steps back.

"Jump," he said.

Confusion spread across our faces.

"You heard me. Jump. I'll catch you."

I turned to look at my nine-year-old cousin Tyler as though to say "Can you believe this guy?" But he was already in mid-air. A minute later, my seven-year-old cousin Carson followed suit.

Now it was my turn. I stood there, knees trembling. Had it gotten colder? Had the house gotten taller? Why did the three of them suddenly look so far away?

They all yelled up at me, "Jump, Katie! Just jump! It will be over with in a second."

I shook my head and stepped back from the edge. "No. No I don't want to jump! I want you to help me down!"

"No dice," said my dad.

After some back and forth negotiations, my dad decided that he was going to back inside and finish watching his game.

"Let me know when you're done being a baby and I'll come back and catch you."

I carefully sat down on the black pebble shingles and watched as the three of them disappeared from sight. For dramatic effect, I really want to tell you that I was up there until the sun came down. But being that I was eight, it was probably more like 15 minutes.

I thought maybe a neighbor would see me and call the police. Maybe I would just wait out the next 24 hours until my mom shows up. Maybe my dad would cave and come help me down the way I wanted.

Realizing that none of the options seemed likely, I eventually yelled for my dad. In a minute, he was back out on the front lawn.

"Ready?"

"No," I said, standing up.

He stretched out his arms to catch me and I bent at the knees.

"Okay," I thought. "One... two..."

I pushed my feet off from the roof and fell through the air. Within seconds I landed abruptly in my dad's arms.

"That's my girl," he said as his hands held me firmly by my armpits.

I turned my head to look back at the roof—much to my embarrassment, it really *didn't* seem as high as it had a moment ago—then I turned back to face my dad.

I realized in that moment just how strong he was, how I weighed nothing in his arms. I smiled at him.

Of course he could catch me. He was always going to catch me.

Then I dropped the smile, released myself from his grip and muttered, "Butthead" as I stomped back into the house.

Over time, the weekend visits with my dad became less and less frequent. Though we've never been estranged there have been times when our relationship certainly was, well, strange.

While he's not going to win father of the year anytime soon, I do believe that my dad is not a bad person. His child-rearing skills fell somewhere on the spectrum between good intention and "good god you did not think that one through."

I've even considered that, in his less than stellar moments as a parent, instilling fear in my formidable years, it's possible George Johnson was trying to bestow something worthwhile to me. Maybe he wanted me to learn early on that life wasn't fair, so I wouldn't be disappointed later. Maybe he wanted me to learn to take risks or learn to not be afraid of anything. My therapist and I would argue that has backfired miserably. Or maybe, in his own roundabout way, my dad just wanted to say he didn't raise no fool.

KATIE BRAVO is a writer-turned-marketer and a co-creator of Bar Flies. You can follow her on Twitter @heykatiebravo.

I'VE BEEN WAITING FOR YOU

ANGELICA LINDSEY-ALI

I HAVE GIVEN BIRTH TO FOUR CHILDREN: two sons and two daughters. I never wanted to be a mother; the Divine had other plans in mind. Before I met the man who is now my husband, I would often proclaim that I would never get married or have children. My plan was to travel the world and live a blissful, child-free life. Mohammed was a blind date. He had a deep voice and gentle, slanted eyes. He looked like a Dogon statue come to life. It wasn't quite love at first sight, but I knew he was my destiny. A mere six weeks later, we were married.

I knew the instant I became pregnant. I spent nine months in alternating states of awe and disbelief. I birthed my first child, a son, in July 2005 with no medical assistance, helped along by my doula and my husband. My second child, a daughter, was born into a pool of warm water, in January 2008. Both of those first births were magical, unusual, and very hard. Witnessing the sheer power of my body to morph, yield, and surrender to the power of birth left me feeling strong but terrified.

We were living overseas when I prayed for her. I had sworn to not have any more after 35 but I couldn't deny the small yearning I had for another child. I walked often and prayed, asking for guidance and ease. I asked the Divine, if it were a good thing, to allow us to expand our family. A month later, I was pregnant at age 37.

The next nine months were abnormally blissful; I had none of the ills afforded pregnant women. My body seemed to rejoice at the fact that it was once again heavy with life. My skin glowed, my energy soared. Even as my belly grew round with the impending arrival, my face remained slim, leaving me with pronounced cheekbones and a delicate collar bone, even at 38 weeks. I made hajj while eight months pregnant, fascinating everyone with the show of strength as I trekked through the rites of the Holy Pilgrimage. I rested and supplicated and bonded with my unborn. It seemed that the third time's the charm, indeed.

That morning she came, I couldn't sleep. The day before, I had worked a full day. At 39 weeks pregnant, I was doing too much but my energy levels were high and my mind felt bright so I went full throttle. My doctor's appointment was scheduled for 9:30 that morning and I had hoped to sleep until at least 8 a.m. Somewhere around 4 a.m., I woke up feeling achy.

For the next couple of hours, I prepared breakfast for the children, prayed, and dozed off intermittently. At irregular intervals, I would feel a wave of pressure, cramping, and pain. I would breathe, drink copious amounts of water, and recite "Allah will not give me more than I can bear." When the pain subsided, I would drift back to restful sleep.

By 7 a.m., Mohammed woke up and was watching a Western on television. I fell asleep somewhere between the opening credits and the height of the action. A gunshot from the television and a simultaneous kick in my belly woke me up at about 8:30. "You should get up and get ready for the hospital," Mohammed said. I tried to slide off the low couch on which I was sitting and, as I moved, I felt the rhythmic pain of a contraction coming. I closed my eyes and breathed through it. It was a week too soon but this was almost starting to feel like the real thing.

I walked to the bathroom and almost made it to the shower before the waves of pain began again. The water was warm, like a womb, and I stood there for several minutes just letting it cascade over my face, neck, and shoulders. I turned so the water could caress my lower back. Painful pulsing gripped my back and lower abdomen, such that I lost my balance and grabbed the wet wall for stability. This might be it, I thought. One after the other, every few seconds, the pain ebbed and flowed. After the fourth wave, I shut off the water; this time, the pain was stronger. I released a loud wail, unconsciously and unwillingly. I could feel myself opening below. My body felt prone and eager. The bones in my spine felt as though they were being ripped apart like a sheet of paper. Mohammed poked his head into the door: "What is it?" "I'm not going to make it," I replied. This was, indeed, it.

I left the bathroom and headed to my room to get dressed, contracting along the way. I tried to slip a gown over my head, but pain seized my limbs and I stopped short. I instinctively got down on my bed, on all fours, with my face on the bed and my bottom in the air. The breeze from the fan was cool on my body and brought welcome relief. By this time, the waves were steady and constant; there was no space between. Mohammed looked in again and, without saying a word, went to call an ambulance. I could hear him in the other room trying to give directions. Just then, a pain so deep and ancient took hold of my body and I let out a long, deep groan. He came running. I told him not to leave me. He insisted that he had to finish something; I can't remember what it was. I reached out and grabbed his hand and begged him to stay. He knew that look and obliged. He got down on the bed and listened. Bring warm water and towels, I said. Close the door and make sure the children are occupied. Come back quickly. He was back in a few minutes with everything I requested. He took his position behind me; I instructed him to press the bones in my lower hips together as my body undulated with each progression. This was it. She is coming. It was a week too soon, but she was here. I felt my body involuntarily begin to push. I breathed with an open mouth, trying to get my cervix to imitate my lips, waiting and full. I wanted ease and openness; I needed relief.

On the third push, her head was suspended halfway between my body and the world. She was stuck. All of the pain had come so quickly, it left me limp and weak. I tried pushing without urge. It didn't work. She didn't budge. I stopped and breathed; I could feel her tiny head moving back and forth. "Please, babe, please try," Mohammed said. I felt the urge to push and surrendered my last bit of strength. I pressed my hands into the bed and steadied my knees. I felt fire as I pushed; her body tore away from mine. She was free. I turned to see her cradled in her father's hands. She was bloody and tiny, but she was alive and breathing.

He handed her to me, still connected to the umbilical cord. I carefully maneuvered my body to a resting position against the wall. I cradled her in my arms. "I've been waiting for you," I said. She opened her eyes and looked at me. Just then, the children came in to greet their sister. She smiled when she heard their voices. The ambulance came and I listened to the doctor aboard marvel at how I must be American because this was "just like a Hollywood movie."

I woke up hours later, alone in a private room. I eased myself slowly out of bed, grabbed a mirror and walked to the bathroom. The torn space between my legs was awkward and bulging. I became lightheaded when I saw it: a tangle of surgical thread and dried blood, swollen, in some places, gaping. I could see the flesh underneath the skin protruding outwards. This was not right. Somehow, the doctor had left me mangled and deformed.

For weeks afterwards, I couldn't sit properly without pillows. I felt shredded and broken. The scar that I was left with reminded me of a crooked French seam turned inside out. It is slanted, running slightly perpendicular to the organic folds of my body.

During my 30 minutes of labor, it was as if all nine months, all three births, had hit me at once. Everything was perfect, but the timing was not my design. Rushed, impulsive, wild, free, this is how she chose to enter the world. When I look at her now, a bright and talkative five year old, I am reminded that once, in a faraway place, I was a warrior.

ANGELICA LINDSEY-ALI is a sex health educator, intimacy coach, and avid storyteller. Follow her on Instagram and Twitter @villageauntie.

DRINKING OUT OF CUPS

ANNA MICHAEL SUSSMAN

GROWING UP with a narcissistic sociopathic drug addict for a father, I never really understood the whole "fatherly love" thing. My friends would go to Daddy Daughter dances, I watched my father throw up in a metal pot while driving me to school. When I was very little, I loved my father. I trusted that he would protect and care for me, because he helped bring me into the world. Narcissists don't want their children to be safe, or to grow up and be happy; they see their child as someone to mold into a replica of themselves. So I was civil but distant toward any kind of father figure that entered my life. I didn't particularly like any of my mother's boyfriends, and I thought of any men in my household as an obstacle and a nuisance, just one more thing I would have to worry about when they inevitably went bad.

It was the same way with my mother's most recent boyfriend, now husband, Neil. While my mother and I are both outspoken and emotional, Neil was introverted and level headed in a way that I couldn't understand. He was an artist that I had first met when I was 10, when I modeled for his sculpture of Alice in Wonderland. He brought me clay to play with and let me read "Twilight" while I posed. He and my mother eventually began dating and I was hopeful, but when he moved in with us when I was 13, I was not happy. I hated having to share a house with this person I felt like I barely knew. And I especially did not like having to share my mother, the one person I felt had always been only mine. We protected each other and didn't need anyone else. So, in my mind I wrote Neil off too. Sure, he lived in my house, he made dinner, he asked me about my day, but I was sure he didn't REALLY care and I was just waiting to bring out the *puke bucket*. It went on like this for a couple years, until one day that I mostly refer to as "The Pot Brownie Debacle."

It was a lovely Wednesday afternoon in November. I was 15. My best friend Shay and I had gotten out of school early, and, while loitering at the Chipotle at CityScape in downtown Phoenix, she and I hatched a devious plan. My mother was in California taking care of my uncle, who had just had major surgery, Neil would not be home until late afternoon. So we decided there, that day in a Chipotle bathroom, to eat pot brownies. These particular brownies (we had two) had been stolen from her older brother, who was about 27 at the time, and Shay had snuck them out of the house and to our school in her backpack.

We were giddy as we used a coffee stirrer to delicately slice a brownie in half. We made eye contact as we bit into them and there was an air of complete excitement, the excitement of doing something you sure as hell know you shouldn't do. The brownies were terrible. But we dutifully finished our halves and put the other brownie back in her backpack. We exited the bathroom, giggling, and ran to the light rail.

Now, those of you who have eaten edibles before probably know that it takes about an hour for the effects to kick in. We did not know that. And after about 30 minutes of sobriety we decided they must be weak and we should definitely split the other one. On the light rail. So we did. And as we got closer and closer to the Mill Avenue light rail stop, I began to feel really weird. I stared out the light rail window and the stations passing by looked swirled together and that made me think of soup and suddenly I was unbelievably hungry.

When we got to our stop, Shay and I stood up and stumbled off the train. We found ourselves standing in front of the Mill Avenue Starbucks which, coincidentally, is building number 420. I laughed loudly. People stared. We went in and I ordered a hot sandwich and a vanilla chai, which I nursed on the bus stop bench outside. At this point, I didn't just feel weird, I was weird. The world was beginning to look sloppy, the people passed by in slow motion, and I was maddeningly aware of each number of chews it took to masticate the individual bites of my sandwich. Eventually, I realized that Shay was sitting next to me whispering, "We gotta get home, we gotta get home, we gotta get home," like a woman possessed. So we got up, at which point I have been told that I looked her in the eyes and announced loudly, "WHAT A LOVELY SIT DOWN" before falling backwards onto the ground. Somehow, we continued on our journey home.

By the time I got to the Subway Sandwich Shop, I was seeing symbols. The world in front of me looked crudely drawn, like someone had scribbled just enough for me to make out a sidewalk, a building, a tree, but the details were entirely lost on me. We finally got to my house, after almost getting hit by several angry drivers. We fell through the front door and onto the floor of the front hall. I crawled around aimlessly for what seemed like hours until I finally realized that the music I heard was in fact coming from the radio on the table. I clicked it off and we collapsed onto my bed. I figured the worst was over.

I guess we must have fallen asleep, because the next thing I know I'm waking up to gagging noises. In a dreamlike state I grabbed Shay and ran her to the bathroom where she began to vomit (see, this is where the puke bucket would have come in handy). In my fucked up state I thought, "Oh god, if she's throwing up I BETTER THROW UP." But since that bathroom was occupied, I ran to the next best place I could think of. No, I didn't go into the other bathroom in our house, conveniently located only one room away, I ran outside to the backyard and made myself throw up in the grass. It was at this moment, on my knees, with my fingers down my throat, that I knew we both needed help. So I called my mother. My poor, tired mother taking care of her sick brother in another state answered the phone and immediately began to panic. Like I said, my mother and I are both outspoken and emotional. So she called Neil. When I heard from my mom that he was coming home from work in the middle of the day, I was ready to get yelled at—no, more than that, I was ready to fight. But he just walked in the door humming. Hung up his jacket. Got Shay and me water (again and again and again, since I apparently could not keep track of a cup for the next 12 hours). And then he put us to bed at 3 in the afternoon. That was it. No yelling. No panicking. No epic fight scene.

The next morning, while slumped over the kitchen table, drooling into my frosted flakes, I realized that Neil did care. Neil was everything a father should be, consistent, wise, and there when you need him. I had spent so long experiencing this one facet of a father: a screaming, sweating, drug-addled man who made my mother cry, but I had never actually had a healthy male role model in my life. I went back into my room and saw all the elusive glasses of water, on the floor, on my shelves, perched on the edge of my windowsill, and I smiled. Neil recently said of the experience, "I just kept coming in and making sure you were alive." See? Not a panicker. So it was that day, that fateful afternoon in November of 2013, that I lost my mind on edibles, but in a way, I gained a dad.

ANNA MICHAEL SUSSMAN is an artist, writer, and musician from Tempe. Follow them on Instagram @_milkbat and find their music at annamichael.bandcamp.com.

JUST CLAIRE

EVIE CARPENTER

I'M GETTING TO THAT AGE.

A few weeks ago, I was grabbing lunch with a friend and she was ranting about the price of things in the restaurant. "How do they think they can charge $10 for juice?" she asked, appalled. Then she stopped, turned to me with her hand over her mouth and goes, "Oh my god, I sound like my mother."

It's inevitable. Nature, nurture, and all that. But for me, it's not my mom I've been resembling, it's my grandma.

Aunt Claire was an... eccentric person. Oh, sorry. You're probably a little confused. I did just say "Aunt Claire." For most of my childhood, I knew my grandmother as my aunt... Aunt Claire.

I'll explain.

Aunt Claire's my dad's biological mother. She gave him up in an under-the-table, made-for-TV dramatic adoption when he was born because she wasn't in a place in her life to raise a child. And to this day, my dad doesn't know who my grandfather was… is? Who knows? Aunt Claire would just say, "He was a public figure."

Thanks to the illegality of the adoption, there were very few rules except that Aunt Claire was only allowed to contact my dad through his adopted mother. She rarely did so.

That is, until my older brother and I were born.

Aunt Claire viewed us almost as a second chance at raising children. Equipped with years of "wisdom," plenty of time on her hands without a family of her own, and the financial means, she couldn't wait to get her hands on us.

But my brother and my infant self already knew a grandma and grandpa, my dad's adopted parents. So we were introduced to Aunt Claire.

This worked perfectly fine until my brother was about 11 and realized what an aunt was. One night at the dinner table, he asked my parents, "Wait, Aunt Claire is really old. Whose sister is she?"

The makeup she slathered on could only hide the wrinkles so much, and it always took her a few extra minutes and the assistance of my dad's arm to get up the stairs.

Aunt Claire and my parents had to come clean, but the title of "Aunt" stuck for a few years, mostly out of habit.

When I was about 10, Aunt Claire decided she wanted to eliminate any memory of the lie she'd been a part of and stop having us call her Aunt.

She thought "Grandma" aged her too much, so we dropped a title all together. From there on out, we simply knew her as just Claire.

If I'm completely honest with you, I hated Claire growing up. And if I'm honest with myself, it's because my pre-pubescent self was jealous of my 60-something year old grandmother.

Claire had a way of grabbing people's attention, and being the baby of the family (both in age and maturity), I did not like this. We rarely got through a meal out without returning a dish to the kitchen at least once and meeting the apologetic manager. And I don't know how many hours of my life were wasted waiting for Claire to finagle her signature flesh-toned pantyhose over her stocky 5'2" frame.

Claire always had a flare for the dramatic. From her oversized designer handbags to the stifling amount of spicy, sweet perfume she'd coat her neck and wrists in, Claire made sure she was noticed.

As a young professional living in San Francisco in the mid-'70s, Claire made a living owning her own business—an "escort service," she told us, handing my brother and me hot pink matchboxes with her company's logo, a suggestive female silhouette, wrapped around them.

At the time, of course, my grade-school aged brother and myself had no idea what an escort was, but my mom's bugging eyes and pressed lips told me it wasn't something I should ask questions about.

But Claire quickly abandoned her business when a tragic accident opened the door to an early retirement.

While Claire was living in the Bay Area, running her "escort service," her car decided to drive itself down one of San Francisco's hilly streets, off the road, and into the Bay while consequently almost severing Claire's foot at the ankle.

Claire lost the ability to point her right foot but gained a slight hobble in her walk and millions in a settlement deal with Toyota.

By the time I knew Aunt Claire, she had used part of her settlement to buy a condo on the 17th green of the PGA West golf course in Palm Springs.

When my family and I would drive from Phoenix to visit her, we would spend the last half hour or so putting bets on what color her hair would be. I would say red, my brother would say black, my mom would say blonde, and my dad would try to refrain from joking about his mother.

Once, we were all wrong, and Claire had dyed her hair a deep brown except for one section framing her face that was bleached completely white. She'd put her hair in rollers and looked like a skunk with a white stripe stretching from the very front to the back of her head.

But no one said a word because Claire did what Claire wanted.

When I was about eight, I crawled into Claire's closet and found what I thought were a magical pair of silver, metallic sneakers. As I reached my tiny hand out for them, Claire found me and snapped at me not to touch them.

They were her pair of designer tennis shoes she only wore to walk her dog, so instead of picking up his poop, she could just kick it into the nearest bush. She called them her shit-kicking shoes.

I have one memory from my childhood of Claire being grandmotherly, or trying to be, at least. I was about six and had the stomach flu. I woke up early in the morning, needing to "get sick," as Claire would have said. I ran into the bathroom, but only made it to the sink before my time was up, if you know what I mean.

I was so proud that I didn't ruin a fiber of her pristine white carpet, but she was still furious that I'd tarnished her porcelain sink. Unable to look at the mess or me any longer, Claire drove off with my dad and brother in her golf cart to the country club for breakfast, leaving my mom and me at the condo.

A few hours later, I woke up to the sound of pantyhose-covered feet shuffling across carpet. Claire hoisted herself up onto the side of my bed and handed me a glass.

"Here, hun, this will make you feel better."

In an attempt to help me, Claire had brought me a glass of the worst thing you could put in an upset stomach—orange juice. She didn't know better, but she was trying.

Claire died from cancer in 2005. At her memorial service, I remembered the time she told me I didn't have a long enough neck for turtlenecks when I was 10 and the time she scolded me for eating unhealthy, salty green olives while making herself a dirty martini. I kept these memories to myself while the other guests talked about Claire's charitable heart, her ability to make any stranger instantly feel like a lifelong friend, and her knack for telling stories.

Now, 10 years later, I'm starting to catch glimpses of Claire in myself. I first started noticing similarities earlier this year when I looked in the mirror and almost jumped because I saw her instead of my own face—the mannish chin she gave me, her round eyes that I try to diminish with liner.

I resented these traits, and promised myself the similarities would stop at the genetic level. I vowed I'd never be like my grandmother, reckless or self-centered. But there's more of her in me than I realized.

Like the ease with which I can now talk to strangers, or my own unintentional, yet lively flare for the dramatic, or even my own not-so-perfect driving. I don't want to talk about that last one.

I'd be lying if I said I was fully embracing my Claire-ness now, strutting into any social situation with her classic silk pants and loose top hanging from just one shoulder. (Claire did always say the shoulder was the most attractive part of a woman's body.) But I'm getting there.

If I could go back, I'd listen more carefully or humor her when she introduced me to an acquaintance as her own child perhaps in an attempt to seem just a bit younger than she was, or I'd ask her what her secret was to keeping those silk pants wrinkle-free, but I'd never be caught dead with a pair of shit-kicking shoes.

EVIE CARPENTER is a photographer, writer and one half of Trader Hoes, a Trader Joe's fan podcast. Follow along on Instagram @evie.hollis and @realtraderhoes.

MY DAD'S A BOXER

JACOB A. MEDERS

MY FATHER MET MY MOTHER in Virginia in the mid '70's. He had an afro, and she had long very long hair just past her ass. She had a horse named Tina, and he was—from what I've been told—an all-state athlete.

-My dad, he's a boxer.

My father would send love notes to my mother in high school using Led Zeppelin lyrics. Any time I hear "Over The Hills and Far Away," I think about my mother and father when they were young.

Hey lady, you got the love I need
Maybe more than enough.
Oh darling…walk a while with me
You've got so much…

Before they were 20, my sister was born. My father named her Ali…. A-L-I.

-My dad, he's a boxer.

My father flirted with the idea of going to college, but my brother was on the way. So joining the Navy ended up being the direction he went—because at 21 he had a family to support. He worked in Intel—Intelligence—and was good with computers.

My father, as I remember, was strong, fast, and showed us love all the time. He'd take us to baseball games and let us ride on his shoulders when walking down the street. It never felt like there were any problems in life, and he would always be there to protect us.

-My dad he's a boxer.

My father liked to have a good time and would drink a lot with his buddies when he was home. He started to get angry, and it would get scary. He wasn't one to back down from a fight and at times was quick to knock someone out.

My father would show us how to hold our fists and throw a jab and a punch. Fists up and feet light, making sure your hips rotate and snap that punch through the target. It would be good for us to know how to protect ourselves at the ripe age of four or five.

-My dad he's a boxer.

My father seemed to have problems at work, because the Navy sent us to Adak, Alaska. From what I've heard, you get sent there when the Navy isn't happy with you. I'm not sure my father cared.

We lived next to a cliff in Adak and one day a young boy hit my brother with a stick when we were climbing the cliff. I think it was an accident, but when we got home, my father was mad. He told my brother that he needed to go find that boy, and hit him real hard right in the face. I was sent to go with my brother to make sure he did what he was told. My brother did what he was told, and I believe he still feels bad about it.

-My dad he's a boxer.

The ground would shake in Adak, and so would the house. It was the first time I remember feeling the house shake from an earthquake. We had two lab puppies when we lived in that house, and my father would get real mad when they shit on the floor. One day he was so mad he picked up one of the puppies and threw it down the hall. It hit the wall real hard. I can't remember if the puppy even made a sound when it hit the wall. I thought it was dead.

My father started to target my mother and would hurt her badly. He would drink so much he didn't even know what happened the night before and would ask her who had hit her. I became afraid of my father and would start to get worried when I knew he was coming home.

-My dad he's a boxer.

My father couldn't stop, so my mother left him and took us with her. We moved to Virginia without him. She would say how much she loved him but didn't want her sons to be like him. He didn't stay in the Navy for very long after that, and he moved to Philly. My father didn't want to lose his family and kept trying to get us all back together.

My father slipped deeper into his drinking and now drug use. He would fight more and once put a man in the hospital because he beat him so badly. I stopped hearing from my father as I moved from elementary school into middle school. Every couple of years, he'd make a phone call when he was drunk and tell us how much he loved us and missed us. He'd even send us birthday gifts every few years when it wasn't our birthday. He tried—when he could—and I respected that.

My father ended up in the hospital once. I came home from school, and my mother said a few men jumped him and took him to a field where they cut him up with a farming sickle, leaving him there to die. It was said that one of the men was a guy my father had beat up and put into the hospital. We thought that my father was going to die, but he didn't.

-My dad he's a boxer.

I go to visit with my father a couple times a year now. He's in his sixties and has gotten a little slower. He still battles with substance abuse and some days are better than others. He works at an olive processing plant in Northern California doing a young man's job. He looks pretty good considering all that he's been through, but his eyes are tired and hands are worn and hard. He rarely talks about the present or the future, just mostly about the past.

-My dad he's a boxer.

JACOB A. MEDERS is an artist and professor at Arizona State in Phoenix. He's also the owner and Master Printer at WarBird Press.

MALCRIADOS

MARISA HAMBLETON

"¡QUE CHINGADOS HICERON!" I yelled at the boys, looked around, and expected to spot my dad. Jonathan, my son, and I lived with him. My nephew David was visiting us in El Paso from Arizona for a couple of weeks. The boys were fond of their summer visits and spending the day with grandpa while I was at work.

I came home that day to find Jonathan and David, respectively eight and seven, tied upside down, one to each leg of the aluminum swing set, our dog, Curtis, pouncing around licking each of their faces. Curtis was hyperactive, naughty, and misbehaved consistently, digging under the fence, getting into the plants, chewing up the garden hose, peeing on the car tires; he was unruly in every way a Springer Spaniel could be.

I had imagined life going so differently. Coming home to yet another crisis no matter how minor never felt normal even if it was a regular occurrence. Being a single mom, living with my dad, and needing his help wasn't exactly the plan I had for my future.

My dad's own stories about being incorrigible resonated in that instant. The story about when the nuns at the Catholic school had had enough of his shenanigans and sent him down to the basement pantry, to el sotano, to pray. He told the story of his expulsion often. Or telling of the pranks he'd play on unsuspecting relatives, where he'd set lady-finger fireworks on the outhouse window sill as they sat on the wooden throne.

It was far easier for me to summon his stories of picking cotton with his grandfather, my great-grandpa, when he was too young for public school.

I can't say for certain which points sparked those deeper emotions. Unlike the spry look he'd get as he told his tales of mischief, the fondness in his voice was palpable when he recollected time spent with his grandparents. He'd go into a focused gaze as if to look for something far away in the distance, then talk about it as if it had happened just the other day. Like his story of enjoying a hot lunch prepared by his grandmother Teresa when he went to work in the cotton fields with his grandfather Francisco.

My dad would recount his pre-school years in a child-like manner, he'd go on about everyone's efforts, "Mí mom, she went to put me in school, but they wouldn't take me because my birthday was too late in the year. So, she left me with my grandma Teresa and my grandpa Francisco while she went to work."

He'd paint a magnificent picture of these pleasant moments during his early childhood years. "My grandpa made me a little basket so I could go with him to pick cotton, a piscar algodon. My grandma would fix us lunch. Sometimes she would make sandwiches, burritos, a thermos of caldo, or whatever. Y vez en cuando she made us tamales.

"We'd break off the stocks del cotton, they were dry, ya estaban secos, we'd put 'em in a pile, and light 'em up. They'd get like coals and we'd put our food there to warm it up, the tamales or burritos, either way.

"Y el cafe— I remember the coffee that my grandma nos hacia. Hijola estaba pero buena, coffee, milk, y sugar—grandma Teresa she'd be a little heavy on the sugar.

"It was SOoo good, mija. Los tamales medio tostaditos bien suave."

I expected poignant facts; instead, he'd share his calculations and the simple things he noticed. "I was around six years old and I remember that first few weeks of picking, I think it took me almost two weeks maybe more to make my hundred pounds. My grandpa Francisco and the other men would make their hundred pounds in a day. But they had regular size baskets, mine was little.

"You know how much they paid you for a hundred pounds? Three dollars. That was a lot of money for me back then. A movie and Coke was a quarter. I'd be able to see a lot of movies for three dollars!"

He was not yet six years old working the cotton fields, enjoying himself, innocently unaware of the situation. Instead, he was absorbed into his keen observations, the camaraderie of the laborers, and the lovely experience of eating tamales with his grandfather, a meal perfectly prepared by his grandmother.

Compelling, yet ordinary for that place, that era, esa epoca, it was the epitome of amistad, that made such sweet memories.

"MoOOom," Jonathan moaned. "Tía Marisa, untie us!" David pleaded.

I shooed Curtis away to examine how they had been fastened to the swing set. They were secured in a combination of knots I had never seen the likes of. Whatever it was they did, I knew it must have been really terrible for my dad to tie them up—easily accessible to the dog. The boys had vivid imaginations, but sometimes their idea of creativity was just plain bad.

My dad received Curtis from a friend and thought he would make a good hunting dog, but the endeavor was short-lived. He didn't retrieve or track very well, he'd run aimlessly into the desert, jump from the back of the truck, and needed too much supervision to be anything more than a family pet. He occasionally needed to be tied up to prevent him from running off when the gates were open. Curtis was my dad's companion and that afternoon another playmate for Jonathan and David.

I wondered if my dad regretted sharing stories of his own tomfoolery with the boys as they ran around the back yard seeing what ill-intentions their imaginations could conjure. Exploring and playing races with Curtis didn't seem like enough fun and the two little malcriados let their inner-maldito get the best of them.

The boys loved their grandpa. They were joyfully oblivious that being a rascal is a family trait along with the long-held tradicion of grandparents spending considerable amounts of time with grandkids while moms went to work. It's what we did, it's who we were. Our familia extended far beyond the nucleus of parents and children, it was neighbors, cousins, friends, everyone—and it never occurred to me that life could be any different. I suspect as much for both my parents and my great-grandparents. My mom with her Welita Bolita. My dad with his grandpa Francisco. The boys with their grandpa Eddie. It takes a barrio.

My dad would tell the tales with a little glimmer in his eye recalling his own mischievous youth. "When I was your age, I was pero mas travieso."

After getting the boys untied, I learned the details of the afternoon and precisely what they had done to get themselves attached to the swing set.

Jonathan and David had grown bored of running around and had decided to include Curtis in their backyard adventures. They put his leash on, led him back to his water bucket—which was held up with its handle over a stake to keep it from tipping over—and thought it would be more fun to make him run in circles so that he'd tangle himself up on the post.

The boys hadn't counted on their grandpa catching them. Nor had the cruelty of the act occurred to either of them.

As my dad retold his version of Jonathan and David's misbehaving incident, he made sure to point out the moment when he caught them in the act, "¡Ande traviesos! ¿What are you doing to el Curtis?" and explained to me that the boys had been warned of what was about to happen next. "¡When I catch you, me los voy a sonar! You're gonna get it."

The boys made it worse when they each bolted off in opposite directions. They were no match for their grandpa, whose legs were as long as they were tall, who ran faster than they did, and was strong enough to scoop them up with one hand. An early lesson on staying put, as it was better to wait and accept the consequences rather than trying to run away.

One at a time my dad had tied them up, upside down at dog-height, so they would know how Curtis felt to be trapped and teased. My dad recounted the incident in a matter-of-fact manner. Surprisingly he wasn't angry. The type of memory this day would create was still in question.

He knew the origins of their mischief. Looking sideways, he whispered under his breath, "¡Chavalos malcriados!"

MARISA HAMBLETON is a technology professional who enjoys telling tales of growing up in El Chuco. Find her online @marisahambleton.

MRS. WISWALL

TERRY GREENE STERLING

SOME OF YOU MAY KNOW I'm a journalist, but few of you know I grew up on a cattle ranch in Yavapai County.

I was the only kid on the ranch.

My dark-skinned blue-eyed father and my elegant blond mother were not your typical cattle ranchers.

They dressed up for dinner every single night and drank Dubonnet and Martinis and played Mozart on the record player and devoured the Sunday New York Times, even though it always arrived two weeks late.

Our life was completely normal to me.

But deep down, I wanted to play with other kids.

So when my mother lugged the heavy yellow suitcases off the top closet shelf, I was filled with mixed feelings of elation and dread.

Elation because I'd soon be playing with my cousins in Cananea, Sonora, Mexico.

Dread because we were going to visit Mrs. Wiswall.

Mrs. Wiswall was my grandmother.

I didn't call her nana.

I didn't call her abuelita.

I didn't even call her abuela.

She was Mrs. Wiswall.

And hanging out with her made me sad, and I didn't know why.

* * *

Our long car trips south, from the ranch to Cananea, began before dawn. I sat in the back seat of the Ford station wagon with Dina and Vilma, our Austrian-Italian-Mexican maids.

About seven hours later, we'd cross the border into Sonora.

The Mexican border agent would sometimes wave us through.

But sometimes he'd be in a good mood, and he'd joke about how we should have asked Mrs. Wiswall's chauffeur to drive us down in Mrs. Wiswall's shiny black sedan.

I was five years old.

I'd translate what the Mexican border guy said, because Dina and Vilma pretended they couldn't hear anything and my mother's Spanish wasn't that good and my dad didn't understand Spanish.

It took us another hour to drive to Cananea, and most of that drive was through Mrs. Wiswall's ranch.

First, we'd drop off Dina and Vilma at their parents' house.

You should know that Mrs. Wiswall had recommended my mother hire Dina and Vilma because they were white girls.

I asked my parents, how come Dina and Vilma and practically everyone else in Cananea lived in tiny houses and Mrs. Wiswall lived in the Big House.

My parents would glance at each other and not say anything.

The Big House sat on top of a hill. It had white pillars and shaded verandas and an orchard in the back and vegetable gardens and a bunch of back buildings that included a carriage house where the chauffeur parked the shiny black sedan.

We'd drive through the wrought iron entryway, past Mrs. Wiswall's beloved rose garden.

Mrs. Wiswall waited for us on the veranda in her tailored dress from I. Magnin and her sensible shoes from Huggins in Pasadena. Her thick curly grey hair was perfectly coiffed.

So elegant. So reserved.

My cousins and uncles and aunts would come for dinner.

We kids were expected to be on our best behavior, all dressed up for these candlelit dinners just like our parents.

We sat quiet as could be at the long dining room table set with a lace tablecloth and Waterford crystal and Victorian monogrammed silver flatware from Tiffany's.

I often sensed a well of sadness in that elegant dining room.

I wanted to fill that well of sadness, so I ate and ate and ate.

There was this one New Year's Eve when I ate way too many tamales with raisins.

Suddenly and without warning I vomited a Niagara Falls of tamale chunks. All over Mrs. Wiswall's lace tablecloth. All over the Victorian silver from Tiffany's.

Oh boy, I thought, I'm in trouble now.

Mrs. Wiswall is going to kill me.

But instead, Mrs. Wiswall pretended not to notice. She glared at my disproving aunts and uncles, my giggling cousins, and my astonished parents.

She rang the bell and a bevy of servants cleared off the table, reset it and served dinner all over again.

No one said a word.

No one dared.

* * *

The only time I remember touching Mrs. Wiswall, she was dead.

Mrs. Wiswall lay in a casket in the Cananea Catholic church.

My father lifted me up and I leaned over the casket and tried to wake up Mrs. Wiswall by touching her folded hands.

Maybe then she'd tell me her secret.

But her hands were granite-hard and she didn't wake up.

I would have to learn the secret on my own.

* * *

Several decades later, I stood on a bluff overlooking the Santa Cruz River.

By then, I already knew that Mrs. Wiswall's family history had been fabricated.

Her ancestors were not prominent white people who traced their lineage to aristocratic European families.

Actually, Mrs. Wiswall was what they used to call a half-breed.

Maria was her name.

She spent her early childhood with her Mexican mother and her American dad and several brothers in a little adobe house on the very bluff where I stood.

The walls of the little adobe were still there. I walked inside.

On one wall someone had spray painted a sign that said illegals go home.

* * *

This is what I pieced together about Mrs. Wiswall's childhood.

She was orphaned at 10. First her dad died of an infected wound. A few years later her mom died of TB.

Maria was adopted by a white couple in Tucson.

She was separated from her dark-skinned brothers and told she must never see them again.

Since Arizona had been part of the Confederacy, the border region had more than its share of Confederate refugees who didn't much like Mexicans.

If there was a crime, you blamed a Mexican. And then you lynched him.

So Maria became Mary.

Mexicans were dirty, stupid, lazy. This is what her new mother told her, day in and day out.

Mary felt she had to be twice as white as everyone else, just so her new parents would love her.

And she did a really good job of it.

She married a very rich white guy. They built the Big House in Cananea, but Mary made sure each of their six kids was born in the United States.

That rich white guy died 11 years later. Mary was a wealthy widow. She married another white guy, Mr. Wiswall, a few years later. Mr. Wiswall died when I was a toddler.

I don't know much about these two husbands, because Mrs. Wiswall never talked about them.

I kind of doubt Mr. Wiswall knew too much about Mrs. Wiswall's secret.

Did Mr. Wiswall know about his wife's dead Mexican mom and the banished brown-skinned brothers?

About the little house overlooking the Santa Cruz River?

About the lonely weight of sacrificing half of yourself just to survive and be loved?

Mrs. Wiswall never let her guard down. She had to pass for white because she had been told so many times that the other part of her was so despicable, she believed it.

Protecting that secret for almost a lifetime fostered the quiet sadness in the Big House in Cananea.

It created the hole I sensed as a child and tried to fill with tamales.

And I know it fueled my father's shame of his Mexican DNA, a shame so deep that he pretended he didn't understand Spanish.

* * *

Every Day of the Dead weekend, I visit the Cananea cemetery to make sure Mrs. Wiswall's grave is clean and well-tended.

In a few weeks, I'll once again wash off her granite headstone.

You know, I feel weirdly close to her these days, now that I understand her sacrifice.

I've forgiven her for her unapproachability and distance, for her reserve.

So I'll get down close to that grave, and I'll lay roses at the base of the headstone. I'll sprinkle chocolate Hershey's kisses around the roses.

And I'll tell her as long as I'm able to write, I will shine a light on the evil that forced her into her secret.

Because that evil still exists today. Especially in Arizona.

Te quiero mucho, abuelita, I'll say.

TERRY GREENE STERLING is a journalist, author and teacher. Find her at terrygreenesterling.com.

HOME ALONE

MARISOL CHAVEZ

I KNEW I WASN'T GOING TO MAKE IT. I was going to be forced to act, one way or another. I was nine years old, I was locked outside, and I needed to poop. Urgently. I wasn't even at my own home. I was at my mom's boyfriend's house. GREG. No offense to any Gregs out there, but Greg is the perfect name for your mom's boyfriend in the late '80s. He looked like a total Greg too: a big paunchy belly, those '80s wire rim glasses, a weird bristly mustache, and graying hair that was combed over to cover his growing bald spot.

As you might be able to tell, I wasn't a huge fan.

Part of why I didn't like Greg was, for the most part, my life had mostly been just me and my mom. I was an only child, and so all her attention was focused on me and making me happy. This was the first time that there was someone encroaching on my bubble of affection. My mom was my whole world. She was perfect and angelic…until Greg came along. Now instead of me and my mom, it was my mom and Greg, with me on the outside, looking in.

I tried to hold back my complaints against this relationship. Maybe it wouldn't last! She had dated a few other men before Greg. They all went away pretty quickly, and maybe Greg would too. He didn't. Soon their dates turned into whole weekends spent at his dumb house. Every trip there felt like a slow drive into the pit of despair for me.

My mom was different during these weekends. Normally, my mom was very straight-laced due to growing up in a very religious and conservative family. But when we were at Greg's house, it was almost like she could feel the need to be just like everyone else in our family fall off of her, and she could relax a little. She could have a drink, which my teetotaling family would never approve of. She could finally feel some physical affection from a man, eight years after her divorce.

But remember, I was also raised in this conservative Christian family. I picked up on the rest of my family's feelings towards the secular world, and I ran with it hard. When I saw my mom drink for the first time, I'm surprised I didn't call our pastor on the spot. I saw my mom and Greg kiss and I knew he was dragging her straight to hell with him.

In order to save my mom from eternal damnation, I started desperately trying anything to keep us from going to Greg's house on the weekends. None of my attempts worked. I tried begging, I tried crying. I'm pretty sure I even developed a psychosomatic allergy to Greg's dogs. Even though I never had a problem with dogs before, I started breaking out in hives when I spent any time at Greg's. It didn't make a difference. My mom would give me an allergy pill and my scheme was shut down.

It was around this time that I started developing a food addiction. Up until then, I was a mostly active kid who may have eaten a few too many Happy Meals here and there. Now I was in full on binge mode. I started hiding snacks to eat when no one was watching. My aunt even caught me once hiding in her kitchen, shoveling down a box of graham crackers. They didn't even taste that great. It was just a way to feel satisfied, somehow. It didn't help matters that Greg started poking fun of my growing chubby body. Yet another reason for me to hate Greg.

One afternoon during one of these weekends at Greg's, he and my mom had left the house to go have some time to themselves, and I was left at home alone with the dogs. So I did what any food addicted nine year old would do. I raided the pantry. Maybe this would be the last straw that would cause him to break up with my mom. One day, he would open his pantry, discover all of his expired candy canes were gone, and he would decide that he couldn't date my mom anymore. I wasn't too picky as I munched my way through his food. My only rule was I would eat anything as long as it had sugar in it. Chocolate that had turned white from crystallization, stale marshmallows, ancient and inedible astronaut ice cream; I shoved it all down. I then filled in any empty spaces by drinking pancake syrup, direct from the bottle.

Stuffed to the gills and a little sugar high, I searched for something to occupy my luxurious time alone. It was a nice Southern California afternoon, so I thought it might be cool if I took my worn copy of "A Wrinkle in Time" and read outside instead of in his stuffy house. Greg had a secluded front yard, enclosed on all sides by tall shrubs, so it would be kind of like reading in my own Secret Garden. I stepped outside, closed the door behind me… and I heard a click. I twisted the doorknob that was still in my hand. No luck. I was locked out of Greg's house. Oh well, I figured. Mom and Greg would be back soon, I assured myself.

The calm attitude lasted about five minutes before it hit me. The mix of expired marshmallows, astronaut ice cream, and syrup started churning in my stomach. If it wasn't a sin to use a curse word, I would have used all of them. I knew what that bubbling feeling was. I was going to have to poop, and Greg did not have an outdoor toilet. I started panicking. I tried the door again. It hadn't magically unlocked itself in the time I was outside. I raced around the outside of the house to find that every possible entrance was sealed. I thought about my choices. I was going to go, one way or another. But there was one option that would take care of business AND be an act of defiance against my mom's relationship with Greg at the same time. I made sure that the coast was clear, dropped my shorts, and left a little pile of protest right on his front patio.

Once the act was done, I felt ashamed with myself instead of proud and defiant. When my mom and Greg got home, I blamed the innocent dogs who were locked out with me. Greg gave me the greasy eyeball, knowing full well that what was left on the porch most definitely did not come out of one of his dogs. But, to his credit, he kept his mouth shut and we all silently agreed that we would never bring up this moment again.

In the end, the protest poop didn't work. My mom and Greg ended up dating for a few more years, but when I was 11, I did something far more shameful than what I did on Greg's front porch that day. Throughout their whole relationship, I had been in my aunt's ear, like a little mosquito, telling her every one of his faults and the sins that my mom was committing with him, like some sort of child narc. Finally, one night when we were at Greg's, I couldn't stand it anymore and called my aunt, begging her to take me away. She came over and had a confrontation with my mom, telling her how irresponsible she was by being in this sinful relationship. I remember sitting in the front seat of my aunt's van while my mom stood by the window, crying and asking me why I didn't want her to be happy. I stayed silent as my aunt pulled away. I didn't have an answer for her then, but I know now that I was being selfish. That day, I forced my mom to make a decision between me and her happiness with Greg. She chose me. My mom hasn't dated anyone since, probably because she never wanted to have to make that decision again.

Once Greg was out of the picture, it was just me and my mom again, just like I wanted. But as time moved on, our tight rubber band of a bond has stretched out. We aren't as close as we used to be. We barely talk anymore, and when we do, it's usually a random text from her about work or her dogs, that I forget to respond to 50% of the time. Now my mom is the one on the outside, trying to find any way to get in to me. I know I need to let her know more often how much I love her. I need to be the one to reach out to let her know that the door is unlocked and that she is always welcome to come inside.

MARISOL CHAVEZ is an improviser in Phoenix. You can usually find her at The Torch Theatre, or at her Instagram @modysoul.

THREADS

CINDY DACH

WHEN I WAS SEVEN, my grandmother tugged at her earlobe and said, "You see these diamond earrings? When I die, these are yours."

When I was nine, my grandmother said, "When you grow up, never be a wife. Be a mistress, because mistresses get jewelry. Wives darn socks. Sometimes mistresses also get a nice apartment in a downtown high rise."

My grandmother was born in Russia in 1910. When she was an infant, her father immigrated to the United States—for opportunity, for the boot straps that our country used to offer. He took a boat to America to find his brother-in-law in Detroit who gave him a job as a carpenter. He sent money for his wife and child to join him, but my great grandmother wasn't interested in leaving her life in Russia. She taught dance, was close with her parents and had a secret love interest.

Seven years later, due to the programs and racism, my great grandmother and my seven-year-old grandmother left Russia by way of Japan. In Japan, when they ran out of money, my great grandmother pulled out her sewing kit, sat on overturned buckets and darned socks for American soldiers. They earned enough money to take a boat to America and find my great grandfather. He was with a mistress who didn't realize she was a mistress. The situation sorted itself out, and my great grandparents had four more children.

My grandmother was fierce and determined and helped raise her four younger siblings. She became a wife, a mother of two—my mother and her brother—a successful interior designer, a divorcee, a woman known for her dinner parties, a mother who survived the death of a child, and a skilled poker player. My grandmother and I adored each other. When I was young, I wanted to be a businesswoman like her. I loved going to the design showrooms. She was known as the lady with the fancy hats, which she did intentionally to be remembered. We would select fabric for the couches and pillows of her clients. At least I believed I had a say in all that.

* * *

When I was 11, my grandmother told me that I should not be a virgin on my wedding night because that would be a terrible time to find out that my husband did not know what he was doing.

My father was furious with her advice. My father was a very religious man. We had an orthodox, kosher home. We did not speak of virginity or the lack of it. My sexual life was up to my future, religious husband. My grandmother was a non-observer and sometimes sinful. My father was a fundamentalist at heart. However, he was a businessman and this was their bond. They admired each other and often sought advice in areas of business.

My grandmother told me that it was just as easy to marry a rich man as a poor man. I just needed to find the right circle of friends. My father mostly agreed, but insisted that the circle should be connected to a synagogue. My grandmother instructed me to always have my own income because a rich husband could take a mistress. My father agreed with the first part.

In college, I pursued a business degree and before graduating, I had a position as a salesperson in a fabric company. I was the first female salesperson hired at that firm, and the established male clients would say to me, "I got ties older than you."

I was 22. I was living in New York in a rent-controlled apartment in SoHo. I had a good income and a fantastic wardrobe mostly purchased at sample sales. My favorite part of my job was walking through the fabric warehouses getting sample cuts for my clients. I loved the colors and touching the textures. It was the most inspiring part of each day.

My grandmother had retired and moved to Florida. She was remarried, going on cruises and still assisting some clients—the ones that had also moved to Florida. We didn't see each other as often, but she was incredibly proud of what I was becoming. We spoke on the phone, and I would mail her fabric samples that she would turn into tablecloths for dinner parties.

* * *

Within four years, I hated my job. I loathed the drama of contract negotiations. I was resentful when tempers flared because of a snowstorm that delayed fabric getting to a cutting room floor. The industry was dominated by men who slammed down phones and kicked doors. It was decades before the Me Too movement, and sexual harassment was a way of doing business. I was 26, and I wasn't prepared. I had financial freedom but no solid footing.

I took a vacation out west, and decided that there, in all that space, I could find myself. I could be a woman who hiked and camped.

I returned to New York and without talking to any family or any friends, I walked into my office and gave 30 days notice. I was moving out west. I told my parents the following weekend.

What was I going to do, every single person asked.

I was going to hike and become a writer, I announced, like a spell had been cast and thus it was true.

I loved to read. I loved stories, and I figured if I just worked hard, I could be a well-published, self-supporting author.

I took my commission check, my wardrobe, bought a Jeep and drove west.

My grandmother was furious.

My father was flustered.

I had everything going for me and there I was throwing it away so I *could go camping*.

I applied and was accepted to an MFA program for creative writing. My commissions paid for graduate school. I then boomeranged for the next 10 years trying to find that balance between talent, purpose, and maintaining a roof over my head. I was a freelance writer, wrote a novel, earned some money as a photographer, worked as a cater waiter, a bartender, a teacher in a hippie alternative high school, taught Comp 101 and 102, and worked as a gardening assistant trimming the heads off of pansies. I liked to hike, but discovered I preferred a bed and a hot tub to actual camping.

* * *

I was 28 when my grandmother died. The first flight back east was the following morning. The man that would eventually become my husband took me ice skating. He had never met my grandmother, but had listened to my stories, and said that ice skating seemed appropriate.

I was living my life picking and choosing from my grandmother's advice. I wasn't a virgin. My future husband did not come from money. I had never found that circle of friends. I was self-supporting, but barely hanging on.

When my grandmother died, my mother inherited the diamond earrings, as originally prescribed. I inherited my grandmother's wedding band, a beloved necklace, and yards of fabric samples.

I eventually found my balance in bookstores and events and management and a way to make a living through the power of words and community.

* * *

The last five years of my father's life was spent in and out of hospitals. His cancer had come with experimental surgeries which led to emergency room visits and overnight stays. My mother would call, and I would fly home. In his hospital rooms, we sat in silence. My father and I had a difficult relationship. He was a good man and had always provided, but our religious difference was a tear too large to mend. I sat in those hospital rooms to give my mother a break. I sat there because my father deserved not to be alone.

Sometimes, breaking the silence, he would ask about my life, "How many cats do you have?" Or, "Are people still buying books?"

I would ask, "How are the Yankees doing?"

The answers were always the same. The Yankees were always doing well and I always had cats.

It was difficult sitting in that silence. I tried to read books, but there were disruptions—a sudden question from my father, a nurse taking blood or the television playing conservative news. The Tea Party was all the rage.

When I could, I went for walks. Memories of my former self materialized on street corners and evaporated down avenues. I went to the fabric showrooms and treated myself to color and texture. I thought of my grandmother and great grandmother and not wanting to leave it behind, I purchased fabric, thread and an embroidery hoop. In my father's hospital room, I taught myself to embroider.

* * *

My father died at home under the care of hospice. I inherited his film camera, his dog tags from the Korean War, and a leather briefcase with a broken clasp. These objects are on a shelf in my studio. I have no use for them, but cannot dispose of them. It's not the sentimentality, but the stories they hold. The ones no one hears.

I continue to embroider. It helps me be still. It helps me stop working after a long day. It brings my grandmother, my father and my great grandmother into my world. My husband makes me custom frames, and I sell some of my pieces. I've seen them on the walls of strangers' homes secretly holding my threaded history.

* * *

My mother lives in Brooklyn, but she winters in Florida in a 55+ active living community. They have art classes, movie nights, and bus rides to shopping centers. They have regularly non-scheduled estate sales, or *estate giveaways*. When I last visited, we went to an apartment where the family had asked the maintenance company to *give it all away*. My mom took a blown glass vase and a swivel chair. We examined silverware, family portraits, and needlepoint pillows alongside the bedpans and oxygen tanks.

I became overwhelmed by my mother's future passing. I was sad that I would wear my grandmother's earrings and I had to step outside to catch my breath. There would be so many things, so much stuff left behind.

* * *

I have no children. I have no nieces or nephews. One day my father's briefcase, my grandmother's fabrics, my mother's vases, and my embroideries will be sifted through by strangers. Some items will be selected for a new origin story. Other things, stuff, will go to thrift stores or the landfill and their stories will go silent.

One day, someone will wear my grandmother's diamond earrings, and will never know that they had been promised to me when I was seven.

CINDY DACH is an entrepreneur, community leader and an artist. She co-owns Changing Hands Bookstore and MADE art boutique. Follow her on Instagram @cindydach.

BELIEF

NO ONE SAID IT WOULD BE DULL

SATIVA PETERSON

MY FRIEND LILAH SAYS, "CHECK IT OUT." We're walking across campus in upstate New York when she points out a flyer. A well-known female performance artist was looking for women who would be around this summer, to participate in a piece. "Sounds like something we should do," says Lilah standing in clogs, a mini-skirt, and a faded t-shirt. I was interested too, but there was a catch: It required getting totally naked in a cave. Was I up to the task?

Lately, I'd been feeling a mild sense of dread creeping in as college came to an end. I wondered how could I inoculate myself against the expectations of the world and my strict mother? Particularly since, in order to launch myself forward, I was going to have to go back (at least temporarily) to my dusty, small hometown Winslow, Arizona. Maybe getting naked in a cave was just what I needed?

I'd spent the last four years here at school in New York's Hudson Valley over 2,000 miles away from home. At first it was hard to believe this place, it was so woodsy and green. The kids here experimented boldly with personal expression. A sociable punk-rock kid,

Tim, from San Francisco, who had a white blond Mohawk and refused to wear deodorant, put it to me most bluntly one day freshman year when he said, "You are just…so …fuck-with-able." Meaning you could fuck with me because I was naïve. I was gullible. Funny thing is, it wasn't a put down. It was just an observation, and I tended to agree with him. I was a rube from the country.

The last thing I wanted to be here was a starchy Pollyanna. I worried that my mother's schoolmarm parenting style might have taken some sort of hold over me, along with her long list of worries. But, as far as I was concerned, this was a place where prudish tendencies could be tested, maybe even discarded.

Despite my late-bloomer vibe it didn't take long before I found my tribe—a lovable gang of goofballs drawn to physical comedy. We liked to entertain each other by making up fictitious modern dance moves and performing them for each other. "This one's called *Canned Corn*," someone would say lunging, then putting both arms above her head, clapping them together in a circle, while the others cracked up.

Along with two friends, I signed up for an experimental theater class taught by Assurbanipal Babilla, an Iranian director and playwright. During each class we improvised rituals and ceremonies where it seemed someone in the group always ended up being martyred, carried overhead on the arms of our classmates. This is where I discovered that I was, after all, kind of a prude.

One time, as a warm-up exercise, Bani had us stand in a big circle. As per his instructions we were to go around one by one saying, "Penis," then, "Vagina." So it started: penis, vagina, penis, vagina. Some people were saying it boldly, operatically. Other people cracked under the pressure. One girl squeaked, "Vaaagiiinaaa" as if she had just found a spider in her hair. It was most undignified. She couldn't get the word out of her mouth without squealing. When it got to be my turn, I knew one thing, prude or not, I wasn't going to make a fool out of myself. I planted my feet, put some energy behind it—"PENIS!"

When I went home to visit I felt caught between my new world at school and my old one at home. When I met my parents at the airport, I knew I better hug my mother first, otherwise the tension in her mouth would reset. Her love was not overly tender. In fact, sometimes it was more like a foundation garment. It gave structure, and a mild pressurizing definition.

My parents may have named me sativa, after *cannabis sativa*, a strain of marijuana, but that was clearly the most outrageous thing they had ever done, and they quickly retreated from such radical hippie behavior. My mom never wanted me to step outside the lines, and I didn't know how to tell her that sometimes I did. That sometimes I felt more comfortable out there.

One night in my junior year I got an unexpected phone call from home. When I answered my mom sounded upset.

"Listen, I don't know how to tell you this, but there are some rumors circulating about you back home."

What? What had I done?

"Mr. B's daughter has moved to Flagstaff. She is working as a dancer in a strip club."

"Okay." I knew who she was talking about, it was a high school classmate of mine, but I still wasn't sure what this had to do with me.

"Well, the thing is, she's using the stage name *Sativa*. Now, don't worry, your dad and I are going to try and make her stop. Even though we support her decision to, um… dance, we thought we'd write her a letter…"

OH NO! *No, no, no,* I think. Not because I've just found out my classmate is using my name, but because I'm mortified of what my parents might do.

"Mom, are you sure about this?"

"She's using your name. People think you are a stripper."

"Well… who cares? I don't even know if I mind."

"Well, I do!"

Far from being horrified, the more the news sank in, the more enjoyable I found it. Plus, if I acted like it was no big deal, maybe my mother would drop it.

"Why should I care if people think it's me?" I said. "It's not. *You* know it's not. Really, Mom, this isn't so bad. I can get all the notoriety of being an exotic dancer with none of the work."

My mom sighed disgustedly. "First, I think we need to verify that it's true. So tomorrow afternoon your dad is going to visit the bar."

"What's he going to do there?"

"Just watch to see if she *is* using your name. So we can move forward with asking her to reconsider."

"*Mom*, we can't tell someone they can't use a name."

The conversation was making me cringe. There was no budging her. I couldn't wait to get off the phone so I could go say to my friends: *Hey guess what? You guys are never going to believe this.* They, of course, thought the situation was hilarious. Especially when they found out my classmate's name: Candy.

"What? Candy! But that already sounds like a stripper name," they howled.

"*I know.* I know."

"Do you know her?"

"Of course I know her! We sat next to each other in Physics. We were on the pom-pom line together."

My friends took turns performing impromptu strip routines with pom-pom moves.

Against my wishes, the next day my mom sent my dad to the strip club to verify whether or not this vicious gossip was true. If so, they must take action. Adding to the total awkwardness, my dad got to the club so early in the afternoon the dancers hadn't even arrived yet. He had to turn around and go sit in his parked car, waiting. Once inside I imagine him sitting quietly in some dark corner while my classmate gyrates.

My parents did write a letter to Candy saying how very distressed they were. Oh, but that's not all. They also sent a copy to *her parents*, and another to *the bar*.

Months passed, and eventually my final spring semester wound down. That's when we saw the flyer for an open call posted on campus. Lilah called the number. There wasn't a big vetting process just, "*Ok, cool, you're in.*"

On the morning of the shoot Lilah and I followed the directions. The casting call was for a re-creation of a piece by artist Carolee Schneemann, feminist and pioneer of performance art.

Today, we would be re-enacting her work *Interior Scroll*. Originally performed in 1975, the piece featured a nude Carolee who extracted a paper scroll from her vagina. As it unspooled she read from it a text that was part poem, part manifesto. For this re-creation she wouldn't be performing the piece as a solo, as she had done originally, but with a group of women covered in mud in a cave.

I could hear my mother's voice, "*Why in the HELL would you want do THAT?*" She wouldn't understand this. This felt not just taboo, but mildly dangerous. It felt like the opposite of the life she was then recommending (become a teacher, move down the street from her, start rapidly producing grandchildren).

If I'd been worried about who I was expected to be, then this was my chance to do something about it. I wanted to cast a spell, put some experience out there in the world that I couldn't take back.

"This is it," said Lilah. We rolled my car to a stop and found a half-dozen women assembled there. We walked over. There were snacks—iced-tea, graham crackers. Like we were getting ready for a quilting circle. Carolee was there, moving about wearing a floral robe. She passed the scrolls out—small squares of paper folded up like intricate origami.

A battle cry went out: "Let's Scroll Up!" and putting aside our snacks, and reaching for lube, we inserted the paper before walking towards the cave.

There were shallow pools of water. We reached our hands down and smeared ourselves with wet mud. Streaking our arms and legs, helping each other cover our backs like it was sunscreen. We practiced our poses, legs hip-distance apart in a semi-squat.

As the filming began, Carolee cued us to begin extracting the scrolls from our "centers." With all our voices speaking at slightly different tempos, I remember it was like singing in the round. *Row, row, row your boat. Gently down the stream. Pull, pull, pull the scroll. Gently out your seam.* During a break Carolee complimented me on my pacing, and I was deeply flattered.

Afterward we rinsed ourselves off in the cave water as best we could and signed release forms. She paid each of us one dollar.

Candy wrote back to my parents and apologized for any confusion. The brief letter was written on fish stationery, little round bubbles decorating the margins of the page. My mom had worked so hard to protect my identity from the careless Candy. Safeguard it—keep my virtue from being despoiled. Meanwhile, I'd been working very hard at something else.

The thing is, I think Candy and I were probably more alike than not. We both wanted so badly to experience the world. If things had gone just a little bit differently, I'm pretty sure it could have been me up on that stage saying my name was "Candy" instead of the other way around.

Lilah and I headed for her mom's house in New Jersey. The next morning we were driving cross-country. It was time to come home to Arizona. I cut all my hair off. It was the worst haircut of my life. *Big deal, who cares?* I didn't. We pulled out of Lilah's mom's carport a day later than expected because the air-conditioning didn't work in my car. Lilah's mom's boyfriend took a look and determined the AC just needed more Freon and hooked us up. The word became a mantra: "Free On!" we yelled out the rolled-down windows as we took off almost immediately going the wrong way—ending up on a bridge to Staten Island, laughing, turning around and yelling "Free On" again once we corrected course.

SATIVA PETERSON is a newspaper librarian and writer in Phoenix. Follow her on Instagram @sativasopapilla and find her at sativapeterson.com.

THE BAPTIST BALLER

DAN HOEN HULL

"PERHAPS YOU SHOULD THINK about getting a teaching certificate. You know, just to have something to fall back on."

It was my junior year of college. I was on the phone with my dad and he had asked me what I planned to do with my English degree once I graduated. I told him I planned to travel, have adventures, and write. He asked how I intended on funding this plan. I told him I was going be a mechanic, of course. At the time, my head was filled with books like "Zen and the Art of Motorcycle Maintenance," "Dharma Bums," and "On the Road."

There was a pause on the other end of the phone. My dad then gently reminded me that I had grown up in a household with a garage full of tools around a family who bought, repaired, and sold cars as a hobby, and I get my oil changed at Jiffy Lube.

"Growing up, you never really cared about cars," he said. "You've always been more of a storyteller. You like writing and books. Perhaps you should think about getting a teaching certificate in English. You know, just to have something to fall back on."

I took his advice. But I never fell back on teaching. I immediately fell into it. When I graduated, I packed the car to start my adventures, wound up in Phoenix, needed to make some money, and took a job as an English teacher. That story happened a quarter of a century ago. I never left.

I spent much of my twenties writing and re-writing my first novel until I finally figured out it was missing something: a good novelist. After five years, I put that book away and fully focused on work. But I kept writing. As a teacher, I spend my working life exploring stories with young people and my summers exploring metropolises like New York, Paris, and Salt Lake City. I found new stories.

I am good at teaching, and I still love my students. They keep me honest in a way that only a room full of 16-year-olds can. That's important to me. Over the years, the only down side to my career has been when I have to deal with adults who do not treat our students with dignity and respect.

The worst was about 15 years ago. We had a superintendent who drove a white A-Class Mercedes with gold trim. Everyone knew whenever he was on campus because instead of parking in the spots reserved for the administrators he would park up on the curb in front of the school and have two security guards leave their posts to stand and watch over it. His arrogance towards the students and staff annoyed me. He was running a school district, not a Fortune 500 company. Whenever I walked by that car to my classroom I always fantasized about keying the side.

It was one of those Monday mornings. The super's car was out on the sidewalk. I held my keys tightly in my hand; I walked by and went to my classroom. I was getting ready for the day and students were filtering in before the bell rang.

A student sarcastically joked that she was excited to see the super was visiting. Another said, "I'd show off my car like that too. It's a lot nicer than my dad's."

Then a student asked me, "Mr. Hull, what do you think?"

"Think about what?"

"The super. That car he drives. Where he parks. How he talks down to us. What do you think?"

Teenagers keep me honest because they're such good BS detectors. But that doesn't mean I always need to tell them exactly how I feel. Still, I didn't want to lie.

Instead, I told them a story:

My grandfather was a Baptist preacher whose yearly salary was never more than $20,000 in his 30 plus years of ministry. But he was also a trader who made money in investments.

Yet, I remember as a kid riding to church with him in cars like the Ford Taurus. And there was no sign at the church that said, "Reserved for Pastor." I once asked him about this. He said that if he wanted a good spot he needed to get to church early.

When he retired in the 1980s he and my grandmother decided they had always wanted to live on the other side of the world, so he took a job with the Australian Security Exchange and moved to Sydney.

Cool for them, but I was a kid. It was the '80s. There was no What's App, Skype, or even email. For over 10 years, communication with my grandparents was only infrequent through thin blue airmail letters.

I don't remember much about what was said in those letters, but I do remember one once came with a photograph of my grandfather dressed in what my dad told me was a black Burberry suit leaning on the hood of a Mercedes S-Class sedan with silver trim.

Years later, when Jay-Z put out "Vol. 2… Hard Knock Life," I saw the cover with him in a black suit leaning on a Bentley I thought, "Hey! Jay-Z looks like my grandpa."

In the '90s my grandparents decided to return stateside to be closer to family and moved back to Ithaca, New York. Grandpa was asked to be an assistant pastor at that same little church, pro bono, of course.

My grandparents couldn't wait to see all of us, so they rented out a beautiful, old hotel in downtown for a family reunion. When they left I was a kid, but now I was a man in my twenties teaching English at a high school in Phoenix, Arizona. He insisted on picking me up at the airport and taking me to the hotel himself. I noticed he was wearing a cheap, grey suit and driving a brown Ford Taurus.

I smiled and thought of that picture I'd seen as a kid. When the hugs and small-talk ended we got in the car and he started to drive. That's when I asked him. "What's up with the cheap suits and modest sedans? My whole childhood you've dressed like that and driven cars like this. But I know you've got money. You rented that whole hotel and bought everyone's plane tickets. And I saw you in that picture with a S-Class Mercedes wearing a $2,000 suit. What's with the double life?"

The car was quiet. Then he said to me, "Well, Danny, you're right. Your grandmother and I are financially comfortable. Over the years, my investments have been good to us.

"But my public vocation is a preacher. I have always seen myself as a servant to my flock. I never wanted anyone in my congregation to feel that how I dressed or what I drove made them feel less than me. I've always made sure I was driving the kind of car most of them could afford and wearing the suits most of them felt comfortable in."

This made sense. But then I remembered the picture of him as the *Baptist Baller* and I asked, "Then what was up in Australia? Dad told me you paid cash for that car?"

"Well," he said, "I've always liked classic suits and wanted to drive a luxury sedan. When I got to Australia, I soon realized that the stereotype for an old American business-man is that he's rich. So I thought, 'Give the people what they want!'"

The classroom was silent. Until, finally, a student in the back raised their hand and asked, "So, Mr. Hull, in telling us this story are you saying that the superintendent is an asshole?"

"No, no, no, no, no!" I said. "In telling this story I'm saying my grandfather wasn't."

DAN HOEN HULL is a writer, storyteller, producer, teacher and Zen monk. He is the founder of the storytelling collective TheStoryline.org.

COMPANHEIRA

KATHY WEST

IF YOU'VE NEVER BEEN A MORMON MISSIONARY, here are some mission rules to set the scene: wake at 6 a.m., pray, study scriptures for two hours, teach the gospel by the book, no TV, no dating, and no personal time to do laundry or send emails except for P-Day (preparation day, which came once a week on Wednesday). Above all, for this story, you need to know this rule, from the small, white missionary handbook: "Stay with your companion at all times… within sight and hearing of each other."

In other words, stay together always, unless using the bathroom.

Missionary life is austere, regimented, not something I'd repeat now. But at 21 years old, full of fire and earnest belief, I volunteered. Arriving in my assigned city in Brazil, I discovered that constant company can become as easy as a habit. I was assigned a fellow sister missionary as a companion, and for a few months until reassignment, she and I ate rice and beans together, crushed cockroaches together, avoided drunk flirts in the street together, commiserated every time we knocked at a gate and saw the person inside sneaking away from the window, pretending they weren't home. We wore through our shoes together, walking miles to visit old women or help new mothers. Round-the-clock togetherness and rule-following created a vivid camaraderie that made us feel unified and saintly.

Ten months into my Mormon mission, I'd spent a few months each with four different companions. So when a phone call announced that a new sister missionary would replace my current companion, it felt routine. She and I would be inseparable saints together, too.

Sister Mahler arrived the next day, 21 years old, suitcase in tow, ankle-length dress, skinny as a ghost. She'd only been in Brazil a month, so I expected the bright-faced eagerness of a new sister missionary.

But Sister Mahler cringed through my tiny tour of our shabby apartment. I admitted that yes, only one person fit in the kitchen at once, and yes, the shower walls did seem to be half rotten and shouldn't be touched if you could manage it. "But!" I said. "We're up higher here on the second floor, so I've only seen one cockroach."

She stared.

I said, "Forget the apartment; you'll love the church members."

I took her to Juliana—a woman with a comfortable home who fed the missionaries generous lunches once or twice a month. When Sister Mahler saw the spread of rice, beans, and liver, she went to the refrigerator and opened it. "Do they have fruit?" she asked in English. I apologized in Portuguese as Sister Mahler pawed through the fridge.

She didn't eat anything for lunch that day. Or the next.

For breakfast and dinner, we ate in our apartment. We each bought different groceries with our missionary stipends. When I downed my cereal in the morning or my sliced mango at night before falling into bed exhausted, I vaguely noted that Sister Mahler seemed to eat only watermelon.

But at lunch time, we ate together in other people's homes. The local church members signed up for a day or two on the monthly schedule, and we showed up at the appointed mid-day time to gratefully eat their rice and beans. Some of the families sacrificed to make sure we sister missionaries had a hearty meal on the day of our visit. Lunch after lunch, *almoço* after *almoço*, Sister Mahler sat at their tables with an empty plate. She refused food, so I ate enough for both of us to not offend our hosts. At one house, Sister Mahler smirked across the beans and called me fat in English.

Her problems weren't limited to food.

During our first two weeks together, Sister Mahler read scriptures, said prayers— typical missionary actions—but behind people's backs, she rolled her eyes or whined about their furniture. If she was too tired for a teaching appointment, she just started walking home. I wanted to ditch her, but the rule: We must stay together. So I stood people up and followed her home, shooting imaginary lasers out of my eyes into her frumpy blonde braid.

I received a birthday package from home that included M&Ms. I offered them to my fellow missionaries, 19-year-old boys who refused, saying, "No, they're yours, from home." Sister Mahler said, "Oh take some, please. Look at her, she obviously doesn't need to eat them." I weathered this insult, like all others, in silence. Contention was of the devil, so I couldn't say a word. Way up on the highest of horses, I considered myself persecuted by my own companion, enduring scorn with patience that Christ himself would be proud of.

Weeks passed and some people at church started calling her Sister Mala. For *mala sem alça*. Translation: suitcase without a handle—a person so inconvenient and irritating that they feel impossible to carry. I could have told them to stop. But I didn't, because secretly, it validated me. On Sundays, church members slipped sympathy chocolates into my bag and squeezed my hand with pity. They could see what I endured, bound to this skinny, grumbly girl who refused lunch each noon, and then at 3 p.m., raged until I found a watermelon she could eat on the side of the road. She only ever acknowledged my effort with a grunt, never thank you. She stumbled over every syllable in Portuguese, unintelligible to every Brazilian. And then, when the Brazilians called her *Sister Mala*, she'd whisper to me in English, "They're so dumb they can't even say my name right."

One day, a month into our companionship, it rained. In our apartment, rainwater leaked down the wall, across the slanted tile floor and out the front door. It really was a terrible apartment. The owner had promised to fix it, but hadn't. And after a year of missionary work, of slogging through rain, of walking miles every day, I was too tired to care. But this was Sister Mahler's back-breaking straw.

She threw socks in her bag, saying, "I'm not living here. We're leaving."

"But it's P-day," I said. Our only semblance of a day off.

She shrugged.

All packed, she walked out into the rain. She'd live in the church until she could find a new apartment, she said. I wanted to stay, but I had obeyed every rule (I never slept in, I wore skirts past my knees, I only called my parents twice a year). So the tether of the always-together rule pulled me. I followed Sister Mahler, thinking—but never saying— *This is bullshit.*

Mormon missionaries don't live in churches, and I didn't even have keys to the building. I called the bishop's wife to unlock the door and I asked her to transport mattresses so we'd have somewhere to sleep until we could find another place to live. We wasted our day off moving and arguing in torrential downpours.

The church in this city was actually a two-story house, repurposed for our tiny congregation. So the wide living room on the bottom floor was our chapel and the upstairs bedrooms were used as classrooms. On Sundays, Sister Mahler and I had moved from room to room as a duo, inseparable. But today, sopping, fiercely angry, Sister Mahler headed to the second floor, where I couldn't see her. And though it seems a foolish, microscopic rebellion now, I felt like an insurrectionist thinking, *I'm not following you, even if I'm supposed to. Watch me.*

In a year, I'd never been farther from a companion.

Downstairs, in the makeshift chapel, I wasn't really alone. As I stewed and paced the tile floor, Sister Mahler seemed to fill the whole space: her pinched face, her condescending sigh, her stupid accent when she tried to speak Portuguese. All the comebacks

I'd swallowed for weeks churned in my chest. I was a good missionary—really, so much better than her. I wanted her to admit it, to feel ashamed for how subpar she was.

A tiny fantasy formed: I'd feel vindicated if she went beyond words to actual physical violence. In my mind, I pictured Sister Mahler lashing out, slapping me, recoiling with a horrified expression when she realized what she'd done, how sorry she'd be—and how I would turn my other, holy cheek.

I went upstairs.

Sister Mahler had washed her clothes in a sink, strung a line in the children's classroom, and was hanging them to dry. She lifted a skirt from a pile of wet clothes and pinned it up.

"Sister," I said in the doorway.

She said, "Leave me alone." She hated help and I knew it. I crossed the room to give her a hand. Part of me warned it would infuriate her; the rest of me said, *good*.

With saccharine in my voice, I said, "You never let anyone help. Here, let me." I reached for the wet clothes.

Sister Mahler puffed out exasperated air and turned. I braced myself for the smack that would prove how awful she was. Instead of a slap, she shoved me with a force I didn't expect from a girl who eats only watermelon. I stumbled backward. Now, now she'd feel penitent. I met her narrowed eyes and waited for the wave of regret to hit her.

But.

She turned back to the table to work. No fight. I sighed in disappointment. I took one step forward to try again.

Wait.

Something caught in me that I didn't expect: I had intentionally tried to provoke a depressed, probably anorexic girl to slap me so I could feel good about myself.

I was supposed to be principled, selfless—a minister of the gospel, a representative of Jesus in every thought and deed. But in this moment, I was a self-righteous, overworked rule-fanatic who hadn't even asked my companion how she was adjusting to a jarringly rigorous life. Sister Mahler faced away from me, turning her wet socks rightside-out in silent fury. I didn't know what to say.

I was supposed to stay here with her until she finished—obligated, tied to her. And as I stood in the doorway, following the rule, the realization flashed that I was her suitcase without a handle as much as she was mine. This fresh, foreign light on our companionship didn't make me like her. But it did make me terribly sorry. It loosened my fetter to her, to the rules. I turned and I left the room—truly alone this time—less the strict missionary I had been, a tiny bit more the person I wanted to be.

KATHY WEST is a writer in San Antonio. As co-founder of minetotell.com, she teaches online courses to help people face their writing fears. Follow her on Instagram @kathy.west.

AFTER PARTY

JULIE HAMPTON

I WAS 15 YEARS OLD when I read about the rapture. The sunlight in my bedroom's second story window was filtered by pink sheers curtains lined with pom-poms the size of miniature marshmallows. The full bed I shared with my older sister, Jen, was covered with the once new, now worn, checkered pastel comforter I had begged for when I was 12, when I finally stopped wetting the bed.

Our room overlooked Beaver Street, and our hometown was named Beaver Dam, after our city's defining feature, built behind the old shoe factory a block from our house. For years, we had a billboard outside of town welcoming visitors to Beaver Dam, home of 15,000 busy beavers. Our high school mascot was a beaver. And yet it would be years before I understood the sexual innuendo. Our town's businesses—Beaver Cleaners, Beaver Liquors, Beaver Floral—suddenly became a celebration of women's genitalia and those who pleasured them.

As a teen, however, I tried to head off my naivety about sex and the workings of the human body with books that would enlighten me on these subjects. We didn't learn much about sex in school, save for the whispered rumors in the bathroom about who made it to what base with whom. And God knows my mom wouldn't talk to me about things she found embarrassing or sinful for a child to know. Raised in the Dutch Christian Reformed church, my mom revealed her own naivety about the female body and reproduction only when I became an adult. Her period arrived while she was riding a horse. She thought she was dying. Her best friend Barbie (a real person, not the doll) explained what the blood was and showed her how to insert a tampon. Two years ago my mother told me, no joke, she believed my oldest brother Phil was an immaculate conception. Perhaps it was shame the Dutch reformers were doling out about sex before marriage that convinced her it was immaculate, or there was a dark secret lurking below the surface I refused to dredge up.

My great aunt Alice, in her eighties, revealed every woman on my mothers' side— except my aunt Betty, an unmarried missionary for 50 years—was pregnant before marriage. She winked: "Ya, we met the boys at church, but we weren't allowed to dance, so we sat in their cars and talked with our hands." The fire and brimstone message of the pastors wasn't enough to stop their libidos, but it gave them the fortitude to preach the hypocrisy of abstinence to their daughters.

When I arrived at the age of menstruation, my mother left a small booklet on my pillow in the same pastel colors as the comforter on our bed. My sister, who had received the pamphlet a few years earlier, smirked.

This was the extent of the recommended reading in our house, except for the Bible and Reader's Digest, to which my dad subscribed. After meals we took turns reading aloud from "Our Daily Bread," a monthly publication written by pastors and laypeople with a daily personal riff on a Bible verse.

We didn't have a lot of books around the house. Certainly no great literature, but I had a library card. The books I gravitated to in middle school were ones that would teach me about puberty and sex.

I started with Judy Blume's "Are You There God? It's Me, Margaret," which covered the basics about buying a bra and menstruation. My Aunt Betty, who lived with us when she was on furlough from her missionary work, found me reading Blume's book and denounced it, along with all of her other books, because someone in the church said they were bad. When I brought home "Forever," Blume's book about teenage sexuality where the teenage lovers nickname his penis Ralph, I hid it inside another book. I feared my sister would turn me in—retaliation for me wearing her favorite clothes.

After Blume, I graduated to adult romance novels. I reread the scenes of romantic pursuit and learned how adjectives and adverbs function in over-the-top description.

But on that Saturday, when I was 15, I found a book in our house called "Raptured." The cover illustration of some ominous clouds backlit by a bright heavenly light didn't look like the covers of the romance novels I'd read, that of a voluptuous woman hanging on the overabundant pectoral muscles of a long-haired man. Yet the title was enough. My parents and sister Jen were away selling our vegetables at the Madison Farmer's market while I watched my seven-year-old sister Heather. Once she was outside with her friend Ben, I found a spot in my room and settled in to be raptured.

The book contained no sex scenes but was a page-turner for the outrageous fictional story within, a 1950s rendering of the end times. It served as a warning for Christians to be ready for Christ's coming.

I had already invited Jesus into my heart when I was five. During a children's sermon, we sat in front of the pulpit. The whole congregation stared at us while the pastor coached us through accepting Jesus as our savior. We didn't really have a choice, but some kid, whose family was new to the church, asked, "Who's Jesus, and why is he in my heart?"

I would ask Jesus in my heart two more times before I was 18, more a function of fear than faith. We were Reformed Christians after all and we just didn't get it right the first time. But this account of the rapture had me spooked.

In college, when I read Margaret Atwood's dystopian novel "The Handmaid's Tale," I thought about "Raptured." Atwood's protagonist, Offred, was a handmaid forced to have sex with the husband of an infertile wife and deliver offspring. She was the victim of a religious regime gone wrong. The "Raptured" protagonists faced religious persecution from the anti-Christ who had come into power. Christians had to decide if they would take the mark of the beast, a tattoo required to receive food and water, or be executed. But then, at the height of the climax, believers disappeared. Raptured by their heavenly father from the fiery end times, they became a reminder to friends and family who were left behind, to not wait. There was still time to be saved.

What disturbed me about "Raptured" wasn't the religious scare tactics. In my upbringing we had one of two options: accept Jesus as our savior and have eternal life in streets paved with gold, or be a pagan and boil forever in the fiery pits of hell. While I couldn't quite figure out what heavenly souls did without earthly bodies—do they float around in angel robes and sing hymns all day or do they play cards?—I was more freaked out by the eternal part. I thought about the concept of infinity. Have you contemplated eternal life or infinity lately? I started to equate the two. Take a moment to imagine them. Never-ending existence. At 15, the idea of going on and on without my body felt more like entering a black hole than some spiritual reward.

So right then I prayed: "Please, God, don't let me think of eternal life anymore. If that's what you are offering, fine. But just let me live out this life," I pleaded, "without having to think about the afterlife."

Since my teens, I've dallied with metaphysics in my thirties and Buddhism in my forties, but have given up most religious views. New advances in neuroscience, and the likelihood of consciousness being a biological process, make the religious fervor of a soul needing to be saved sort of moot. I still believe there is a divine order to the universe that is more complicated than I can possibly understand, but my morality no longer comes from religiosity. While reincarnation as another human or a large feline would be welcomed, I've decided this life, the one that I'm in right now, is my last, and only, dance with life. I was too scared at 15 to accept it, but now, this beaver is going to get busy, dammit.

If there's a rapture, I'll be left behind. And if an afterlife presents itself at death as a bright light, the voice of God, or pearly gates, I'll consider it a surprise invitation to an after party I have the free will to accept or decline.

JULIE HAMPTON is a writer, performer, business woman, and teacher (currently at Phoenix College). Find her @juliekatherinehampton or @casadijulie on Instagram.

THE ROCK GODS

RAY STERN

I WAS PUTTING ON MY CLIMBING SHOES at the base of a cliff when I noticed a dark-red blood spot on my left ankle.

It was smaller than a dime, yet uncomfortably large. "What the hell?" I thought, staring at it for a second like a rookie medic. I tried to recall—did I scrape myself, or bang into a rock? That was the usual source of minor injury on this sort of outing. But I felt no pain.

I wiped the blood off and was surprised to see unblemished skin. Another blood spot then appeared on my calf. I realized what was happening and looked straight up 60 feet of granite to the overhanging top of the route.

"Mike, you're bleeding on me!" I yelled.

My friend had led the route, taking the rope to secure at the top. He'd struggled on the tough climb and cut himself without even knowing it. A second or two passed.

"Damn, you're right!" he shouted down at me. "The rock gods will be pleased!"

It wasn't the first time we'd spoken of these strange deities.

This was in the early 1990s, two or three years after I'd started climbing. We were book-taught "trad" climbers, and created the concept of the rock gods organically, in the midst of a wonderful exploration of the art of climbing. We spent our weekends and vacations surviving adventure after adventure.

My climbing friends and I all happen to be atheists and agnostics—the very last people you'd expect to be talking about any sort of gods. But it seemed natural, and I wasn't surprised to find out that other climbers talked about rock or mountain gods, too.

Superstition and risk-taking go hand-in-hand, and not just in climbing. (Nor just because Arizona is home to the Superstition Mountains.) Anyone faced with the possibility of imminent death may cling to an irrational belief—something that's expected to control the one thing they have no control over: luck.

For most climbers I know, that irrational belief is usually manifested as a belief in self. You will make the next move, however risky, because you can, because you're you. That's what Jon Krakauer is talking about in the book "Eiger Dreams," when he says a successful climb might be "held together with little more than chutzpah, not the most reliable adhesive."

Still, my friends and I did indeed talk of something else at work.

Our mythology grew around the idea that the rock gods need a small blood sacrifice in order to be truly happy and ensure everyone's safety. Of course, we didn't really believe in such gods. The idea was an entertaining fantasy set in the context of a chosen activity in which scratches and "bloody flappers" on hands and fingers are common, and some climbs are rated PG, R, or X for their potential to kill or maim you.

We must have left enough blood for these fictional deities over the years, because something sure helped out my dad the day he almost lost his life during a climb with me.

My father's in his late seventies and looks like a former athlete. He's in good shape for his demographic, but he has to limit his cardio exercise, because a long time ago, before he moved his young family to Arizona, his lungs were seared by chemicals and smoke as a New York City firefighter. I'd persuaded him to climb with me as a Saturday lark, picking a classic route I knew he could handle. We'd been to a local rock-climbing gym twice before this.

Before his firefighting days, he was in the Navy. He's an ex-boxer, spear-fisherman, and sailboat owner.

He was psyched about the day's adventure, a climb up the Praying Monk on Camelback Mountain. The Monk is a free-standing, fat pillar of pink sandstone about 100 feet high. The route is called the East Face—I've climbed it 30 or more times. It's easy and fun, but always a thrill. In several spots, the hand- and footholds are not at all obvious.

As the name indicates, it's a face climb. It's not 90 degrees vertical, but to give a frame of reference, climbing the flat plane of the outside of a skyscraper would be a face climb.

The route's first known ascent was made in 1951 by Gary Driggs, who was 17 at the time and already an accomplished local climber. Before he did it, locals—who didn't have modern, rubber-soled climbing shoes—spoke of the "Impossible Monk," and considered it unprotectable and just too sketchy to be climbed safely. Driggs took a memorable lunge about halfway up, risking his life for the glory of being first.

To get to the Monk, you first have to ascend a lower climbing area called the Headwall. That was Dad's first outdoor rock-climb, and the Monk—far more technically difficult—would be his second. In retrospect, I should have spent a little more time on instruction, considering what we were about to do. But fathers usually do the instruction—it's tough to instruct one. Mine, anyway.

Typically, when I take a newbie out to the Monk, there are at least three people involved. That's helpful because climbers at the top can't see those at the base. In other words, I, the leader and only one with experience, would not rope in my father before his climb and double-check his harness before he started up this no-BS route.

No problem, we agreed. He felt confident he knew what to do. He would belay me as I climbed up first.

"After I set up the anchor on top, I'll pull up the slack in the rope," I told him. "Tell me to stop pulling it up when there's about 20 feet left, then tie yourself in. Tie the double-figure-eight knot into your harness. Then I'll have you on belay and I'll let you know when you can start climbing."

"Got it."

"Tie a double-figure-eight knot."

He confirmed he would. I had extra anxiety as I led the route, climbing higher and higher above him. He would have to do everything right, because he'd have to, I thought. Of course he would.

I couldn't banish the worry entirely—it was standard practice to check your partner's knot, no matter the experience levels, and I hadn't done that.

I attained the summit, slung the chain-anchors, and called down to Dad, "On belay!"

"Climbing!" he called back. As expected, I couldn't see him 100 feet below because of an overhang of rock. I slowly pulled up the rope as he climbed. Usually, the climber on top rope is in no danger at all. If Dad slipped off the rock face at any point, he wouldn't fall. He would find himself suddenly dangling on the belayed rope, like the fish he used to catch on his boat.

The route was well within his ability, and he climbed smoothly up the first 30 to 40 feet. Soon, I was relieved to see his face appear on the moonscape of rock below, then his whole body, the rope clearly running from his harness up the face to my hands. I pulled methodically as he kept climbing. He was smiling and having fun. He got to the blank spot where Driggs had lunged, and without knowing about Driggs, he saw a chance to show off. He sprung off his footholds, launching himself straight up, his hands outstretched. His fingers grabbed a lip of rock well above him and locked tight. Then he hauled himself up to the next good footholds.

"Awesome!" I yelled.

He was beaming as he made the last few moves and joined me at the small summit for the amazing, 360-degree view of Echo Canyon Park. I took in the last few feet of slack from the rope, Dad now seated beside me. That's when I heard him say, "Oh. Look."

He was looking down at his own harness. I stared at it. The horrible reality came at me in a rush. Instead of the double-figure-eight he had only recently learned, he'd chosen instead to tie a standard sailor's knot—the bowline.

Useful as the bowline is, in climbing it's notorious for coming undone. As his bowline had, somewhere on the climb. The end of the rope hung loosely overlapped through the harness. It would not have held his weight for even a second if he had slipped on his climb. He had scaled the Monk unprotected. My insides churned.

"And you did that lunge move."

If Dad had missed his handhold on that totally unnecessary lunge move about 60 feet off the deck, he would have died. Little question about that.

I've had a few close calls in climbing myself. But it's easier to process my own risk-taking. Even years later, no climbing memory fills me with as much dread as the thought of what could have happened to my dad that day, and how I would have been responsible for it.

There's no good explanation for why he stuck the move. Sure, he's my dad—the one who gave me my adventure gene. He can do things like that. But I'm also glad for all my scratches and scrapes over the years—and the blood offerings left on boulders and cactus needles across Arizona.

Just in case.

RAY STERN has worked as a journalist in Arizona for 23 years, and is currently the news editor for Phoenix New Times. Follow him on Twitter @RayStern.

ADVEN-
TURE

BAMBI, A GERMAN BAR, AND THE EARLY DAYS OF THE INTERNET

R. BRADLEY SNYDER

I DO NOT RECALL exactly what I was wearing. I assume my shirt had an absurdly wide collar, because most of the pictures of me from the summer of 1976 show me in shirts with absurdly wide collars. I also assume that the shirt was tucked into very short, pocket-less shorts that had white piping along the seams. I assume this because boy's fashion of the time was to wear what today would pass for jogging shorts with striped tube socks pulled up to right below the knees. I also assume that I was wearing shorts because I remember cold air hitting my upper thighs as my eyes adjusted to the dark velvet interior of the movie theater's lobby.

I instantly knew that something special was happening. For one thing, my mother ushered me and the other kids from our north Phoenix neighborhood *to* the snack counter, not *away* from the snack counter. In my house, candy, like they had at the snack counter, was limited to Halloween and Easter.

I also was impressed by the reverence of the theater itself. Neat rows of chairs sat in the dark and pointed silently at a giant, white screen. It was like Christmas Eve mass with a sticky floor.

The movie was "Bambi." It was being shown as part of the theater's summer discount program for kids. "Bambi" was over 30 years old at the time, but I did not know that or care, and I still remember everything about it.

For those of you who have not seen "Bambi," I'm about to reveal an important scene from the movie.

Bambi's mother is shot and killed while fleeing with Bambi from a poacher. At first, Bambi does not realize what has happened. From the safety of the thicket he yells out, "We made it! We made it, Mother!" When no response comes, Bambi is left calling out for his mother into the falling snow.

Tears poured from my five-year-old eyes, snot from my five-year-old nose. I was devastated. Moreover I was confused and angry. At five years old, I was aware that "Bambi" was a story that people had made up and drawn for me to see. What I could not figure out was why those people had killed Bambi's mother? It was their story. They controlled it. Why hadn't they saved her? Why had they deliberately made me feel so horrible after making me feel so good?

This could be the story of the first movie I ever saw, but it isn't. I needed to tell you that story to help explain this next one.

"Bambi" started my love for the transformative power of media. I grew up fascinated with how one person could evoke emotions from countless strangers with a song, a painting, or a play. Towards the end of my high school years and well into my college ones, that fascination was focused, in part, on the golden age of Hollywood. Movies like the "The Thin Man," "Casablanca," "The Maltese Falcon," and "Cyrano de Bergerac" became incredibly important to me. They affected my mannerism, helped form friendships, and even influenced the way I dressed.

Still, I do not recall exactly what I was wearing as I sat with my friend Mark at the bar of the old German restaurant near downtown Phoenix. I assume we both were in oxford shirts, khaki pants and blue blazers because my friends and I always wore blazers to this particular old German restaurant. It was a tradition that had started when we were too young to drink legally. We thought the blazers made us look older. Whether we were right or whether the owners of the establishment did not understand American consumption laws remains unknown, but we were wearing blue blazers the first time were served, and we were not about to mess with a good thing. It was the winter of 1992, I had just turned 21, but the blazer remained.

Mark and I were discussing "Lawrence of Arabia." It was a favorite of ours and had recently shown in theaters, allowing me to experience the scene at Ali's well as David Lean had intended; with Omar Sharif's character appearing as a speck on a vast sea of dessert and approaching steadily… menacingly… on his camel until he is close enough to shoot and kill Lawrence's companion for drinking from the well.

Mark and I were discussing that scene and repeating favorite lines from "Lawrence of Arabia," when the man sitting on the other side of me interrupted, "So you boys like old movies?"

He and his friend next to him both appeared to be about 65 years old. The one who had interrupted us had a round face, glasses and reddish brown hair. His companion's face was gaunt, and his hair was fading from blonde to white through yellow. Apart from these differences, their appearances were quite similar. They both had on dull western shirts with pearl snaps that they had tucked into Wrangler slacks. Their faces were wrinkled and tan, and each wore his hair slicked back with pomade. Holstered on their belts, they each carried a pocketknife and a Zippo lighter. Overall, they gave the impression of men who might have been greasers in their teenage years.

"Yes, we like old movies," we replied.

"Have you ever heard of Sonny Tufts?" he asked.

We said we had, and I was being truthful. It was a name I knew but had a hard time attaching to specific movies or specific roles. In fact, "Sonny Tufts" was kind of synonymous at the time with "bit player." I knew that Sonny Tufts had been in a lot of things, but I didn't know what.

The man who had interrupted us straightened himself and proudly motioned to his friend (who had remained quiet, staring down his drink) and said, "This is Sonny Tufts!"

Being near someone who, while not known for being in the greatest films, certainly worked with people who were in the greatest films was a real thrill. We began to pepper him with questions.

"Was Humphrey Bogart really as shy as they say?"

"Yes, but exceedingly polite."

"Was Mickey Rooney as big an asshole as they say?"

"I don't have firsthand knowledge, but I have heard stories."

"Who was the most beautiful actress you ever met?"

"Elizabeth Taylor."

"Who was the coolest actor?"

"Steve McQueen. Undoubtedly, Steve McQueen."

Mr. Tufts seemed embarrassed by the attention we were giving him and answered in short sentences spoken softly. His friend then would happily fill in details.

We shared cigarettes, toasted, discussed the transformative power of cinema, and at closing time agreed that they don't make movies like they used to.

When the bill came, Mark and I grabbed it immediately. Mr. Tufts and friend were reluctant to let us pay. We had been there a very long time and had drunk many, many rounds. Mr. Tufts and friend pointed out that they were retired while Mark and I were just college students, but we insisted. It isn't every day that one gets to buy a drink for a Hollywood legend.

This could be the story of the first drink I ever shared with a celebrity, but it isn't. I needed to tell you that story to help explain this next part.

Over the years Mark and I talked about that evening frequently. There were questions that we regretted not asking. There were answers that we regretted not remembering.

One afternoon seven and a half years later, Mark called me at my office. I do not recall what I was wearing, but at this point of the story, it is irrelevant. Mark and I were living and working in New York City, and he was calling to make plans for that evening. He asked, as he had often done in the interim years, where we might go to share a drink with the likes of Sonny Tufts. However, this time it struck us both simultaneously: Why not share another drink with Sonny Tufts? We were both going home to Arizona for the holidays. Maybe we could just look him up. Maybe he would be pleased to learn how much that evening meant to us. Maybe now that he was seven and a half years older himself, he would enjoy interacting with two younger people who appreciate his role in Hollywood history.

"He might even remember us, right?" I asked Mark over the phone.

"Sure," Mark said, "We did talk for a long time."

We both went to work at our separate computers to try to locate Sonny Tufts. In 1999, online phone directories were less than complete, and we quickly hit dead ends. Mark turned to IMDb for clues, while I thought of other places to look. I was about to suggest that we call someone in Phoenix to look in the White Pages for us when Mark said, "Sonny Tufts died in 1970."

This is, in fact, the story of the first time I was conned, and, for a brief moment, I had the same reaction as I had after the death of Bambi's mother.

When he is not telling stories, **R. BRADLEY SNYDER** explains children to adults and to clients ranging from the U.S. Justice Department to Cartoon Network.

THE GARAGE DOOR

SASHA HOWELL

I CAN COUNT ON ONE HAND the number of major lies I told my parents when I was younger. I don't mean the little fibs about whether I'd finished my homework or cleaned my room. I mean the big, fat lies, the kind that would get me grounded. For life.

I've begun to divulge these to my mom and dad over the past few years. They can't ground me now that I'm almost 40 (at least, I don't think they can). Plus I have my own child and I'm hoping that these confessions can somehow absolve me from any future lies she might tell me. At least it's worth a shot.

But there's one story I just can't quite share with my parents, as it's bound to tip the scales of a decades-long battle between them over who is the worse driver. It's really a toss-up. My mother has a lead foot and a complete inability to park within the lines. My father's brilliance somehow does not transfer to merging onto a highway, and he's a little punchy with the brakes. But for them the score comes down to one thing: Who has backed into the garage more often than the other.

In 1996, when I was 15 years old, my neighbor Katie Fouts came over to hang out while our parents went out for dinner and a movie. We watched TV while we gossiped about boys and who was going to make the varsity tennis team. Then, at some point, Katie turned to me and said, "Let's take the car out."

"Umm, Katie. We only have our permits."

"I know. Let's do it anyway."

Maybe my 15-year old brain thought that two permits might equal one driver's license, but I'm pretty sure I agreed because I wanted to seem cool in front of Katie. Then she threw another idea at me.

"Let's have a beer first."

She sounded so confident, which was strange. Neither of us were rule breakers; that's why we got along. Katie and I were both the kids that came *after* the troublemakers. Our brothers had been partying and boozing it up for years. We were *good* girls. This entire plan felt foreign—and really, really exciting.

I grabbed a beer from the fridge and we split that can of courage, swallowing down any nerves with each swig.

"I'm ready."

We grabbed the keys and got into the baby blue Buick LeSabre parked in the garage. I turned on the ignition and then as I lowered the gearshift into reverse and checked my mirrors, I realized I had never, not even once, backed out of the garage. Any time my parents said it was my turn to drive, they'd already gotten the car out and pointed it straight ahead to make our S-shaped driveway easier for me to navigate. This should have been a sign for me to stop and to cast this craziness to the side.

"What are you waiting for?" Katie barked.

"Nothing, just making sure the mirrors are set," I lied.

I took a breath, took my foot off the brake and started to back out. CRUNCH. We froze. I hadn't even made it out of the garage. I put the gearshift into drive and slowly took my foot off the brake again. We inched forward into the parking space, metal and on metal screeching with every move. I shifted into park, and we sat there for a minute in total silence.

"I'm going to go see what I hit."

I took the long way around to the passenger side of the car. Without even looking at the damage, I had already resigned myself to punishment. I wasn't going to be grounded. I was going to be cast into the dark well of children who disappoint their parents, which, for me, was worse than death.

And then I saw it. A dent the size of a giant fruit platter scooped out of the front quarter panel, the baby blue paint scraped away along with my out-of-state-college dreams.

Katie sat there, staring at me through the glass. She didn't move until I started crying, then she jumped out to see the wreckage for herself.

"This is bad. What are you going to do?"

"I. Don't. Know. Let's go inside. I can't stare at this any longer." We walked to the door, and I hit the bright lighted button to close the garage. It got about halfway down then shot back up.

I figured it was probably the cat running in front of the sensor and hit the button again. This time we watched as the garage door made it halfway down then reversed back up to the fully open position.

It wasn't the sensor. Katie and I went to look at the garage door track that used to be straight but was now smashed into a sideways V. My brain immediately switched from flight to fight. I scanned the wooden shelves along the wall for a can of WD-40 and a crowbar, and I muscled and lubed that track until I got the garage door to go down.

Katie bailed and I went to straight to my room. We both recognized that getting the garage door closed was not enough to get me out of trouble.

That night, I lay in bed, tossing between torment and torture. Do I wake my parents and get it over with? Do I say it first thing in the morning? How much should I tell them? Do I mention the beer? I only drank half of it. Do I tell them it was Katie's idea? That's mostly true.

I stared at the glow-in-the-dark stars on my ceiling and whispered a prayer to the God of teenage hopes and dreams. And while he hadn't come through on my requests for bigger boobs or Johnny Marynowski's affection, he would clearly see how much I needed him now. "Please help me and I'll never lie to them again. I promise."

The next day, I woke to the usual Sunday morning sounds. My mom was in the kitchen and my dad was puttering around the house before it was time to leave for temple. I had almost forgotten about the prior night's events until I heard the garage door open and the car start up. What followed was another awful yet familiar crunch, then the slamming of a door and a string of swear words I don't even dare to repeat.

I ran down the stairs, almost tackling my father in the process. "What happened?"

"I HIT THE FUCKING GARAGE DOOR."

My mom burst into laughter. Two weeks earlier she'd done the same thing with her car, so this crash made them even.

It was not funny to my father. "I don't even know how there could be so much damage."

We all went outside to look at the car. The dent was even worse than the night before.

"Oh, and the fucking garage door is broken now, too!"

I stood there between them, both of their faces bright red, my mom's from laughter and my dad's from anger.

I gave a big smile up to the skies above and then turned to my parents and asked, "Do you want me to drive today?"

SASHA HOWELL is a writer, mother, wife, marketer, goof and more. But of all the titles Sasha holds, her favorite is eternal optimist.

BAD HOMBRE

NATE NICHOLS

SINCE I WAS IN HIGH SCHOOL, my family has taken near-annual trips to Mexico with my best friend Campbell's family. His mom, Jackie, was born and raised in Leon, Guanajuato. When her parents divorced, her father's alimony was to build her mother, Maria, a rustic bed and breakfast in a small pueblo in Jalisco called La Manzanilla. Nestled between the jungle and the Pacific Ocean, the town of 2,000 is friendly and sleepy, pacified by the constant breeze. La Casa de Maria, as the small inn is known, has been a staple of our trip each year. We always bring back souvenirs: powdered mole, art, replica Mayan figurines and, as I got older, tequila. However, last year, at New Year's, our collecting graduated to arguably its most impractical height: live animals.

Being in the jungle, La Manzanilla is full of life. One year, the bugs were so pervasive one of our less hardy travel companions threatened to book an early flight back to her Arcadia mansion just to escape. The owner of a small pizza parlor keeps a capybara, the world's largest rodent, as a pet in a small enclosure behind his restaurant. Side note: Mexican pizza is nothing like Italian pizza or what Taco Bell has dubbed a Mexican pizza, and somehow manages to fall short of both. However, watching a capybara pick up and drink a beer straight from the bottle while standing on its hind legs does make this particular pizza parlor worth a visit.

The epicenter of all this life is a nature preserve full of mangroves. Similar to a cypress tree, the mangroves grow out of what is essentially swamp or bayou. The area is teaming with birds, fish, and hundreds of crocodiles. The man who oversees the preserve, Primi, is a friend of the family. On our first visit, he delighted in explaining how, before the preserve was fenced in, crocodiles used to stroll down the main street in town, or wander the beaches, which came as quite a surprise for sunbathing tourists. Primi lost part of his arm in a car accident as a child, but likes to tell tourists and newcomers that it was a brush with a crocodile. Just as the fish and birds lay their eggs in mangroves, setting the stage for new life, so too began the life of what I have dubbed my Mexican refugee cat.

The majority of our New Year's trip was spent in the palapa, a large shade structure with a roof made from intricately woven palm fronds. It's filled with hammocks and lounge chairs, and we spent the days napping, reading, playing corn-hole, and enjoying beers while watching the water. On our fourth or fifth day, we had an unexpected visitor. At first we just heard a soft mewing. Then, through the fence from the adjoining palapa, emerged a newborn kitten, no more than six weeks old. He was very shy at first, darting back through the fence any time one of our group approached. Eventually, we shared some of our tuna sandwiches and made a friend for life.

The group next door explained that they had been walking back to the beach past the crocodile preserve when they saw the kitten inside, apparently thrown over intentionally. They found a gap in the fence and were able to pluck the kitten out and save him from becoming an appetizer. Since then, they had been caring for him, giving him milk and letting him sleep on their deck. They were about to move on to their next destination and weren't sure they would be able to bring the kitten with them. We played with the cat on the beach for the next few days. He loved to chase strings, sample ceviche, and nap with us in our hammocks. Then the group next door moved on, and the cat was still there, solo with nobody to care for him.

We decided that he shouldn't stay on the beach alone at night. Unfortunately, my friend's aunt didn't allow any animals other than her own dogs in the inn. My mother and I smuggled the cat into the house in a cloth tote bag. Luckily our room was off to one side, so we didn't have to pass the main house with our inexplicably meowing bag. A cardboard box full of beach sand was his litterbox and we were able to find some cat kibble at a local store. It took him a day or two to warm up to his new surroundings: hard floors, no ocean sound, fewer places to run and hide. One of the first nights he was there, the sight of his own reflection in a mirror had him terrified for an hour.

Then he started to get a little too comfortable. I came back to the room and found him hanging six feet in the air, claws dug into the metal screen on the window, crying. It wasn't going to be possible to keep this cat's presence a secret much longer. Eventually, the girls from across the street, who clean the rooms, were our downfall. They almost let him escape, and the commotion made the cat's presence known to everyone. Luckily, my friend's sister, Carson, was able to persuade her aunt to take pity on the cat and let him stay.

We took him to the town's only vet for a checkup. The large dusty office had garage doors to accommodate horses, one of main means of transportation in town. The kitten was entranced by the cage full of chickens out front. When the time came to get his first shots, I had to hold him while he howled in pain, although I think he hated the worm pill they forced down his throat even more.

A day or two later while we were all enjoying the warm sun on the patio, my friend's sister decided she wanted to give the cat a chance to enjoy some time outside. It was an innocent enough thought, but it led to the loss of the cat's second of nine lives. One of the dogs that lived in the house burst through the screen door and grabbed the cat in its jaws. Carson leapt into the fray, screaming and crying, trying to separate the two. She saved the cat, but one of the dog's teeth went through the nail on her thumb. The cat puffed up to twice his size, like a puffer fish, every hair on end. Miraculously, the cat was unharmed except for a slight limp.

As the end of our trip drew near, we began to think about how we were going to get the cat back on an airplane to the U.S. The cloth bag we brought him to the house in didn't seem like it would pass muster with the airline and the vet in town didn't have any type of carrier. I went to Manzanillo, the biggest town in the area, with Jackie. After visiting several stores and finding nothing, we were running out of options. Finally, we went to Soriana, basically a Mexican Target. We went up and down the aisles until we found the pet section. Amongst the disorganized piles of merchandise, including a can of wet dog food that had somehow been opened and dumped out, I spied the last pet carrier left in the store on the very top shelf. It didn't have a door. After asking three employees to bring us a ladder (one refused to hang up a personal phone call and the other two never returned), Jackie grabbed a broom and began scraping the tops of the shelves in search of the missing part. No luck. We took the door-less carrier to checkout. After explaining our less than stellar customer service experience and the defective quality of the merchandise, an argument in Spanish ensued between Jackie and the manager. I speak enough Spanish to be conversational, but this argument was so fast and loud that I was lost. I don't know that I ever felt like more of a gringo than I did as a hapless bystander in front of a growing audience of employees and customers. In the end, we paid full price for the carrier without the door. As we left, Jackie turned to me and said, "This is why I left Mexico."

The morning of our departure we put the cat in the carrier, wrapped some mesh around the front, and secured the whole thing with duct tape. Not the most elegant solution but the cat made it back on the plane. He passed through customs no problem and was off to his new home in Los Angeles with Carson. She had taken an instant liking to the kitten. The only problem was that she knew her boyfriend wanted a dog and she had already adopted one cat without his permission. After a week-long trial, the cat hadn't grown on the boyfriend, and I got the call that the cat was coming to live with me. For the first time in my life, I was going to be a dad.

The first order of business was giving him a name. Carson had wanted to call him Coco, an homage to his origin story, plucked from the jaws of a cocodrillo. However, my dad pointed out that the cat had swagger and confidence more along the lines of LeBron James. I went with Killer Mike. The human Killer Mike is half of one of my favorite rap groups, Run the Jewels, and it seemed like a better fit. Little did I know, the cat would take the name literally.

Life with Killer Mike hasn't been a cakewalk. Most of the time, he's sweet and docile, but then he flips a switch and it's like he's back fighting for his life with the crocodiles. He has a penchant for sneak attacks, emphasis on attack, that include scratching and actually sinking in his teeth.

From what I've read online, cats that are weened too early, raised alone, and have experienced trauma are more likely to attack their owners. My mom and a co-worker independently sent me an article that said housecats really do want to kill their owners, and would if, they were big enough.

I'd like to believe Killer Mike doesn't actually want to murder me, despite the increasing number of scars on my arms, legs, and face. I couldn't imagine coming home and not finding him waiting for me. I hope he remembers we saved him, twice, and spares me for that kindness. And that our future holds more snuggling than bloodletting.

NATE NICHOLS is a native Phoenician and former Phoenix New Times freelancer. He's currently a full time DJ.

THE UNDERTOW

DANIEL MILLS

IT WAS THE MONTH OF JUNE and life appeared filled with possibility. We passed the time with games of kick the can and water balloon fights, nourishing ourselves on the sweet nectar of Capri Suns. The days were long and stayed light out almost until bedtime. Summer vacation had barely begun.

With a caravan of neighbors, my family travelled south to a foreign, exotic land where people spoke in a different tongue. Not even the water was safe to drink. Rocky Point was the farthest from my world I'd ever been as an eight year old.

Today, as an adult, such a tourist trap is much less frightening, but I'm not so naïve to think it isn't still dangerous. Paying a stranger on the beach 20 dollars only for him to return with a small baggie of baking soda, or buying some of the shittiest weed you've ever smoked are a few of the horrors recounted to me by friends.

But back then, eight years old, the world was small, a Rocky Point vacation filled with adventure, and the ocean something to be marveled at.

Early that Saturday morning, my family combed the beach as the tide fell back, exploring an underwater city of crabs, starfish, and various cephalopods. We then set up camp with neighbors, staking our claim and continually refusing offers of puka shells and sunglasses from the local entrepreneurs. If I remember correctly, some of the women were enticed into having their hair made into cornrows, a decision they would first regret while smearing sun tan lotion onto their scalps, then a second time when trying to remove the braids.

To adults, few things are more relaxing than a day spent lounging at the beach flipping through magazines as you drift in and out to the rhythm of the ocean. But to a small boy, lying on a beach towel for hours is perhaps the most boring thing imaginable and should only be considered as a home base for when you need to replenish supplies of Capri Suns and potato chips.

The afternoon lingered on in the sweltering heat as Tyler and I watched the waves grow larger, their crashes coming louder and foaming at the mouth. All along the beach people gravitated toward the water, wanting to get closer and to be filled with excitement by the force of the movement.

Tyler was my next-door neighbor and best friend at the time, and neither of us could resist the thrill of the waves. Promising to stay within eyesight, we ran off basking in independence our parents seldom afforded us. The Sea of Cortez opened wide.

* * *

A rip current is a strong, localized flow of water that moves away from the beach at a 90-degree angle. It occurs spontaneously in any body of water with breaking waves, varying in size and speed, but mostly narrow, around 20 or 30 feet across. It exists for short durations before petering out and is relatively easy to escape so long as you swim horizontally across.

It was exhilarating to feel the current pull me, and I laughed, imagining I was on a kind of roller coaster. When I realized we were too far out I yelled to turn back, but Tyler was already out of earshot. Despite being two years my junior, he was the stronger swimmer.

Within a few minutes, I had been pulled so far out that the beach now looked dotted with tiny figures, unrecognizable to me, their muffled voices reaching over the sound of crashing water.

At first, I didn't admit to myself that I might be in trouble and swallowed the urge to yell, thinking that if I did, I would turn around to see Tyler, or another one of the kids, looking at me perplexed for an honest display of panic. "You're fine," I told myself, "You know how to swim."

But the open water was something different entirely. It moved in great swells with a momentum I had never encountered, and I suddenly felt very small—and afraid.

So I was forced to focus attention on the towering waves and struggled to keep my head above water, timing my breaths for the intervals in between each one, as they lifted and washed over me—seawater entering my stomach with each poorly timed gasp.

I shouted for help once or twice, but my voice was thin and insignificant against a backdrop of white noise.

In desperation, I swam downward, thinking as it happened I could claw my way along the ocean floor and escape the relentless procession of waves. But no sandy bottom greeted me beneath the surface, and sunlight from above gave way to the cold darkness below.

With no energy to fight the tide back to shore, and the onslaught of waves against me, my only resort was to keep my neck turned upward against a piercing blue sky, the sun and salt burning my face, while my mouth remained inches above the water.

A slow, creeping fatigue approached. Floating in the Sea of Cortez, I waited for one of two outcomes—rescue, or the alternative.

* * *

At eight years old, the future is a strange thing that doesn't truly feel real. Playing with your friends, trying to escape your parents and the freedom of summer is what you think about. You know in some vague way that one day you will grow older, into an adult, perhaps go to college, become married, but it's a future that doesn't really belong to you. It belongs to someone else, someone who shares your name, your childhood, but that person is a stranger.

Floating in the ocean, staring up at the sky and feeling the burn of saltwater in my eyes and on the edges of my lips, all those things felt real to me for the first time, because suddenly they were being taken away. As my body started to fail in exhaustion, and my limbs began jerking involuntarily because they couldn't understand there was nothing to grab on to, I felt a deep sadness that I'd never get to know the person I'd become.

And now as an adult, I often feel so jaded. I feel disillusioned by a world that was once filled with wonder, accepting too easily that this is synonymous with growing older.

When I bring myself back to that time, it's not the fear that has stayed with me, but the sense of how badly I wanted the future I now find myself in. And all the possibilities that come along with it.

I remind myself, don't take this for granted.

* * *

When my dad reached me, I remember him giving a pep talk of sorts, like he would on the other side of the dugout fence at my baseball games, telling me to float on my back, emphatically saying that I could do this. His face had a panicked, bewildered look I'd never seen before. I didn't have the energy to respond, let alone swim.

My dad belongs to a rare breed of people called endurance athletes. If you're not familiar, they enjoy waking up at 4 a.m., or earlier, to run, bike, and swim absurd distances. To normal people, putting your body through so much pain might be regarded as a form of mental illness not properly diagnosed. But they seem to enjoy it. It's also probably what saved my life.

I'm not sure how long it took for us to get back. I only remember the slow progress, the feeling of him shoving me forward with each wave, my neck flinging backwards against the blow. The details become lost, because I was either in shock, or my mind blocked them out.

There was the feeling of solid ground beneath my feet, then the long walk with my dad back to the hotel. I laid down and fell into a deep asleep, dreaming of a summer filled with games of kick the can and Capri Suns.

DANIEL MILLS is a writer in Phoenix. You can find more of his work at danielmills.co.

MAGIC VENU

MIRIAM WASSER

LIKE SO MANY ACCIDENTS IN LIFE, my story begins with a vodka-soda, a cute boy I was trying to impress, and a magician.

It was November 2012, and I was working for a nonprofit in southern India. I spent my days interviewing and photographing migrant laborers and people who scavenge in garbage dumps, so when my boss invited some of my friends and me to a kick-off party for an international children's film festival coming to town, it seemed like a great way to unwind after a long week.

Despite being on a small boat that cruised around a very smelly, and very polluted lake, the party was really fun—I mean, come on, it had an open bar. The night got even better when a friend and I were introduced to the aforementioned cute boy, Ankit, who was working for the festival and spoke English with an adorable British accent. We had a few drinks with him and some of his friends, laughed a lot, met a Bollywood star, and exchanged phone numbers at the end of the night so we could all meet up later in the weekend to see a documentary they were raving about.

It's for that reason that I got really excited the next morning when I woke up, just slightly hung-over, to a text from a number I didn't recognize.

"Hello, Ms. Miriam. This is Magic Venu. We met last night." Not Ankit, but a classic Saturday morning text nonetheless.

Then it continued: "Please tell me your address and I'll come pick you up around noon. We have a lot of practicing to do before tonight's show."

I'm sorry, what?

It took me a minute to reconstruct, but I finally remembered one, meeting Magic Venu, and two, that in a misguided effort to impress Ankit I may have made some off-hand comment volunteering myself to be cut in half during a future magic show.

Apparently that show was the next day.

In hindsight, I probably should have made up some excuse. But because he was supposedly southern India's best magician, not to mention a good friend of my boss, I panicked and did what any normal person would do: texted my address to a stranger so he could send a car to come get me.

When I got to Magic Venu's house, he introduced me to three lanky men wearing sequined vests and a very grumpy little person dressed in a clown costume—aka, his four assistants.

He then led me to what looked like an upright yellow and red coffin on wheels.

"*Ta da!*" he said.

Suddenly Magic Venu's smile disappeared, and he began shifting his eyes between the coffin and me.

"It's going to be tight," he declared. "But I think you'll fit."

He walked over to the side of the contraption and opened the top and bottom hatch that served as a door into the box. Then he stared at me with that look of, "Come on, idiot, we don't have all day.

"I should get inside?" I asked.

"Yeah," he replied, beginning to sound annoyed.

A few words on the contraption: In addition to the upright coffin portion, which was actually two separate parts, it had another box attached bottom right side. At the risk of ruining a magic trick, I'll tell you that the top portion of the coffin slides back and forth across the bottom two boxes via a metal runner, which is how you create the illusion of cutting a person in half.

But back to Magic Venu's basement.

To call the process of getting my body into that thing a "tight squeeze" would be a huge understatement. The whole contraption had been custom made for the person who normally served as his assistant: his 12-year-old daughter.

Now I'm only about 5'6", not particularly large in the grand scheme of things, but his pre-pubescent daughter, who I later learned had graciously agreed to let me take her place that night, couldn't have been taller than 5'1", maybe 5'2".

I maneuvered myself into the rolling contraption, a feat that required Magic Venu to hold the coffin steady while I bent my knees, scrunched my shoulders, and tilted my head to the side.

"Good," he declared, adding—as if it were no big deal—that now all I had to do was align my face with the hole that was cut into the top of the coffin like one of those head-in-the-hole wooden boards you take pictures with at a carnival, and then somehow extend one hand and one foot through other holes on the front face of the coffin.

"Are you fucking kidding me?" I thought, my leg muscles already starting to burn.

But somehow I Cirque de Soleil-ed myself into position.

With my right foot peeking out of the hole at the bottom of the coffin, I maintained balance by standing on my bent left leg and pushing my butt up against the back wall. I then found that if I curved my torso into a sort of U-shape, I could align my face with the top hole.

Satisfied, Magic Venu began describing how we would create the illusion. All I had to do, he said, was gently push my shoulder into the right side of the coffin and contort my body into an S-shape as the top portion of the coffin slid on the runner and locked in place over the other box.

Simple, right?

I mean, maybe when you fit in the box.

My first few attempts were utter failures: I fell against the wall and moved the top part too quickly; then I moved it too slowly, too inconsistently; then my facial expression was all wrong; and so on and so on until a very frustrated Magic Venu let me out of the box and told me to go try on costumes with his wife for a while.

He and I would resume our rehearsal later.

Upstairs, Magic Venu's wife opened a closet full of sequined gowns and handed me a pile of things to try on. But immediately, we had a problem.

Like the box, the costumes were tailored to fit her 12-year-old daughter.

After vetoing a sequined shirt that wouldn't fit over my chest and a long red dress that wouldn't zip in the back, we settled on a tight yellow kurta and pair of matching elastic-waist pants that gave me a rather large muffin top.

Yes, this ill-fitting pajama outfit would have to suffice, she decided.

She gave me a pair of white gloves and sent me back downstairs to continue practicing.

By the time we had to the pack up the van and head over the theater, I had managed to figure out a technique for moving in the wooden box that, while painful, was deemed "good enough."

As the cheerful show music began, I stood near the stage entrance and watched Magic Venu greet the audience with a cheesy smile and wild gesticulations. He never spoke, but wearing a sparkly yellow robe, a gold and red cape, and a sequined turban atop his head, managed to work the crowd.

I wish I could give you a detailed play-by-play of what turned out to be a terrible— and I mean absolutely terrible—magic show, but I've apparently blacked out most of the memory, perhaps in an effort to not re-live the trauma every day.

However, lucky for you, my future grandkids, and all of posterity, my roommate filmed it. As such, the following description has been reconstructed from repeated viewings of a shaky and cringe-worthy video that may or may not exist on YouTube.

After I walk out on stage and take a bow with Magic Venu, he leads me to the box, opens the side hatch doors, and helps me inside.

He then walks back around, and taking hold of my chin, gives it an awkward little shake. Next, he spends a few seconds waving his arms and wiggling his fingers for the audience before finally adjusting the sleeves of his robe and beginning to furiously wiggle his fingers at me.

I take my cue and start moving the top portion of the coffin.

Though the video my friend recorded has no sound, I'd like to think—and I'm going to tell you as if it's fact—that the crowd went nuts.

Meanwhile, I just stand there grinning like an idiot who is probably developing scoliosis.

I'm handed a bouquet of fake flowers to wave while Magic Venu opens various trap doors cut into the contraption to prove my legs and torso are no longer attached.

Eventually, he snatches the flowers back and begins to prance around the stage, and finally—finally—he faces me and begins wiggling his magic fingers, allowing me to shift back into place.

Then, of course, we do the entire trick over again—weird chin wiggle, trap doors, and all.

After I'm finally released from the coffin, I take a bow, and as gracefully as my cramped body will allow, walk off the stage.

I remember I was in the process of taking off the long-sleeved top, under which I was sweating profusely, when Magic Venu's wife handed me a blue sequined dress and some black stockings.

Go put them on quickly, she told me because—surprise—I was going to be in the show a few more times.

What follows on the video *that totally doesn't exist on YouTube* is an incredibly awkward montage of me looking confused and skipping on stage while holding various props—scarves, flowers, top hats.

Unbeknownst to me, the blue sequined dress had a huge slit up the back, and at one point, I flash the entire audience as I turn to skip off stage; at another point, I'm pushed on stage without any direction and made to stand there while the little person in the clown costume dances around with an umbrella.

And then later, after a wardrobe change into a slightly longer yet equally ugly black and silver sequined dress, I'm instructed to go on stage and hand Magic Venu a big top hat and wait for further directions.

For about four awful minutes, I stand there as Magic Venu puts a top hat on my head, then takes it off and magically removes scarves from it. Then he puts it back on my head and starts removing scarves and other foam objects from a different top hat. He hisses at me to smile and hold all the objects, or to skip around, or to, well, you get the picture.

Maybe you all are wishing right now that I could tell you that this night was the beginning of my illustrious career as a magician's assistant, and that I quit my job at the non-profit and toured the world with one of India's most famous magicians. But alas, for reasons unknown to me, Magic Venu never asked me to be in a show again.

And trust me, Magic Venu, the feeling's mutual.

MIRIAM WASSER is an environmental journalist with WBUR, Boston's NPR news station. Follow her on Twitter @MiriamWasser and find her at miriamwasser.com.

LAST LAUGH

ROBERT ISENBERG

MY BEST FRIEND CALLED ME, right after school. He said, "Hey, I did something. And I'm not sure how I feel about it. Can I run this past you?"

Let's call him Ron. We had a lot in common. We were both 16 years old. Both juniors in high school. We both took Latin. We were both on the fencing team. We both read "Dune" in the seventh grade. And everybody thought we were "the smart kids."

But there was a key difference: Ron actually was smart. Painfully smart. He took classes at Middlebury College and had already earned the equivalent of a minor in higher math. He read the journal Foreign Policy for fun. Everywhere he went, Ron wanted to press buttons, learn a new skill, make a mess, turn the music louder.

And he *loved* practical jokes.

New England is legendary for its pranksters. Maybe it's the long winters, or the tough-guy demeanor, or the general sense that nobody really likes anybody else. But jokes are an almost tribal rite of passage. MIT dedicated a "hall of fame" to its most creative shenanigans—like putting a cow on the roof of a building, or taking apart an entire

Volkswagen Bug and rebuilding it in a friend's living room. I've heard that playing jokes on people is addictive. Once you've placed a bag of dog shit on somebody's porch and set it on fire, you just want to do it again.

I wasn't one of those people. I hated—and still hate—practical jokes. I grew up in a wood-heated house in the forest, and my parents are even-minded and literal. Their idea of a joke is usually preceded by "knock, knock." Plus I was a wallflower: If I ever entered the practical joke game, there would be no getting out. The cycle of revenge would be endless. And I wouldn't be savvy enough to keep up. The paranoia alone would've killed me.

The thing was, Ron's jokes weren't really "jokes," just destructive things he'd do to pass the time—like convince a friend that someone she had slept with now had an STD, or leave a dead fish in someone's air duct at a party, or walk out of a department store with the leg of a mannequin. (The trick, he said, was to make it look like you were *supposed* to be walking out the door with a mannequin leg).

(Side-note: Ron never did the fish-air-duct prank, but other friends did, and he would have appreciated its uncomplicated awfulness).

He rarely tried these jokes on me. I was his best friend, so I was more valuable as someone to brag to. I listened to his stories, and I laughed as convincingly as I could, but mostly I was grateful that I wasn't the victim.

When Ron started dating Liz, I thought the games were over. She was cute, spunky, and fun. They were an odd couple: A tall and gangly guy with a Jew-fro, and a petite girl with flaming red hair. (Imagine Pippi Longstocking shacking up with Weird Al). But somehow they hit it off. They went on actual dates at actual restaurants. He ordered flowers for Liz on her birthday. It was official. It was real. The mad genius had found his muse.

But then I got that phone call.

"So you know how it's Valentine's Day, right?" Ron began.

"Oh, yeah, I guess." I had never been on a date, much less *dated*, so Valentine's Day was as meaningful to me as Arbor Day.

"Well," Ron went on, "I decided to write Liz a love letter."

The love letter was cheesy, and he knew it: *When I see you, my heart throbs with desire... I feel butterflies in my stomach... my mind reels with happiness...* stuff like that.

"So you know Liz gave me her locker combination, right?" Ron said.

"Right," I said. I was too polite to reveal my impatience.

"And you know how I'm in Advanced Human Biology, right?"

I froze. *I* was also in Advanced Human Biology. The class was nondescript, except for the one thing that made it infamous: Students had to dissect a fetal pig.

For me, adolescence was a test of endurance and will power—could I avoid interacting with every football player in the school? Could I ride the bus for an hour and a half through sub-zero temperatures and still have the energy to do my homework? Most relevantly: Could I saw open the skull of a fetal pig and pull out its brain, then reconstruct it on a folded paper towel?

I had done all that, and more. I had hacked and slashed my way through the pig's body, until all that remained was a spine and some limp skin. I had overcome my nausea, my disgust, and—like every aspect of my high school life—I had numbed myself to the experience, turned passivity into obedient and unthinking action.

"Well," said Ron, "see... I taped the love letter to the back of the locker."

"Okay," I said. "Did she read it?"

"Well, here's the thing I feel weird about..."

When Ron taped the letter to the back of her locker, he had also used safety pins to attach the organs of the fetal pig to the paper.

"You did *what?*" I cried.

"Yeah, but isn't that funny?" he said, as sheepish as I had ever heard him.

The joke was this: When the letter read, "*I feel butterflies in my stomach,*" the pig's intestines were actually attached to the word "stomach." When his heart "*throbbed with desire,*" chunks of fetal heart were stuck to his sloppy cursive. And so on—an anatomical horror, left in the dark recesses of that locker, waiting for Liz to discover it—which she would do sometime this afternoon, right after her afternoon choir practice.

"I don't... think... that's... a good... idea..." I said.

There was a pause on the phone. A long, hollow silence. I was a pushover, after all. A yes man. I had never contradicted Ron. No matter how repulsive the idea, no matter how cruel or pointless, I always submissively approved. And as the silence stretched, I could sense Ron's growing apprehension.

"Maybe... I should... go back," Ron stammered.

"I mean," I said, "that's what *I* would do." (Knowing that I would never have stuck pig guts in my girlfriend's locker in the first place).

"Okay, I think I gotta go," Ron said. But he paused: "You think it was a bad idea?"

He had never really sought my judgment before. In many ways, our friendship seemed boundless. I always admired his tenacity, his brilliance, even his savage sense of humor. In turn, Ron respected my friendliness, my diplomacy, my pleasant optimism. Now the tables had turned: Ron was quiet and anxious. I was—well, what was I?

"I don't think... it was a great idea..." I said.

"You're right," he said quickly. "Oh, man, what did I do?"

It was a good question, because "what he had done" was actually worse than he could possibly have imagined.

Because a fetal pig, used in dissection, is stored in embalming fluid. When Ron attached the note to the locker, he had underestimated how much of that fluid would ooze out of the organs, saturating the paper. Eventually, the paper was too fragile to stay put, and it tore away from the wall, slapping against Liz's books.

The fluid also ruined the ink. Ron's handwriting had always been sloppy, but the fluid had made it completely illegible.

So when Liz arrived at her locker, she opened the door, and found this: a mound of animal guts, wrapped in notebook paper, with unreadable writing scrawled across it. Before she even saw the mess, she probably smelled the formaldehyde that was seeping into her textbooks.

After Liz screamed... and called the police... and her parents showed up... and her panic attack was so severe that she could barely breathe…and Ron confessed…and everyone reprimanded him for his psychotic stunt…and he apologized profusely…*somehow* Liz found it in her heart to forgive him. And their relationship continued—for another six years.

But after that, Ron calmed down. His pranks tapered off. The tension that followed him dwindled. And for the first time, he would ask my advice *before* he acted. He weighed my answers carefully, more so every year. The wallflower had been right, and the mad genius had been wrong. For me, in the great joke that was pubescence, this was a welcome punch line.

An erstwhile Arizona resident, **ROBERT ISENBERG** is a staff writer for Providence Monthly in his native New England. Feel free to visit him at robertisenberg.net.

FULL CIRCLE K

ANWAR NEWTON

YOU REALLY HAVE TO HAVE A "GLASS HALF FULL" VIEW of the world to find being carjacked fortunate for all parties involved as I do. Now, while victim blaming is frowned upon in most cases, this was mostly my fault. I had just finished the night working the door at the bar, my second job. The clock lurched past 3 a.m. as I plopped into my 1988 Honda Civic LX. I started the five-mile drive back to my place when I thought, around mile two, that I could eat, and fortunately there was a 24-hour Circle K at mile three. I parked directly in front of the glass doors and suddenly had a fantastic idea: What I was going to get was right at the counter. I could just pop in, grab it, and you know what? I could even leave my car running. There's nobody here except for me and this cashier. Now, there was a point when I was standing at the cash register, snacks in hand, when I thought, "This cashier sure is taking a long time to walk from the fountain drinks over to here." I glanced back at the car through the glass doors now filled with an uneasiness. I finally pay and, sugary garbage in hand, returned to my car to a surprise. There was a man sitting behind the steering wheel. Upon further inspection, that man was definitely not me, so this was all wrong. My heart's BPM punched up as if it were the drop in a popular EDM song. This party had just gotten started.

I waved at the window, three bags of Haribo gummy bears in hand, in a surprising amount of calm seeing as how my entire net worth was this car. The arrogance of leaving it running. He didn't notice. I tapped at the window even more politely than the wave, as if I was apologizing for the inconvenience. My eyes darted back and forth, maybe looking for the camera crew? This is a joke, right? He finally looked over and with utter apathy, shrugged. "What do you expect, buddy?" is what it screamed into my stupid face. I stood there mulling over whether I should jump onto the hood of the car in all the uselessness that would be. The car flew into reverse. This was it. I held my phone high and mouthed the words "calling the cops" to him. My hands were shaking from the adrenaline. The car shuddered and the engine died. My car thief restarted the engine as I dialed nine. The car lurched and shut off again as I dialed one and then the car door opened.

"Hey, hey, hey, man, hold up!" he yelled. I froze. I figured he was going to shoot me for calling the cops.

"Hey… Teach me how to drive this!"

I couldn't have heard that right.

"Teach me how to drive this, I don't know how to drive stick!"

He didn't know how to drive stick. The greatest anti-car theft device in modern America had just saved me. It's here where my friends ask me why I didn't beat him up. Rush him and knock him out. I don't exactly look the part of a victim when it comes to the world of crime, quite the opposite actually. But I looked him over as he stood one foot out of the car in his goddamn cargo shorts. The pockets looked weighted and heavy. He could still be carrying a weapon, who knows. I reluctantly tried to appeal to his human side.

"Do you need help, man, what's going on, you're trying to steal my car, is everything okay?"

He looked 17 or 18, like a young poor Harry Belafonte. He asked desperately if I could drive him to 24th Street and Indian School. We were at 13th and Indian School. I agreed, not because I wanted to help him. Part of me did. But I was more hoping he would get out of the car to let me drive and I could lock him out and flee. He instead got back in and scrambled across the center console to the passenger seat. I let out a deep sigh and got in, a little skittish that he might just start stabbing me or something else nightmarish. I put my seatbelt on and actually began teaching this asshole how to drive my car he just tried to steal.

"You gotta put the clutch in and shift, see?" I said to him.

He had a hospital bracelet on like he just escaped from a mental facility. He rifled through my glove compartment asking what CDs I had to listen to.

"I don't really have any CDs… hey, so we're almost at 24th, do you want me to drop you at the corner?"

He rubbed his face nervously and then told me it's not 24th Street he needed to get to, but 48th and Baseline Road. An understandable 15-mile miscalculation on his part.

I needed to start thinking of an exit strategy. I looked over at the door locks on his side. Locked. Shoving him out on the highway was not only out of the question, but extremely inhumane. He's just going to keep pinging you further and further away from civilization until he's found the perfect place on the outskirts of town to slice you open and take your car with all the new shifting lessons you've just given him, I thought to myself. The next cop car I see, I'm the drunkest driver on the road. We barreled down the highway exceeding the speed limit by 15 miles. The one time I wanted the cops to be behind me in my entire life, and not one. Teenage T.I. had turned the volume on the radio so high that my speakers began to blow. I started asking him questions about himself. A trick I picked up from the movie "The Negotiator" with Samuel L. Jackson. Become their friend and they'll surrender maybe. Or something like that, I hadn't seen the movie in over a decade. I pulled off the highway at 48th and Broadway, baffled that no cops had crossed our path, and began to figure out how to end this hostage situation. Another Circle K came into view and I bluffed, telling him that I needed gas although the tank was full. The 20 minutes we spent on the highway was filled with scatterbrain responses to my questions but through it all, I could tell that he was just a troubled kid and a bit mentally ill at that. I pulled up to a pump and suggested he go grab a water for himself while I filled the tank. He refused as if he knew I was going to speed off as he walked up to the door of the gas station. I pretended my card wouldn't work at the pump and told him I'd go inside and staying in character asked if he wanted anything. Cigarettes. As if he didn't already cost me enough.

Inside the Circle K, I realized my phone was dead. Perfect. I grabbed a water and at the cash register I calmly told the elderly woman working "Can you please call the police, there is an unstable man who has carjacked me. If he comes in here, pretend like you're not talking to the police. I'm not sure if he's got a weapon." She dialed 911. I explained very quickly to the dispatch what was happening as I tried to obscure my view from the door as to not give myself away to my carjacker as we all realized he was entering the gas station. I dropped the phone and the elderly woman and I played along. He asks her for some cigarettes and in the snarliest response she had in her, she retorted, "Do you have ID?" Before he could respond, in came three police officers. I pointed directly at T.I. and the officers restrained him, removing the contents of his pocket. The little punk had my things squirreled away.in his cargo shorts but no weapon on him. I went outside with the officers and one of the officers walked me to my car. He helped me make sure I had everything and nothing was stolen, although I'm sure he was also scoping to see if I had drugs or anything criminal. He asked if I wanted to press charges. I told him no and that I just wanted to go home. They had the kid sitting on the curb and were talking to him as I got back into my car. As I pulled away I looked back over at my carjacker one last time. He was standing, unrestrained and the officers surrounded him. He looked over at me driving off and yelled, "Thank you for helping me."

ANWAR NEWTON is a comedian in Phoenix and creator and cohost of This Week Sucks Tonight. Follow him on Instagram @theanwarnewton.

HOW YOU GONNA DIE?

SALVADOR LEE BRAVO

THERE WAS THIS ONE TIME A COUPLE OF YEARS AGO while I was traveling the Ukraine when I was pretty fucking sure I was going to die, and I thought this because I was also pretty fucking sure that I had just been kidnapped by Ukrainian auto mechanics. I thought all this as I was in the backseat of a taxi cab in a tiny shitty town on the Ukrainian Romanian border called Novoselystya.

I remember thinking, "So, this is how I go."

I was unimpressed with my own death.

I wasn't alone in this cab. Next to me was one of my best friends, Josh.

During the previous two weeks Josh and I had an adventure through Ukraine, we'd both been arrested for public intoxication and held overnight in the worst jail cell on Earth, had an overnight trip on a bus with no shocks and half of its floor missing, had an old woman watch us defecate into porcelain holes in the ground because I guess that's normal at bus stops, and had someone diligently try to recruit us into the Ukrainian Fascist Party.

We ended up in this town because heavy rains had flooded all the roads into our destination, Northern Romania. Unfortunately we didn't find this out until our bus had stopped in Novoselystya. So we were stranded for a night.

As we stood there trying to make sense of bus schedules our would-be taxi driver saw us.

"Hotel?" he said.

I turned to Josh, he shrugged his shoulders.

"Sure, thanks," I said. "How far is this hotel?"

Silence. This was a typical Ukrainian response. We brushed it off.

The taxi pulled out onto the street. I expected to see adorable small town life come into view. The Ukrainian small towns we had seen were bustling with life, filled with fruit vendors, kids skateboarding, old men playing chess. Instead, what appeared was a dump. The town was filled with grey bland buildings, empty sidewalks, and empty streets.

After driving for 20 minutes we saw absolutely no one, which made me feel uneasy. I felt more uncomfortable as the nondescript buildings we passed turned into nondescript junkyards, and then nondescript oil refineries. We kept driving until there was nothing in our view but out-of-commission smokestacks.

And then I realized, at first calm, but then quickly followed by a deep dark impression: He's not taking us to a hotel.

"Josh, we need to pull over."

He looks at me. "You sure?" He was worried too.

"Does this look like a place where they build Marriott's?"

This whole thing didn't feel right at all. I remember thinking, this isn't even a cab, all the cabs I had been in during our time in the Ukraine had these weird looking meters and taxi licenses, this one barely had a floor, it didn't even have seatbelts… we had to tie ourselves in.

"Where is hotel?" I ask the taxi driver.

He responded by accelerating.

"Can you stop here? No hotel! Here is fine!" we say.

He stepped on the gas harder. The car was speeding

"No! Stop! Stop here!"

I was right. Something was wrong. We needed to get out of that car. As I undid my seatbelt I tried again. "Please stop now."

I tap his shoulder "Please…."

"No!"

The car slowed and he pulled up to a rusty and broken chain-link fence. He honked and a man that looked like a mechanic appeared and opened the fence. We rolled into a dirt lot surrounded by stripped and broken down cars. Into our view three other figures emerged smoking cigarettes and mumbling in Ukrainian.

"Damn, this is how I go," I thought. "Kidnapped by Ukrainian auto mechanics."

I looked at Josh. "Dude, where are we?" As though he would know.

"I don't know," said Josh, keeping his eyes on the mechanics.

I could tell he was in utter disbelief. I was feeling it too. I closed my eyes. I knew we had royally fucked up.

I turned to Josh. "Look...I think we should..."

Before I could finish my sentence the taxi driver turned around and looked at Josh. "You! Out!"

The men opened the door on Josh's side and pulled him out.

"You go, you stay," said the taxi driver

"No, I'm coming with him," I said.

"You stay!" he yelled at me.

I jumped out of the car and followed them to a door.

"You stay, he go!" he yelled again.

"No we're leaving!" I pulled Josh's arms. They pulled back through the doorway. "No!"

I tried pulling Josh away but I was already through the threshold with them. We stood in a bare, dirty, and narrow hallway. A space where there was barely enough room to turn around. The door was blocked by two of them. There was no way out.

"Look, man, whatever happens we'll stick together."

They stared at us. Sized us up and then walked down the hallway. We followed.

I thought about my mom. How in a couple of weeks after not hearing from me she'd panic. I thought how her initial efforts to email me or call my hostels would fail to produce any information about where I was. Then she'd get on a plane and fly to Ukraine. This little El Salvadorean woman would be running around Ukraine without a clue of where to look for me. She might never find out what happened. I realized that no one actually knew where we were. This stop was a last-minute change to our trip.

We walked through door after door, it felt like we were walking in circles. They started talking to each other, then yelling.

"Sal, I think we're fucked."

We walked through more doors. My mind raced to find a solution.

We approached another door. I stopped and thought, I can't believe I got us kidnapped. I'm smarter than this. How could I be so careless. We couldn't fight these guys and we didn't have any money. I'd heard stories that the mob here kidnaps for no reasons other than to cause terror. This was real kidnapping.

"What do you want? Whatever you want we'll give it to you."

The taxi driver looked at me and said,

"Hotel."

He opened the final door to reveal the front lobby of a four-star hotel. A clean and beautiful four-star hotel.

An attractive Ukrainian woman approached us and said, "Eh-llo, we heard your bus stuck. We have room for you and two tickets for new bus tomorrow to Romania. Welcome to Novoselystya."

SALVADOR LEE BRAVO is a market researcher in Phoenix and regular Bar Flies DJ. Follow him @saleebravo.

GOD SAVE THE QUEEN

BRAD DeBIASE

"WHATCHA DOING DECEMBER 4TH?" the text read. Knowing full well that on the other end of this message I would be asked to volunteer for something, I coyly deflected with a bulletproof:

"Dunno yet, what's up?"

"Doing a charity turnabout show…you should be in it. We're raising Christmas money for the children," Afeelya instantly replied. The exchange was a gay Verizon spaghetti western standoff. Opposite me stood my friend Rich, better known to the Phoenix drag world as the one and only Afeelya Bunz. Cowboy emoji. Sparkle emoji.

Now for those of you not familiar with the term "turnabout show," this refers to taking non-performers, getting them dolled up, and putting them onstage in front of a jury of their peers to buck and twirl around in, ideally, a radically out-of-character display of drag performance. Most often this happens in the context of fundraising, so the prospect of witnessing select individuals assume a drag persona has the leverage to produce a very lucrative profit margin.

"Lemme make sure I'm good that day," I offered. Partially to legitimately make sure I was available. Partially to weigh this potentially impactful decision. I consulted with my friends for all of a few hours—What do you think, should I do it? What would I even do? The usual considerations. I feigned hesitation, but in my heart of hearts, this moment was too good to pass up, and lowkey, it was an exciting prospect. Impact be damned.

You see when I moved from Connecticut to Phoenix in 2012, I put my creative self away in a box on the shelf, to collect dust that I would hopefully brush off down the road when I had time to. The life of a Ph.D. student offered little, if any, time for extra-curriculars, and so I always trusted that my creative flame could be relit when the window of opportunity presented itself. And honey, this was not just a window. This was a rhinestoned, double French door with a waterfront view of Elton John's Pride weekend yacht party. But I digress. The dormant creative self that I knew dwelt in me was stirring. I'd been a theatre kid since high school and felt comfortable in front of a crowd. So while I might consider myself to be an extrovert with a half-decent sense of comedic timing, my new Phoenix friends still hadn't ever really seen me *perform*.

"Sure, count me in," I told Bunz, sealing the deal. And it was done. The initial adrenaline rush of the decision quickly wore off and was supplanted by the endless possibilities of what I had just signed up for. What am I going to perform? Who's gonna put me in drag? Where do I get fake boobs? You know, the typical questions a 28-year-old man asks himself on a Tuesday morning. "One thing at a time," I told myself, "there's plenty of time and plenty of resources." First things first: WHO am I? The blank canvas was mine to paint, and the options were literally endless. I can't pick between two restaurants, much less have limitless creative control over every attribute of a gender-bending fictitious entity. 'Twas time to confer with the tribe.

Cut to: a small gathering on my friend's pool deck, considering aloud all my lady-options. And so, from a cloud of brainstorming and pot smoke burst forth what will forever be known as "THE LIST", a.k.a., the cursory pool of drag name options that befell me, including but not limited to: Annie DeVito, Patty O'Furniture, Val Qaeda, and Summer Clearance. Honorable mention to my friend Tyler, who is otherwise known as Jon Benet Rams-Me. The show was still a couple weeks off, and there was plenty of time to decide on details, but the train was running full steam towards Afeel-ya's show, and this had become a team effort.

It was the night before the show, and most of the pieces were in place…except for one, well, maybe three, very…external pieces that had to migrate north for the winter. *gestures toward groin area* It didn't escape me in this moment that I *could* have simply put on a billowy ball-gown for tomorrow's performance and avoided this entire inquiry. But alas. I was here to achieve greatness, and greatness happened to include a skin-tight three-piece black leather ensemble that left little to the imagination. So, after wandering into some saucy corners of the internet for a very particular tutorial, I mastered the art of building an indoor play-place and went to bed. She was in for a big day tomorrow. All that was left to do was to transform.

December fourth. Eight a.m. I reach for my Schick Norelco trimmer with great trepidation to fully use and abuse it in ways neither it nor I had ever anticipated. Suffice to say, I'm half Italian but I'm hard-pressed to tell you which half. "You can do this," I whispered to the rudimentary grooming instrument, "I don't want this for you either." *Bzzzzzzzzzz.* An entire play of the "Lemonade" album later, my thumb finally clicks the trimmer off and the silence was deafening as I looked up at myself; intrigued, alarmed, and reintroducing myself to the naked mole rat staring back at me. And while I wasn't altogether bothered by the extent to which I had trimmed, it was just a little lame that by the time I put on three pairs of dance tights and the remainder of my costume, 80% of the grooming I had done was rendered completely unnecessary.

It was time. My friend Nik, otherwise known as Piper, agreed to meet me at the bar to assist in the transformation. I was the pre-stretched canvas to her Barb Ross, and after a seemingly endless three hours of makeup later, and those same three pairs of dance tights, there I emerged at six foot three, cherry red hair, serving full Hot Topic hooker. She was ready. It was time.

I could see Afeelya's silhouette through the curtain, and my head began to spin with the countless ways the next five minutes were about to go down. To be honest, I was less fazed by the drag transformation itself as I was more anxious about making good on a performance. Though, all T, Piper did me right with that mug. [*Translation: Piper had done a superb job on my makeup.*] And then it happened.

"Welcome to the stage, Kim Etiquette from Connecticut!" Afeelya roared, and the cheering quickly drowned out the introductory thumping bass of Britney's "Work Bitch." I opted to lip sync to a hyperactive dance mix involving all songs "Work": Work Bitch, Work From Home, and so on. My knees buckled as I waited for those first lyrics to hit, at which point I whipped open the curtains and it was time to slay the children. [*Translation: it was time to put on an amazing show.*] A reminder to myself that drag slang can sound quite alarming out of context.

I had forgotten the feeling of being face-to-face with stage lights, the warmth, the deliberate chaos of doing eight things at once. The adrenaline, however, was all too familiar. It was this chemical reaction, these fired synapses that I had put away, in a box, on that shelf back in 2012. My primal performance instincts began surfacing one by one. Hit every beat. Improvise. Make that eye contact. And we were here to raise holiday money for LGBT youth after all, so I should probably collect some dollars.

I worked my way through and around the 80-person showroom, sharing cheeky exchanges with both friends and strangers as they gawked at this newborn creature before them. Every dance move extended beyond the ends of my fingers and toes and I knew every syllable of that goddamn mix. I was winded, and growing very ready to call it a day. Several fistfuls of cash later, the mix was rounding out of Nicki's "Anaconda" and into Beyoncé's "Formation" and I knew I was in the home stretch. I found my way back to center stage for my final act, and literally without missing a beat, the mix slid right back into those opening thumps of Britney's "Work Bitch." What was happening? Something had surely gone wrong. The DJ knows the song is almost over, right?

"Keep gettin' that money, girl!" Afeelya's booming voice came out of nowhere over the mic. And she wasn't wrong. People still had money outstretched. "Make them believe you planned that shit," I recall thinking. So: lather, rinse, repeat. Somewhere in the primal depths I found the stamina for an encore, and when all was said and done, they were using a push broom to clear the stage of dollar bills. I was finally ushered off, and collapsed off stage into a well-deserved vodka soda, trying to process the blur of the previous 10 minutes. I wasn't exactly sure what I just did, but I knew I had accomplished whatever it was that I had set out to do. Hashtag triumphant. I was later told that my one number raked in somewhere around the $250 mark, so we'll call that a success. The glowing feedback I received was a lovely ego boost and all, but feeling like I could still stick the landing onstage after all this time was that much sweeter.

Later that week I arrived at my office as per usual. Not two minutes into my opening routine my pocket buzzes. It's a text from Afeelya, "Hey girl. Whatcha doing March 13?"

BRAD DᴇBIASE works in grants and programs at the Arizona Commission on the Arts and is also a Phoenix-based drag performer. Follow Brad on Instagram @audubon_street.

SELF

IT'S A BOY!

LAUREN GILGER

I KNEW IT WAS A BOY before the ultrasound tech checked to see, before she put the picture of his little penis in an envelope for the Big Reveal. I knew it before my mother put our present in a blue gift bag and said the blue didn't mean a thing, really. It was just the only bag she could find on the way to our shower.

I knew it before my five-year-old niece opened the envelope in front of the crowd of friends and family and said, "It's a boy!" and then burst into tears.

She wanted a girl. So did I.

* * *

I have always called myself a feminist. And, yes, I realize that being a feminist has nothing to do with having a son. And yes, I realize that men can be feminists too. But, that's not my point. Hear me out.

I grew up with a mother who worked a lot and a dad who stayed at home and let my sister and me paint his fingernails. They were nice and big and round—so much easier to paint than our own. He was great at Chinese checkers but no good at side ponytails. "More *side*, Dad," my sister and I would complain.

My mother was—and is—a powerhouse. She has been in journalism for more than 30 years. She worked her way up from being a farm reporter in St. Cloud, Minnesota, to running one of the top journalism schools in the nation.

Stories about her work ethic are legendary in newsrooms across the country. The best one: While she was the bureau chief in St. Tammany Parish for the Times Picayune in Louisiana, she dictated a story *while she was in labor* with my sister. IN BETWEEN CONTRACTIONS.

She didn't want to let all of the notes she had taken at that night's parish council meeting go to waste.

Unlike my mother, I have always embraced all things girly—from those side pony-tails to the Spice Girls to makeup to "Sex and the City" to high heels... which I wear to work every day, thank you very much. I like to shop, get dressed up, put on a good face mask, drink rose. Sometimes I like to put on a good face mask while drinking rose in a bubble bath. So what?

But, like my mother, I have a deep-rooted belief in women—in our power and equality.

When I was a sophomore at Xavier, the all-girls Catholic high school here in Phoenix, I goaded my religion teacher (a former nun) into calling me a radical for arguing that women should be able to become priests. In college, I chaired the Women's Empowerment club, performed twice in "The Vagina Monologues" and hoped our college chapter of the Knights of Columbus would protest us again. I also fell in love with Sister Elizabeth Johnson's class on women in the Bible and every feminine image of God she had rooted out. In grad school, I got a tattoo of one of them—three soaring birds. I'm not going to show them to you.

As a journalist, I've championed women's issues and worked to tell their stories. I went to the maternity wards of the Dominican Republic to find out if Haitian immigrants there knew their babies would not get birthright citizenship. I documented the suffering of thousands of women implanted with a medical device meant to prevent pregnancy that also sometimes happened to result in a 25-year-old woman needing a hysterectomy.

I married a musician who has no qualms about the fact that I am the breadwinner in our family. When we were dating, I told him how much money I made. Instead of being threatened, I think he was relieved. He cheers me on, pushes me to achieve, and makes me lunch to bring to work every day.

I have always looked at the world with a kind of defiance. *I dare you to underestimate me because I'm blonde and five feet tall. I dare you to talk sports and negotiate your salaries in the men's room. I dare you to interrupt me in a meeting, or take credit for my ideas. I dare you.*

(I realize I sound like Elle Woods, but I was never in a sorority.)

* * *

So, when we decided to have a baby two years ago, I pictured a girl. I assumed it would be a girl. It only made sense.

I would have a little girl who I could dress up, who I could watch musicals with, who I could teach to be strong in the face of sexism, a girl who would achieve and excel and stand up for herself and for other women.

I would have a baby girl and buy her one of those onesies that say "The Future is Female." I would sign her up for Girls Rock Camp and let her run wild and play in the dirt and teach her that she can be whatever she wants to be.

But, instead, I had a boy. A beautiful blonde boy with chubby cheeks and bright blue eyes who has so much love in his heart—and no idea his mother wanted a girl.

And, now that there was a baby boy with a tiny penis growing in my belly, I had to wonder: What about the boys?

Conventional wisdom right now says American men are in crisis. Boys are more likely than girls to get in fights, they're more likely to smoke, to die young, to be victims of violence. They don't do as well in school and they're less likely to go to college. When there is yet another devastating mass shooting in this country, they are the ones pulling the triggers.

We read about men using their power to put women down, to hold them back, to demean them and even assault them. We read that men are clinging to privilege by their ever-sweatier hands.

But then I look at my boy.

Nathaniel is so beautiful. He has round eyes and soft skin and his cheeks turn the most perfect shade of pink when he's been running around in the sun. And his hair! This kid has hair I'd kill for. It's smooth and wavy at once, golden blonde and already—at one-and-a-half—runs past his shoulders. We keep it in a baby man bun most of the time that makes almost everyone over a certain age uncomfortable with his baby gender-bendiness.

Nathaniel is strong and confident and stubborn and gutsy and incredibly sweet. He fights hard for what he wants—like "up!"—and often wants nothing more than to be held, probably while dancing to "Barbara Ann" on loop.

He just learned how to say the word "love."

When my mother was pregnant with my older brother—her first child—in 1980, she said she was determined to raise him to be a feminist. She bought him gender-neutral toys, including an anatomically correct male doll.

He was not interested. When she refused to buy him a toy gun, he came up with an ingenious alternative: He would simply eat his peanut butter and jelly sandwiches into the shape of a gun, point it at someone and make "pew, pew pew!" noises.

And he didn't become an angry misogynist. He became a priest. That's not an analogy—he's actually a Jesuit priest, an academic at the New School who texted me the other night to tell me he cried three times when he went to see "My Fair Lady" on Broadway.

He is a man not unlike my father, who often used his gentle giant hands to pin up my dress-up prairie skirt so you could see the ruffle-y bloomers underneath. No complaints.

And he is a man not unlike my husband, now also a stay-at-home dad, whom I have seen cry exactly three times. But who spends his very little free time writing songs about love that make ME cry.

Nathaniel has two favorite things in the world right now: One is a tiny, plastic Buzz Lightyear figurine that is constantly clutched in his left fist. The other is the garbage truck that stops at our house on Friday mornings. He'll stand outside and wait an hour for that garbage truck if he has to.

I know what you're thinking. "He's such a boy!" People are always saying that when they see him playing with a truck or kicking a soccer ball. Maybe it makes them feel less uncomfortable about his long, luxurious, girly hair.

When they say that, I think back to my baby shower and my niece's tears and that sinking feeling in my stomach. "It's a boy!" everyone cheered.

All I could think was: "What in the world am I going to do with a boy!?"

Now all I can think is: What would the world do without him?

LAUREN GILGER is a journalist in Phoenix and a host at local NPR station KJZZ. You can follow her on Instagram @laurenmichellegilger and Twitter @laurengilger.

MUCHO SUPREMO

JULIA FOURNIER

I KNOW A WOMAN WHO CRIED ALL NIGHT on the first Tuesday after the first Monday of November, 2016—and well into the next morning.

Between asleep and awake, she went back and forth through every stage of grief but acceptance. At some point, in the bargaining phase, she promised to become vegetarian and do meaningful service work, if only. . . .

She believed that in becoming a better person, she might somehow offset the atrocities that would surely begin occurring.

When she was young, she cried so much that people called her "crybaby."

She wonders now if this could be how anxiety manifests in children.

She dances often with anxiety.

Adopting twins with serious cognitive and behavioral issues has made her a worst case scenario person.

She immediately switches to problem solving mode, even when hearing complete strangers in the checkout line. She wants to fix their troubles.

Her boys are 21 years old now and she knows with certainty she will be at least a partial caretaker for one until her death... or his.

She used to speak in front of large groups of people about what she did for a living. People thought she was extraordinary at her work. This embarrassed her, but how could she turn down free trips to Toronto, New Orleans, San Juan? In those days, she took a beta blocker for the anxiety, to keep from making stupid mistakes... and vomiting.

And then somehow it became impossible to get on an airplane without her heart feeling like it had become the size of a basketball pounding up through her chest and into the seat in front of her. Alcohol on planes made her nauseous. Finally her doctor prescribed "The Big X."

But when her sons stopped following even the most basic rules, began doing bad drugs and getting arrested, and her husband was caught cheating, Xanax didn't help much.

She couldn't breathe.

When the kids turned 18, she got them places to live and left her husband.

She tried the soothing sounds of Hawaiian music, stopped listening to the news and drinking coffee. She found a lover, and dependable sex twice a week helped. A lot.

But when Trump happened, there was nothing that could keep away the anxiety she felt for the future; marginalized people, the entire planet.

Becoming vegetarian and her work with The Phoenix Restoration Project, helping refugees at the bus depot get to their families across the country, makes her feel like she has control over *something*. She can make *someone's* world better, if only for a short time.

* * *

And then, a friend sent her a picture of her daughter's mouth and asked what she thought about the little bump pushing through her gums. She never imagined that two years later, despite all efforts, the cancer would still be growing and winning. One of her oldest and dearest friends, a woman with whom she had spent the last 30 Thanksgivings, developed a rare form of lymphoma.... Then her lover was diagnosed with cancer as well.

It seemed to her that Trump and the Republicans had unleashed not just a metaphorical cancer on the U.S., but an actual cancer on many people she loved.

At work she had a hard time focusing. She let deadlines pass. One day, she told a friend that she wondered if there was any reason to go on trying with so much ugliness, stupidity, and cancer in the world.

This friend, sober for the past three decades and caring for his mother with dementia, looked her in the eye and said, "Interesting that you should say that. I think I'm on to something."

And that is when she was introduced to micro-dosing.

She had done mushrooms a few times in her twenties, once, notably, at a Joan Armatrading concert.

While Joan strummed Van Morrison's "Moondance" with Taj Mahal during the lunar eclipse, the man sitting next to her turned into a tree.

With only this experience to go on, it was hard for her to imagine that mushrooms could help with the anxiety that welled up inside all day, every day, and made her extremely irritated when people complained about minor issues like why Trader Joe's stopped carrying their favorite cookie.

* * *

The worry about her sons kept her awake at night, and she could feel herself headed towards complete non-functionality if she didn't try something different.

She contacted a shaman, made a "donation" and received her "gift."

After putting the fungi through the coffee grinder, she began a routine of taking the tiniest amount, sub-perceptual, twice a week before going to bed.

She waited for something to happen.

Something happens.

At some point, after a week, maybe two, she realizes that the tightness in her chest, shortness of breath and knot in her stomach are gone. She doesn't want to fix things any longer because she now knows most things are out of her control, so why bother. She slows down to talk to people, appreciates nature and makes room in her life to exercise every day. She laughs more frequently. She feels more creative and productive, she *is* more creative and productive. It's easier to say, "I love you" and give hugs. She doesn't mind waiting in line. There is a positive, rather than negative tinge to the world.

Was this that "feeling of wellbeing" she had heard about?

Life seems amazing and great, despite the fact that it is still as fucked up as ever.

Months pass. Extremely impatient at a stop light, she finds herself curious about the strength of her dose.

It seems like the sparkle is wearing off. She talks it over with her "mush-buddy." He suggests she double up, but she decides on increasing by just a half to see what happens.

* * *

Sometimes, at her volunteer commitment, newly released ICE detainees need overnight housing until their bus or plane leaves the next day, so she will host refugees at her place.

The night she brings home Efrain is the same night she is going to increase her microdose. Efrain is reluctant to accept her hospitality and she doesn't blame him. It takes weeks to get to the U.S. border from Guatemala on foot. People are robbed and abused along the way. Then there are months in detention before release. Staying with a stranger is risky.

She listens to Efrain and his brother talking in a Mayan language called Mam as they discuss whether or not Efrain should stay with her. She loves the sound of Mam.

After getting Efrain situated, she climbs into bed at two a.m., takes her dose, puts on Coltrane and closes her eyes. As she drifts off, she thinks about the time she waited in line at a film festival with a friend, a Coltrane freak, to see the premier of "Chasing Trane." She had asked him to tell her everything he knew.

He first pulled a little metal box out of his front pocket, opened it, and began to talk. Inside was dirt taken from the yard of Coltrane's childhood home. Then he showed her a video of the celebration of mass at the church of St. John Coltrane in San Francisco. This was when her fascination with Coltrane began.

Later that night she wakes from a dream into a dream. A large green and golden hexagonal prism rotates above her bed, a giant eyeball watches over it. Pinpricks of light show through the walls of the prism as Coltrane's "Naima" plays. The perforations of light make symbols that represent the meaning infused in the music. At that moment, asleep or awake, having obviously ingested more than a sub-perceptual amount of mushrooms, she knows with certainty that Coltrane is love.

She wonders if the Mayan, sleeping in the next room, can hear Coltrane playing and also knows that Coltrane is love. She thinks it is possible that Coltrane would not be love to him, that perhaps pipes playing, birds singing or the sound of his baby laughing in the highlands of Guatemala might be love instead.

She closes her eyes and goes back to sleep. When she opens them, the music is gone as well as the prism. She gets up and makes breakfast for Efrain.

She plays "Love Supreme" while he eats his eggs. He is curious about why she helps people. She tells him about her feelings for Trump, the government, the Republican party, and the people who elected them.

He reminds her that the governments in the countries most refugees have left are much worse.

She tells him her standards for her own country are very high.

He points to her phone where the music is coming from and says,

"Coltrane es el mejor."

Later that day, home after getting Efrain through security at the airport, she texts both her Coltrane friend and her mush buddy about the "dream."

Mush buddy texts back… "Too much!"

Coltrane friend texts back, "Lucky."

JULIA FOURNIER—Phoenix native, mother of twins, former school teacher, and happy grandmother—is co-owner of The Hive Gallery and Bee's Knees Resale Boutique.

#THELINE

STACY PEARSON

THE CALL FROM THE BOSSES CAME on a picture-perfect December afternoon, just a week or so before Christmas.

"Stace, can you get up here tonight? We have a new crisis client that we need your brain on. Total fucking disaster."

I called my family, booked a 5-something p.m. flight, swung by my house to grab a jacket and jeans, and went to the airport.

I work for a multi-state communications firm. When important people get into trouble, they call attorneys for legal help and they call us—me in particular—to manage what comes out of their mouths.

I credit my functionally fucked up childhood for this professional ability to talk my way out of trouble.

Our team huddled the next morning, walking through the potentially devastating, and currently cliché, issue—a high-profile, politically-connected, White, wealthy businessman was being accused of some nasty #MeToo behavior. A reporter was sniffing around.

A few hours later, on the 49th floor of the most impressive office building I've ever been in, the client's lawyer passed out non-disclosure agreements and began telling the back story.

A decade ago, the guy was accused of sexual assault by a woman who claimed he held her head down, and choked her, while she blew him in his car outside of a bar. He said it was consensual, she said it was not. She called the police the next morning. Then, two days later, she filed a massive sexual harassment claim against her employer, with whom our guy did a ton of business. Her criminal and civil claims were investigated and debunked. The final report, written by a woman mind you, stopped juusssst short of calling the accuser crazy. The chosen term was "diminished credibility." Charges were never filed. Media never reported any of it.

Now, 10 years later, and in the heart of the #MeToo era, a second woman is claiming this guy rape-raped her, almost two decades prior, after he snuck into her bedroom and climbed on top of her, despite her protests.

He denied both accusations, but the math is simple. One false claim can be false. Two claims make both true. And if there's a third, this guy is toast.

The men in the room offered their support during this "trying time" in his life.

Our client shook his head and held up his hand to silence them.

"Just stop. I was a huge asshole for a long time, I admit that. But I'm not a rapist."

"Humpf."

Like, I really humpfd at this guy in the meeting.

Then I said, "So, hey, look, I want to believe you. I do. And I'm the only person— only woman—here who can defend you in the court of public opinion. So I'm sorry, but I need to ask some really uncomfortable questions about where you draw the line between *huge asshole* and *rapist*."

And for the next two hours, I grilled him.

"Were you in the front seat or the back? Did you grab the back of her head? Did you pull her hair? The whole time, or just when you were finishing? You finished, right? *Could* you choke her—like is it anatomically possible for your dick to block someone's airway? Did she gag? Bite you? Cry? Swallow? Who knew about this? Who else knew? Why would this second accuser come forward now? Why were you in her room, at all? Does she have other reasons to hate you? How much did you drink, then? How much do you drink, now? How do you define consent? What did it mean 10 years ago?"

I was impressed. Dude never flinched. Short story: He owns bars. Spent the better part of 20 years drunk and/or high, trying to get laid as often as possible with as many women as possible. Often, in a grab-her-kiss-her-drag-her-to-a-private-corner kind of way. He owned it. And had I met him in his heyday, I probably would have liked it. He looked pinched between being sincerely mortified by his behavior in hindsight, and occasionally being proud of his most creative conquests.

I listened without judgement. And without mentioning my own freakishly relevant history.

For example, I got his whole bar thing—I was raised in a tavern owned by my swearing, drinking, divorced (three times) grandma. I learned to smile at the friendly, atta-girl grabass and recognize the creepy/rapey grope.

And there was that time, in high school, when that dude I met at a party dropped me off at my house at curfew, lurked maybe an hour, popped off my screen, climbed in my open bedroom window and jumped into my bed, without any kind of invitation. At all. I didn't even kiss him goodnight in the car. But I had to choose whether to scream and get my parents involved, or just fuck him and get him out of there. At least he was quick.

I didn't mention that time at a work conference, when I swung by my male colleague's hotel room. No biggie, we planned to walk to the big group dinner together. He opened the door wearing a towel, and asked me to come in. He just needed two minutes to get dressed.

I knew better than to go in.

But I did.

He dropped his towel. And started—perhaps continued—jacking off.

And like an Olympic hurdler in a sundress, I ran up/over the bed to get around him and out the door. His parting words were hauntingly weird. "Did I scare you? Did I?" he said with a grin, without skipping a wank.

And I didn't mention my shitbird boss, the one who thought Blackberry messenger was invented so he could tell subordinate female staff, "your talent inspired me, hard, this morning."

After all, if #MeToo taught me anything, it's that these are the typical stories of a 40-year-old woman, right? I'd even go as far as to say I fared pretty well.

Hell, there's a part of the creepy hotel-wanker story that's still funny. The part when I ran downstairs and told a woman I was travelling with what happened. Her eyes bugged, she yelled "Holy shit!!!!!" Then she leaned in and asked, "Was he circumcised?"

What!? Yes? What the fuck?

Bottom line is that members of the sisterhood have dealt with—and continue to deal with—way worse than I've had to.

So where was this client on the #MeToo spectrum? No worse than my worst stories? Better? Dirty-fun dude? Aggressive guy who's scary as shit if that's not your thing? Rapist? Victim of some elaborate smear campaign?

For the next six months, we waited for a reporter's call and I worked on that calculus.

He's thrown lots of grabby patrons out of his bars. Good guy. Has a shit ton of female executives in his companies. Points to the plus. Looks kinda weird. Some-might-wonder-if-he's-circumcised weird. Slide the marker toward rapist. But the first accuser seemed so, incredibly, full of shit. Move the marker again in his favor.

I also tried to reconcile his era—the same one I came up in. "Sixteen Candles"? Loved that movie. Remember that part where the jock gave the nerd his hammered girlfriend to bang in Dad's Rolls Royce? That was so…fucked up. "Revenge of the Nerds"? Great waterbed scene where the nerd puts on a mask, pretends to be the cheerleader's boyfriend, fucks her, but because he was so good at the ~~sex~~ rape, she wasn't even mad. Great love story.

And, today, if some trenchcoat-wearing, lovesick boy showed up outside my daughter's window blasting music, I'm not going to encourage her to appreciate the grand gesture. I'm going to call 911, John Cusack, as god is my witness.

I worked through the fact that I really _want_ to believe every woman's worst story in a feeble attempt to make right for the ~~hundreds~~ thousands of years we weren't believed enough. And for every time someone said, "But look what she was wearing." But the increase in baseline belief can't mean the blind ignorance of truth.

That's how #MeToo dies, right?

A reporter finally called. I coached my client through two very tough interviews. I shared with the reporter my deep thoughts about '80s movies and lobbied that this guy was likely in the ignorant, selfish, bad-sex zone of the #MeToo spectrum. Jerk, yes. Rapist, no. But the reporter did not give a shit about my spectrum, the first accuser's "diminished credibility," or rapey coming-of-age movies.

I struggled with the hellfire I knew was coming for him. Legally, the statute of limitations had long-since expired. But I predicted people would call for his castration, boycott his businesses, and ultimately hurt his majority-female staff. Dude has plenty of money. But the bartender needed to make rent. He seemed genuinely distraught about that. I know I was.

The story ran and was absolutely brutal. More accusers. More credible-sounding details than I could have imagined. But I was okay with my role as his named, paid defender. The guy was getting publicly shamed. But he deserved to live and learn.

In fact, I started to believe that maybe this situation would create an opportunity to talk about what's missing from the #MeToo movement. Space has to exist between absolute fucking flogging and turning a blind eye. Where's the time-out corner where we can stick Al Franken, and this guy?

I brainstormed with the client about the best ways to fill that void. Advance the conversation. I told him to keep his head down, take his lumps, but that when the mob turned their attention to the next asshole in the news, maybe we could create space where bad behavior can be acknowledged, sincerely apologized for, learned from, and…maybe forgiven?

A place that I can even say this out loud without being called a rape apologist or get my feminist card pulled.

Then, I got a call from a friend who worked for him in her early twenties. She'd just seen the story.

Her voice cracked when she confirmed it was me who was helping him.

"I'm one of his victims," she began.

Turns out…the line between huge _asshole_ and _rapist_ is clear.

And I'm the asshole.

STACY PEARSON is a political consultant with a journalism background. She can usually be found on Twitter @StacyPearson or at Circle K buying scratchers.

KNOW THY ELF

AMANDA KATE KEHRBERG

ATLANTA IS SWELTERING with late summer heat as crowds descend for Dragon Con, a massive media and comics convention that draws about 80,000 people annually. Or, as unsuspecting tourists know it, "why our waiter is dressed like Spider-Man in September."

The convention takes over downtown, scattering programming from panels to concerts to parties across all the major hotels. Imagine you're squeezing past a conga line of Deadpools when you run into a spontaneous jumble of people cosplaying as Rick from Rick and Morty, along with one guy dressed as Morty shivering as he whines, "Aww, jeez, too many Ricks." In the distance, you hear a Key & Peele fan shouting, "Meegan! Meegan, your sweater!"

That's basically Dragon Con: just one big, warm pop culture hug.

My best friend Angela and I are here for the first time. We met 15 years ago as Harry Potter fans, but since then my experience with fandom, as a graduate student and teacher, has been more study than practice.

The trip to Dragon Con is part of her scheme to get me out of my current funk. And she's not wrong: I've barely been out of the house in months, adjusting to a new role as a caregiver to my dad after his ALS diagnosis. I got the news in 2014 about a month before the Ice Bucket Challenge went viral, precipitating a personal media blackout just to get a moment's break. When my dad finally wrote the email sharing the diagnosis with his siblings, it began, "This is your ice bucket."

As we check into the hotel, next to a couple towing a full rack of immaculately pressed gold Star Trek uniforms, the guy at the front desk admires Angela's hair.

"I love this color!" he coos, referring to her mint green and teal highlights.

He turns to me, giving me an appraising sweep of his eyes.

"And what about you? Do you have a fun tattoo or something?"

I shake my head.

"Nope, sorry."

I know what he's thinking: From the outside, Angela and I look like when the cool, artsy kid at school gets paired with the austere German exchange student, and in the end they both learn the true meaning of work and play, and, I dunno, Christmas. If I already look a little out of place next to her, I *definitely* look out of place next to a few thousand other people in town this weekend.

Angela is determined to fix that. She has plans this weekend to drag me out of my style comfort zone; and drag is the right word, since I've been known to go from zero to drag queen in about 60 seconds with only a simple berry lip. It's a plot founded in the philosophy of so many movie makeover montages that transform women's lives the way boxing montages do for men.

And I'll be the first to admit, I'm a pretty blank canvas to work with. My local sandwich shop was not wrong when they started labeling all my orders "bland." My favorite part of "The Lego Movie" is the first 10 minutes when they sing "everything is awesome" and everyone follows the instructions. Growing up, my hairstyle was the timeless "just released from a polygamous compound." When I watch "The Handmaid's Tale," I know I should feel more fear at the dark vision of a fascist state, but I can't help envy government regulated, monochromatic wardrobes.

Like anyone, I sometimes experiment when I travel. Like, I wear a hat.

For herself, Angela has packed three bold lipstick colors to try out on different days: black, green, and purple. But for me, someone who reserves mascara for births, deaths, and weddings, she's chosen a more daring accessory: elf ears.

I don't know why she settled on elf ears, but I am, as always, along for the ride. Over the years, I've let Angela drag me along to everything from psychics to tarot readings and even past life regressions, which is how I know that advising me to "focus on my root chakra" and "learn to receive" is my spirit guides' polite way of saying, "Girl, you need to get laid."

A sprightly young man dressed like a Lord of the Rings extra, whose nametag reads something like Kringle or Caraway, applies the pair of silicone elf ears to mine with sticky spirit gum. I admire my new pointy ears in the hand mirror while Angela transforms into a high-born night elf, and even I have to admit: I make a pretty cute forest elf.

We haven't walked far when my vision blurs and my view of the busy hall skips like a busted film projector. Angela grabs me a soda while I sit for a moment, trying to ease the spinning room. It must just be the humidity, I'm sure, or the closeness of the crowds and the hours on our feet.

We haven't eaten since a late breakfast of blueberry bagels, so I'm convinced if I can just make it to dinner I'll be fine. There are restaurants only a block away, so we head down the escalators and out onto the street.

Outside, I lean on Angela, heavier and heavier, until I slip unconscious to the pavement and have the first—and thankfully, only—seizure of my life. I'm told later that my head thrashes back against the concrete and my jaw is pulled wide, my feet shaking so hard that my sandals fly off.

The thing about having an emergency at a comic-con is that there's a high probability you'll be rescued by people in superhero costumes. Heroes who, on an average day, are more likely to save day-old donuts or fight bad grammar, but heroes nonetheless. Several rush to hold my shaking head and call 911, creating a strange tableau for a growing audience of onlookers, who break out in applause as I'm lifted onto a stretcher.

I come back to consciousness slowly on that stretcher, and I don't know where or when I am. It's a terrifying feeling. The first thing I see is the silver-painted face of a street performer, sat on his upturned bucket and staring at me with the same disdain Bette Davis throws at Marilyn Monroe in "All About Eve," like my young upstart act is trespassing on *his* territory. The second thing I see is Angela's face—and that, thank goodness, is familiar.

"Where are my shoes?" I ask, as I wriggle my toes freely in the Atlanta air.

She holds up my sandals, her expression frozen in that sort of cringing pity that is all teeth, topped with raised eyebrows trying to signal some measure of hope.

It's a short ride to the nearby Grady Hospital downtown. On the way in, the security guard asks Angela if she has any weapons and doesn't laugh too loudly when she pulls out a replica of Rey's gun from "Star Wars: The Force Awakens."

Later, as I wait on the stretcher for a room, I can hear Angela on the phone with my mom. "Yeah, she's fine," she says, "but she's kinda mad she's in the ER in elf ears."

In the hospital room, I'm questioned by a steady stream of nurses, doctors, and residents. They take a urine sample, then realize later they never actually needed one. Angela laughs so hard at this that she can barely hold her phone straight to take a picture of my now superfluous pee cup, a shot which some perplexing Apple algorithm will later memorialize as her "2016 Photo of the Year."

In between examinations, we watch a series of documentaries on the history of Marvel Comics, airing serendipitously on the local PBS affiliate. Angela gestures wildly at the tiny hospital TV as she cheers on the company's leadership in representing diversity and emotional depth.

You don't have to be strapped down to take Angela's Marvel Master Class, but it helps. I'm so grateful for that education, though, since without it I wouldn't have fully appreciated what a marvel Stan Lee was.

After I'm discharged, we take an Uber back to the hotel while the driver regales us with stories of growing up with Will Smith and impassioned, gleeful predictions that Donald Trump will be our next president.

Crumpled in the dark backseat in September 2016, I can't say which I believe less.

Back home in Phoenix, after a fresh round of tests, the cardiologist is as confused as everyone else. Everyone except Angela, who is convinced I am "allergic to whimsy."

As the doctor explains, sometimes the brain can overreact to certain triggers and tell the rest of the body to man the lifeboats over nothing. He's seen triggers from a too-cold soda can to a high-pitched noise, but finds most incidents are sparked by anxiety.

"Anxiety?" I ask. "Anxiety about what?"

"Well," he says, with a withering sigh, "were you anxious about wearing elf ears?"

AMANDA KATE KEHRBERG is an instructor, writer, and occasional stand-up comic with terrible taste in movies. Find her at byamandakate.com.

SPEECHLESS

TREJON DUNKLEY

I'M SITTING in an impossibly chic little cafe in downtown Phoenix, sipping at my too-bitter latte. Baristas in these places spend more time working on their foam art than their brewing, and charge accordingly.

Five years ago, I wouldn't have imagined myself in this spot. I wouldn't think I'd still be in Arizona, a Sun Devil alumni. It seems like every fear 17-year-old me has had, I've fulfilled. An even bigger disappointment is who sits across from me, pretending her tiny egg sandwich is substantial.

Amanda Courier. The demon of my senior year nightmares, my rival, my enemy. And now my friend.

She's still impossibly beautiful, but softer, more natural, more confident. I remember her at Speech National finals, looking like Jackie O Jr, in her powder blue suit, her rouged cheeks. A pageant doll. A goddess.

She's living her version of my dream: living and working in L.A., getting published in Vogue Italia, photographing web series stars. It's still easy to hate her, want to be her.

"I hate what they did to us," she says, almost out of nowhere. I don't need to ask who "they" are.

"I wanted to be your friend so badly. I thought you hated me. My coach told me you did."

"Mine too." The Capulets and the Montagues, an ancient feud played out with speaker points.

I joined the speech team my sophomore year of high school. At that point, I was the certified "weird girl" at school, and had a hard time finding my place. The friends I'd had in middle school were floating away and I couldn't find new ones to fill the void. I spent most of my lunches in the library, with the books that would always be there. When auditions for the musical came up freshman year, I jumped at the chance, hoping the theatre would be where I found my footing. I didn't get in, but I was a shoe-in for the student-directed one-acts, where my less than stellar dancing skills weren't such a huge deal.

My director practically begged me to join speech after my performance in the one-acts. Even then, I think he saw his golden goose. The Charger girl that would show the circuit we were more than just middle-class underdogs, floundering next to the prep schools and their National Championship coaches.

I wanted to prove him right. I wanted to prove everyone else wrong. Everyone who thought I was just a bookish loudmouth weirdo. My dad, eternally disappointed in my gender. My peers, who only noticed me to mock me. I wanted to be someone great.

For two years, I was. When the out-round banners flew down, my name always appeared at least for semis, usually for finals too. I took my wins with gracious pride, and the first few times, an extreme amount of tears. I earned the loving moniker "pterodactyl face" after an ugly cry during the awards ceremony found its way on Facebook. My team loved me. My opponents feared and respected me. I was the pride of Division One. To this day, one of the schools I challenged remember my pieces, my skill, me, 10 years on.

My senior year, after a mix of increased school funding and a circuit-wide encouragement of our skills, our team got moved to Division Two. The big dogs. The winter and spring invitationals that had once been such a piece of cake for us would now be overrun by the prep schools we so feared and loathed. I had no fear though. I knew I was their match. What would stop me from quickly crushing them?

The first practice of the year, my coaches presented me with a list of competitors to watch out for. This one had gotten to finals at Harvard. This one had gone to George Mason that summer, the MIT of speech camps. I was ready for them all.

They didn't tell me about Amanda. I met her for the first time in a round, and her piece brought me, and herself, to tears.

I saw her silently weeping, trying not to muss her mascara.

"I'm sorry. It's just. I miss my cousin." He'd died of AIDS, and her piece, about a Midwestern mother mourning her dead boy, was in commemoration of him. I hugged her then, and thought he'd be proud.

After prelims, my coach came up to me, compared my scores to hers, and said "She's the one to beat this year." Ambition overtook compassion from that moment on.

I saw in her everything I wanted to be. She had her perfect speech boyfriend, and her beautiful tailored suits (her secret, she said: clearance sales at Macy's). She could afford the camps I never could, had the rich friends I'd never have, had her own car. I scrolled through her Facebook and Instagram and tried to find the secrets of her beauty, find the chinks in her facade. I thought if I could break her open, all her falseness would come spilling out and she'd stop winning every tournament, stealing my well-deserved limelight.

"I was so fucking bored of that piece by the end," she said. She's swirling her iced coffee, finding the last drops of caffeine amid the melting ice. "They cut all the soul out of it by the end, it was manufactured to win. It didn't matter what I said, as long as I paused for five seconds in the right place."

I knew the feeling. My piece was chosen to win championships. A famous memoir by a wealthy widow. I barely understood the words of the book, but I knew where to cut to manipulate judges. I knew how to pantomime taking off a wedding ring, have my tears stand on my eyes, but never fall (tears were a prop, and props were forbidden). But where was the soul by the end? My coaches lambasted me for being stiff, for forgetting the character. "Where's the soul? Do you even like her?" They took it from me. You don't need a soul to win. Just clean pops.

As Amanda won firsts over me, and I kept floundering, all I could focus on was getting to Nationals. If I got to Nationals, the first McClintocker of my generation, I'd prove myself, it'd all be worth it. It was the only thing that mattered. It was the only way I could justify my existence.

I didn't even make it out of sems at the qualifier. I walked into school the next day, unable to speak, a cloud hanging over my eyes. Every time one of my well-meaning friends or teachers asked how Quals went, I had to stave off tears and barely whisper, "Fine," although it was anything but. Three years of work and sacrifice, wasted. My glory gone. And of course SHE was going. She was going to Nationals, and she was going to triumph and my life was over. I didn't get out of bed the week of Nationals. I found out she got 2nd in the Nation, and through my bitter tears, all I could think was "Thank god that bitch didn't win."

I found her Tumblr that last summer of our senior year. That blogging site where all the sad girls went to vent their troubles. I found the most shocking things imaginable on her page. She had painful periods, and acne scars, and a troubled relationship with her mom. She felt too big some days, too short. She was a dork in her high school as well, only had friends in speech. She worried her art wasn't good enough, she hated her college. I found out, to my eternal horror, that she was just a girl. Like me, she was just a lonely, anxious strange girl, who wanted to prove everyone wrong.

So I started messaging her.

Anonymously at first, about how I loved her page and her art and related to her. Then I finally attached my screen name. And then "I don't know if you remember me, but we did speech together. I did the Joan Didion piece?"

We had all the hallmarks of internet friendship. Sharing memes back and forth, silly

Snapchats in face masks and filters, sad girl singer song-writers, encouraging messages to sad posts, endless heart emojis on each other's selfies. She became my friend. A truer friend than I'd known in years.

I coached for my old high school for years, and when my coach found out I was talking to Alexa, he looked quizzical and asked, "How can you be friends with her? She was always such a bitch."

I thought back to times she actually *had* been a bitch. We only talked rarely but she was always kind. Complimented my suit, gave me small pointers. The monster I saw her as was of my own creation, exacerbated by my coaches and teammates. I went home that night and wondered how a teacher could call a 17-year-old girl a bitch. I stopped coaching after the next tournament.

She grabs my arm as we walk out of the cafe, hugs my shoulder. "I'm glad we did this. I always wanted to do this with you. I always thought you were so much cooler than me, I never thought you'd want anything to do with me."

I can't help laughing. "We're speech kids. I don't think any of us actually qualify as cool."

She laughs too. Not her stage laugh, not her gracious winner's laugh. Full-bellied, a cackle of sorts. "Thank god. Thank god."

TREJON DUNKLEY is a Phoenix writer, actress and comedian who just wants her niece to think she's cool. Follow her @trejondunkley wherever media is socialized.

THE WAITING ROOM

DIANA MARTINEZ

IT'S COLD.

Air conditioning that breathes 68 degrees and a stiff pink gown isn't very soothing on the nerves. The walls around me are painted shades of dull and bland, holding still-life paintings in equally mute color schemes.

As chalky and outdated as they are, they're the only things my eyes seem to land on.

A couple weeks ago I came to grips that I needed to see a doctor. For this lump. I actually noticed it years ago, but, like other things in my life, I prefer to accommodate passive dangers.

Like the once-committed, on-again, off-again dude. I'm convinced he'll come around and we'll work things out. Who cares if he's verbally and mentally abusive, right? I keep trying. Keep going back. Maintaining the cycle.

Wrong, actually. You don't welcome egomaniacs back into your life or leave tumors alone and hope for the best. That passivity is what they feed on. They have to be removed. So long as you know they're there.

And, that's why I'm here, I guess. Waiting for a biopsy they say I need, but if it were up to me, I'd still be walking around with it intact, like a little sidekick cheering on my refutation. I like the blindness too much.

67 degrees.

This "second" waiting room is always the worst. At least in the first one, you're fully dressed and maintain a little connection to the outside world.

Man-handled magazines are left on empty chairs, an aloof receptionist hands you an interrogating clipboard, and daytime television spouts in the background while other numbers—I mean, names—share in the waiting.

Everything in here looks like it was taken out of an attic. A quarter inch of dust covers a stack of nameless books, a wooden end table holds a non-working lamp, and plastic plants pose as if they were told "this is what the real ones do." Like two-foot-tall actors, who were just alerted "It's showtime."

This is all an act.

All of these old and off-putting things, in this in-between space to the right of the hallway and in front of procedure room, are placed.

Trying to comfort its unwilling attendees. I manage to stare long enough at the all-star cast and its stage hands to keep from running out and far away. Or worse, facing the fact that I have to be cut open.

I almost came to this realization recently. That something needs to change with my tolerance of these hazards. Like when the aforementioned ex yelled in my face, hit the wall behind me in a heated argument, and then hours later all was as normal.

I've had my moments too though. Too many. From refusing to leave his house because I couldn't handle the fact that this plug finally had to be pulled, to wanting to jump out of a fifth-story window one day because it was the only thing that made sense to stop this broken record from spinning.

I'm sitting uncomfortably straight, too untrusting to let my guard down.

I'm the one who doesn't like this duality? Ironic.

But I'm onto it. It takes me for a fool, trying to mask its purpose. It knows why I'm here. It's expertly woven reality and a weak facade into the wall-to-wall carpeting.

It's like the formal living room that some houses have. A sitting room, I should say. You sit and look, but you don't live there.

It shows you what life looks like, without being able to enter into it. And this room, brisk, dry, and clever, knows a different life is just what the doctor ordered.

Cut out the tumors. Stop the cycle. See. Heal. Don't be still-life, like we are. Be alive.

And I think that's the point of this whole production. I'm distracted by its staleness. Not comforted, not leisurely waiting. Just here, bothered by its performance. Preoccupied long enough to make it through the necessary wait. The wait that leads to life.

Damn. Bravo, room. Encore.

The creak of a door and a human voice breaks the blaring silence.

"We're ready for you."

DIANA MARTINEZ is a writer of many forms and a Phoenix native. Follow her business @reqreading on Instagram and find her @dnmrtnz on there, too.

VOICE

ZAIDA DEDOLPH

I'M A HIP PERSON. I know how to groove. And as such, I read my fair share of internet think pieces.

Recently there have been a lot of internet think pieces about women's voices and the many, many ways that they can be scrutinized. I can relate to this. For as long as I can remember, my voice has been subject to criticism. I've been told I speak too quietly. I've been told I speak too loudly. Nicer people have called my voice "squeaky." Evil troll monsters, like my grandmother, have called it "shrill."

This story isn't about those people. Those people are why I have a great shrink to tell stories to. Instead, this story is about the time that my body tried to shut me up entirely.

I graduated from college—magna cum laude, no big deal—smack dab in the middle of the recession. Here is a list of things that I graduated with:

-A 3.87 GPA
-Excellent time management skills

-Excessive amounts of type A energy
-$40,000 in student loan debt
-Zero job prospects

Throughout college I had worked full-time in the specialty coffee industry. So, to pay the rent and blow off some surplus piss and vinegar, I kept it up.

I'm not talking about Starbucks. I'm talking about a different world: one where people compete with coffee to see who has the better palate, who can pour the prettiest latte art, who can brew a coffee within a certain extraction yield with the most accuracy.

On a typical morning I'd hit snooze around 4 a.m. I'd brush my teeth using unflavored toothpaste, then use a tongue scraper—it's supposed to improve your palate. I'd eat bland foods all day, nothing too spicy or salty or sweet, and stay away from zinc and vitamin supplements, because all of those things would interfere with your ability to taste. I spent my days measuring solutes, cupping coffees, and smiling endlessly. If I hadn't been so caffeinated, I would have been exhausted. But obsessive compulsive disorder is kind of my spirit animal, so I thrived in a world where things had to be and look and taste perfect, or else you got fired.

I worked my way up to be a barista trainer. Then I was a shop manager, then I directed operations for a roasting company. But what I really, really wanted was to be a coffee buyer. I thought, on some level, that if I could travel to other countries and get paid for it then maybe people would stop making fun of me for getting an anthropology degree.

The problem is, coffee buying jobs are hard to come by—especially for women. In coffee, as in many industries, women are grossly underrepresented. In regions of origin, women are often responsible for tending farms and maintaining crop knowledge, but rarely own the land they work. In regions of consumption, women—and people of color, I might add—are all too often hired as pretty, friendly faces in retail and low-level management, but rarely bridge the gap into roasting or purchasing or executive positions.

On top of that, coffee-producing regions are some of the poorest places in the world. They're generally remote, rural, and mountainous. Some areas are controlled by drug cartels, who inflict fear and terror. Access to preventative care and urban amenities can be difficult to come by, so women routinely die from totally treatable things like cervical cancer.

When a management job opened up at what we'll call Fancy Coffee Company, I leapt at the opportunity. Fancy Coffee Company not only had coffee shops and did roasting, they were among the first companies to develop relationships directly with the growers who produced their coffee. They had a whole team of buyers that visited the farms. They knew the families. They built commerce on these relationships.

When I was hired at Fancy Coffee Company I was told my chances of becoming a coffee buyer were fantastic. The company was huge by industry standards, but didn't have any women working in buying or roasting roles at the time. They told me they wanted to change that. All I had to do was earn my stripes by opening a new store.

This is where this story really begins.

I unwittingly adopted the company's problem child. This store was a tire fire. It was in one of Chicago's wealthiest neighborhoods, and as it turns out, rich people hate spending money, except on dogs, and they all think their dogs' dirty butts belong everywhere, like especially in coffee shops, where the city of Chicago most definitely does not allow dirty dog butts. My office was 95 degrees at all times in the summer, and 30 degrees in the winter. The ventilation system once sprayed dirty snow into the cafe and onto our customers. I'm still not sure how or why that happened. There was also an electrical problem that caused our hot water spouts to spurt steam at random intervals, so you were liable to get burned at any point in time if you were behind the bar.

They had high expectations at Fancy Coffee Company. I routinely worked 60- to 80-hour weeks. The staff had to be trained. The store had to be stocked. They had strict benchmarks for management—more so than at any previous job, my life became a constant battle to keep waste and labor low, customers happy, and profit margins high.

The week my store opened, I came down with a cold. The cold turned into bronchitis. I couldn't take a day off work, so I went to the urgent care center by my house and got a round of antibiotics. But I couldn't stop coughing. I'd go to work, sneak into the back to cough for a few minutes, then waltz right back behind the bar to smile and chat with customers.

After a few weeks I was desperate. I went back to the doctor. He called an ambulance. I was taken to the emergency room hooked up to a tank full of oxygen. I called my boss to tell her I was in the hospital. She asked if I was healthy enough to handle this job, or if she should be looking for my replacement. I slept for two hours and went to work in the morning.

Over the next few months I was put through the ringer. I took round after round of antibiotics. My lungs were x-rayed a billion times. They drew buckets of blood. They thought I had pneumonia. A lung tumor. Tuberculosis.

But mostly they thought I was having asthma attacks. They gave me about a thousand steroid shots, right in the butt! The steroids helped some—they gave me loads of energy. They didn't shrink my testicles, because I didn't have any, but they did shrink the rest of me. Over the course of a year I got an inch shorter. My feet shrank by a size and a half. I never stopped coughing.

I tried to reframe my perspective. Sure, I couldn't stop coughing. But! In my life I have been on no less than three buses where there was a man masturbating, and two of them were wearing scrubs, and one of them was looking at a picture of a foot on his cell phone, and I hate that I can rattle off these statistics, but you don't forget stuff like that. I have also been on one bus where a man NO FUCKING JOKE cut off a lock of my hair with scissors and then ran out the door. I can safely say that if you sound like you have the black lung at least like, 10% of the creepiest men on the bus will avoid sitting next to you. So, that's nice.

Also, sure, I couldn't stop coughing. But if I had been born in coffee region it could have been so much worse! I don't have to worry about drinking the water or having a drug cartel kidnap my kids, because I don't have any kids, I have cats. I have cats, not kids, because I have safe and reliable access to contraception. Also, the cartels wouldn't even want my cats. Because they're assholes. And they eat too much. And Ruby has to have her Prozac by 8 p.m. or she turns into a literal demon.

And sure, I couldn't stop coughing. But I had a doctor to cough on. And an education. And a job. And so many other countless privileges that come with being born white and American, which I will never be able to fully articulate or appreciate. So sure. I couldn't speak for all the coughing, but I still had a voice in this world that a lot of people will never experience.

I kept working endless hours, I kept cutting costs, I kept waking up early, I kept my palate clean. But I coughed any time I opened my mouth.

Finally, a team of doctors stuck a tube down my nose and into my throat and discovered that the problem wasn't with my lungs. My vocal cords were having spasms, clapping wildly when they should have stayed open to let me breathe. The only remedy for this was speech therapy: one hour, three times a week, for at least six weeks.

My boss said there was no was no way I could miss that much work. And I wouldn't want to. After all, a coffee buying job had just opened in the company, and I was certain that after nearly a year of excellent performance, despite all odds, I'd get it. They said they wanted to hire more women! I had worked so hard! I had coughed so much!

I submitted my application, nailed my interview, and waited.

I didn't get the job. Instead, it went to one of the barista trainers. He started around the same time as I did, after the cafe he owned went bankrupt within months of opening.

I asked what I could do to improve my application. "You should make time to just hang out with the boys in the roasterie more," they said.

"Plus, we felt like he really needed a win. He's had a rough year."

ZAIDA DEDOLPH lives in Phoenix. She is a retired barista and present-day nonprofit professional. She likes cats, coffee, and procedural crime dramas.

JUST GO AHEAD, LET YOUR HAIR DOWN

TIARA VIAN

YOUR SELFIE IS 90% HAIR. That's the caption I see all the time in my Instagram feed. Hair is a big deal. And hair is technically a dead collection of keratin cells tumbling around your face and those cells make you who you are. Or at least that's what I had believed my entire life.

When I was maybe six or seven, I had long, wavy-curly, fine hair. My mom tied it in twists and braids with brightly colored barrettes on the end that always got lost on the school playground. My hair was healthy and shiny and I could not have cared less about it. Wash days on Saturdays were a nightmare, mostly because it consisted of Mom combing through the puff ball for an hour, then washing it in the sink while I lay on the counter, finishing it with a healthy dose of Palmer's pink oil and some fresh braids. But that routine worked for me. My mom would probably disagree because I have two sisters and they each had thicker hair than I had.

When I was 11, Mom had had enough. I was charged with taking care of my hair as she had done for the last 10 years. I was completely unprepared and my hair suffered.

I grew up on Davis-Monthan Airforce Base in Tucson, and my school had few people who looked like me. Most of the kids were White, Asian, or Latino. I started to notice all the straight-haired girls at school had beautiful, hip-length hair that flowed in the wind. While my hair was frizzy and mainly stood up instead of cascading down my back. It was breaking off, my scalp was always itchy, and no one thought it was pretty. I was so depressed and started begging for a relaxer.

If you don't know, a relaxer is a potent chemical hair treatment, much like a perm, that makes kinky-curly hair straight. To me, straight hair was pretty hair, and I wanted pretty hair. When I was 12, we were going to visit my Auntie in Greensboro that summer and she was a hairdresser. So I convinced my sisters (who were also suffering equally dry hair) that we should all get Auntie to relax our hair. Against their better judgment, our parents caved. And we each got a relaxer that summer. We had also moved off-base so it felt like a brand new beginning. Seventh grade was going to be awesome.

That fall, I walked into my middle school with LAID hair. It was about shoulder length and it blew in the wind. It was shiny, stick straight, and perfect. But of course, as a high functioning introvert, I said nothing to my friends when they asked how summer was. I stared blankly at the boys who said I looked different, and I sobbed internally when the White girls said I looked bald. My fine hair was FLAT. Almost like I had no hair at all. Which is what one boy said to me when he touched my hair. Side note: Never touch a black woman's hair... you all have been warned.

So my little heart was crushed. I still didn't have hair like everyone else. Kids thought it was odd that every eight weeks I got a touch up relaxer. Ya know, because my hair was still growing in curly. But with no guidance on how to take care of my hair I didn't know what else to do but to keep relaxing it.

A few years later, I attended high school with about the same mix of kids—mostly White and Latino. Like seriously, at lunch nearly *all* the Black kids hung out at three tables clustered together. It was in high school I discovered the curling iron. Ironic that I relaxed my curly hair to make it straight and then used a curling iron to make it curly again. I clearly had no idea what I wanted. But everyone else had what they called "barrel curls"—long, straight hair lightly curled to give you Mila Kunis vibes. Anyone else watch "That '70s Show"? That's what I wanted... but what I got was more like Reba's hair in the '90s (without the bangs). I fried my hair every morning like that. Flipped out to the sides, wispy, dry, and damaged. Can you guess how long my hair was? Yep, still shoulder length....

When I graduated, I wanted a fresh start—away from all the kids I went to high school with. They all went to the U of A, so I went to NAU in Flagstaff. Flag was much more relaxed—meaning, way less pressure to look a certain way. I met this Black girl who told me that she wasn't going to relax her hair anymore and just let it grow. She said she was embracing her natural hair. Her hair was shorter than mine, only half of it was curly and the other half was straight. Her curly roots and straight ends looked strange to me. I couldn't bring myself to walk around with funny-looking hair so I kept up the relaxers.

By the time we graduated she had cut off her straight ends and was feelin' herself in a cute curly fro. I was still hiding behind the relaxer.

After college, I moved to Tucson and back into my parents' house because every millennial does it these days. My younger sister, who has always had thicker, longer hair was trying something new. She was relaxing her hair less and letting some texture back in. It looked fabulous on her. It was about to her shoulder blades but it wasn't dry or fried like mine. She had discovered leave-in conditioner... and hair oils... deep treatment masques... and didn't use heat! I had to see what it was all about. So I Googled and YouTubed everything I could about letting texture back in while still relaxing... it's called texlaxing, by the way. You just leave the treatment in for less time so it's not fully processed straight.

Through all of that Googling I stumbled upon "natural hair" videos. Black women were growing out their hair, just like my friend was in college. And as they grew it out they hid the evidence of the two textures with cute, unassuming hairstyles. They made it seem easy, even fun. They said things like, "I'm ready to be who I've always been." Really, just by growing out your hair? And they all had healthy, gorgeous hair. I was tired of having ugly hair in every photo I took, because at this point, selfies were a thing. So I decided to give this "natural hair" thing a try. I stopped getting relaxers and my roots started to curl up and get thicker. I used conditioner like it was my job, I stopped using a curling iron, and I started dreaming about long, curly hair.

It wasn't an easy process. My hair was uneven, unruly, and unbelievably tangled. The two textures did not play well together. Sometimes I'd be in the bathroom for two hours finger-combing through knots. I could have just cut it off and started over but I was too insecure to have short, or rather, *shorter* hair. I was transitioning to natural so I could keep the length. I started video recording my "wash days" because it really took an entire day to get it washed and styled. Literally, it was just me sitting in a bath robe applying as much conditioner and oil as possible so I could comb through the knots. From that, I started a YouTube channel so other people might learn how to survive transitioning from relaxed to natural hair. And it was fun. People started to subscribe to my channel and even thanked me for sharing my journey.

I found this whole community of women trying to figure out the natural hair thing. I made videos about the different styles I wore to disguise the two textures. I started to learn what worked and what didn't, and others learned along with me. I gained confidence because I finally felt like I knew how to do my own hair. It was a huge victory.

My YouTube channel didn't start out glamourous, and I certainly wasn't confident that this natural hair thing would work out. But after two years of transitioning, I was ready to chop off the straight hair. I also discovered that hair is just hair. While it tells a story, it's not the end of my story. Social media can and does make a lot of people self-conscious about their looks, but it did the opposite for me. I found a community where everyone cheers each other on in their "hair journey," which is more like a journey of self-acceptance. And even though my selfies are 90% hair, my hair doesn't define me.

I wear it how I like and I no longer want approval from anyone. I'm done hiding behind that relaxer and embracing who I've always been.

TIARA VIAN is a public radio producer and on-air host. She also blogs about natural hair and lifestyle on YouTube as 'Ko'lana Kurls.'

ATTACK OF THE 50 FOOT DISH QUEEN

ROBRT PELA

I AM *NOT* A HOARDER. There are no flattened cats or buckets of last year's turds in my kitchen. I don't keep every crayon drawing I ever did in fourth grade. I am living proof that it's possible to own 17 separate sets of dishes, two of them with service for 36, and not be a hoarder. One can devote an entire wall of one's guest bedroom to 43 vintage alarm clocks, none of which keep proper time, without being a hoarder.

What I am is someone who loves inanimate objects. I like stuff. I always have. I'm what is known, in polite circles, as a "collector." It's a nice word that means I can't seem to stop buying things.

Seriously, don't bring me holiday cookies on an attractive plate, because before you've pulled out of my driveway I will be on eBay hunting up an entire set of that dishware pattern. My favorite department store aisle? Any alleyway on bulk pickup week. The words *endcap, discontinued,* and *box lot* cause me to levitate with joy.

If I were smart I would get a job at Target, for the employee discount. I'd have a booth in an antique mall, volunteer at a thrift shop, become a garbage collector. But I'm not smart. I am instead a person who owns three dozen 1930s pencil sharpeners shaped like airplanes.

And anyway, I don't want to work for a living. It'd cut into my acquisition time.

I like items. Objects are great companions. They don't talk back or shit on your rug. They require minimal exercise and they never complain if you handle them. And they would never ever hurt you or steal from you or sleep with your boyfriend while you're at the car wash. Have you ever heard of a vintage Mrs. Beasley doll running off with your husband? That's because it doesn't happen.

So, yes. I want *everything*. I want my stuff, I want stuff I see in stores and in photographs on internet auction sites. Do you have nice stuff? I want it. Do you have a good mid-century nightstand? I want that, too. Honest to god, lock your front door tonight; I'm coming with a truck for your coffee table and lamps.

The problem is, this is not really a great time for me to be someone who loves having things. Culturally, the world seems to be embracing this whole less-is-more thing. Minimalism is back. Tiny houses are in. Decluttering is a lifestyle now. Marie Kondo is the new Martha Stewart. You've heard about Marie Kondo. She wrote that book about how you should hold every item you own in both hands and thank it for bringing you joy, and then give it away. She's the Harvey Weinstein of stuff. You can't treat things like they are just… well, *objects*! Give away my signed first editions of the works of Jacqueline Susann? Not on your life. And why am I thanking my vintage shoeshine kit or that sweet, 1940s gold-trimmed Tom and Jerry set? It can't hear me. Which is one of the reasons I love it so.

Worse than the Marie Kondo crap is this thing called Swedish Death Cleaning. Seriously, it's a thing. The idea is you get rid of all your stuff now so that other people won't have to do it once you're dead. First of all, you know what? I *want* people to be inconvenienced when I'm dead. I didn't make it easy for them while I was alive. Why would I start after I'm gone? You don't want to deal with my pristine, complete collection of Plasmatics 45s? Tough shit. Take them to Zia. Don't take them to Zia. I don't care. I'm dead.

Nope. While I am breathing, I am *not* giving my stuff away. And I may own far more 1930s movie magazines than I will ever be able to read, but you won't find me *talking* to them. I display them on shelves in my home. I organize them neatly into boxes that I place in my basement. Or my carriage house. Or one of two attics.

Okay. That's sort of the other reason it's a lousy time for me to be a collector. My husband and I are downsizing.

I hate that word. *Downsizing*. But we decided that we should start spending time in our other houses. It's obnoxious, I know. But we have other houses. Did I mention I also collect houses? They're good for keeping your stuff in. Anyway, we can't afford to both live in the one we have here and visit the other ones, which—do I have to tell you this?— are both full of my collections.

So we put in an offer on a little tiny apartment in a central Phoenix highrise. I have coat closets in my home that are larger than this apartment. *Where will I put nine different* tea services in this Barbie-sized home? I wonder. How many oil paintings of total strangers can I fit onto the walls of my tiny new condo? Because I own many oil paintings of total strangers. Don't judge me.

So, we're going through our stuff and we're getting rid of a lot of it. No…We're not bidding it adieu, Marie Kondo. I'm not cradling any of my 11 vintage Proctor Silex chrome toasters and whispering "Thank you for making my bread so stiff and warm!" before packing it off to the Salvation Army. We're just, you know. Sending the toasters off without any farewell.

It's horrible.

I say to my husband, "Look. You've seen the 17 Rubbermaids full of old toys I moved here from my parents' house 20 years ago. You've shared space with my tens of thousands of books with funny titles that I have absolutely no intention of ever reading. You know my Melmac collection isn't going anywhere other than with me to our new home. Where am I going to put 4,000 record albums, 274 green plastic army men, my grandmother's drum table?"

We looked first at a unit that was nearly the size of our house now. It was glorious. I could keep everything and even get more (this place had some *big* closets). My husband looked at me and said, "Exactly what part of downsizing do you *not* understand? It's just stuff!"

When he said that, I thought, *I have been happy with my husband for 20 years. But I've only been happy with that plaster cherub lamp for six years. Maybe 20 years is enough happiness. Maybe it's the lamp's turn.*

So we looked at a much smaller unit on a nicer side of the building. My husband said, "Look at that view!" And I looked at the view and I thought, *Yes, but that view can't hold my collection of vintage greeting cards.* Sure, the view can accommodate the sun and the moon, mountains and a bustling skyline, but can it stash 86 vintage Bakelite Brownie cameras and a complete collection of mint-condition Pyrex? No. It cannot.

It's a difficult time for me, but my friends are trying to help me through. They're bringing me helpful magazine articles about how to distance yourself from a lifetime of collections. The only problem is that now I have a collection of magazine articles about not collecting.

A friend who is opening an antique store agreed to buy a bunch of our cool old things from us. He came for the first load about a week ago. And this afternoon, I stopped in at his shop with a box of ashtrays shaped like Mae West that I couldn't bear to part with but know I will very soon not have any room for.

I was standing there in my friend's antique store, and I spotted a French Deco armoire that I'd bought in 1983 and that my friend had just taken off our hands. He'd priced it at $250. I thought, *Really? That's a lot less than I would have sold that for. That's a really good price.*

And I got up real close to it and ran my hand across its smooth veneer finish. I felt silly, but I told my old armoire how lucky I was to have known it, and how great it was at holding my collection of vintage suits. I thanked it for years of servitude and devotion.

And then I took out my credit card and asked my friend if he would take $225 for it. Fuck you, Marie Kondo.

ROBRT PELA is a Pulliam Prize-winning journalist and longtime columnist at Phoenix New Times. His essays appear regularly on NPR member station KJZZ's "Morning Edition."

HOLIDAYS

SWEET POTATOES, TWO WAYS

JENNIFER LONGDON

I WAS AWAKENED BY A TEXT MESSAGE about 2 a.m. following Thanksgiving of 2014: "911!! 911!! I'm not bringing the rolls for Christmas. I'VE BEEN ASSIGNED THE SWEET POTATOES! WHAT AM I GOING TO DO?"

I had no idea who it was from.

I'd heard of families this organized, that assigned shared dishes early so they could be planned. In my own family you might get several green bean casseroles and no potatoes at all. This family had it going on. Whoever they were. I was a bit jealous.

I typed "wrong number" but paused before sending. There was a person in crisis on the other end. I texted on a lark, *I think you have the wrong number. This is Jennifer. BUT, I have a TON of great sweet potato recipes. I'll send one if you want. You can do this!*

I waited and got nothing. So, I went back to sleep.

Hours later, I was enjoying a breakfast of leftover pecan pie and coffee surrounded by the silence of my little house. My own Thanksgiving dinner for one had been a bit bleak but it was tasty. Rather than a huge turkey meal with all the trimmings, I had indulged in a nice steak, sautéed onions and mushrooms and a lovely bottle of wine. My pie came from box in the freezer. While I imagined my texter had spent the evening surrounded by family, I finished not one but TWO intricate pages in my adult coloring book.

"I don't really cook." My cellphone dinged.

"Oh God!"

"This is awful."

"Frowny-face emoji"

I finished my pie and coffee.

Ok, Let's start at the beginning. I'm Jennifer. I live in Phoenix and I DO *really* cook. What's your name?

I learned that Sara was 23, lived near Branson, Missouri, and worked as a scheduler for the local cable company. She had meant to text a 660 area code and somehow got my 602 number instead.

"Dinner is at my sister's house. She knows I don't cook."

* * *

"Bitch."

I love family dynamics.

Ok Sara from Branson. Let's show your sister what you can do. Shall we?

Nothing. I figure Sara's gone away.

It's now 2 in the afternoon.

"Would you really help me?"

Sweet or savory?

"What?"

What's on the menu? Do you want a recipe that's sweet like with the marshmallows and stuff or do you prefer a savory recipe?

"I don't know what savory is."

Oh goodness, Sara cannot cook.

Savory means it's not sweet. It's salty or spiced… Just not sweet. You can make them both ways.

"Like 2 dishes?"

"I don't know. That would be hard."

I have some unresolved sibling rivalry issues perhaps. I'm really feeling for Sara.

Well, you could do one or the other but if you really want to show your sister, 2 simple dishes would do it. They're both easy.

I thought a second and then followed with:

SUPER EASY

I typed in all caps to emphasize that this would indeed be SUPER. EASY.

Personally, I was having a little crisis. What if I led poor Sara astray? Could this person really cook by text message? I pulled out my recipe books and began to search through them and even Googled sweet potatoes.

Evening fell, and I took the second half of my Thanksgiving bottle of wine outside to watch the sunset when Sara sent a volley of texts.

"Do you mean it?"

"It's easy?"

"I really can't cook."

I sipped my merlot and watched the sky change and wondered about Sara. I created this image of this young, Midwest girl—probably a bit of a rebel—now sweating the intrigue of the family holiday dinner.

EVERYONE can cook. You just haven't learned how.

I mean it. SUPER. EASY.

"Why would you help me?"

Now, that's a legit question. Why was I getting involved with some girl halfway across the country? Why should I care? She can Google as easily as I can.

I was lonely. I was bored. I was disconnected. I struggled with the holidays for years, choosing to spend them alone in my self-imposed solitude. I NEEDED my Grinch-sized heart to have a reason to keep beating. Sara was going to get me through.

Over the next weeks—all by text—I taught her to infuse olive oil with garlic and rosemary and then brush it over par-baked sweet potato spears, generously add fresh cracked pepper and kosher salt and roast them to perfection. She under cooked the first one and then over cooked the next. But, by the third try, Sara had it down.

It would have been easier to talk I suppose. Neither of us ever dialed the other. I feared it would somehow mess with our mojo. One text at a time, we got through. We made her shopping list, strategized on what to do the day before and what to finish at her sister's place on Christmas day. We talked about how to present her dish at the table. I knew the savory sweet potatoes would be unique and she'd score big points with that plate.

Now, the minefield of the holiday meal is the sweet potato casserole. Every cook has their own recipe.

Sara, tell me about your favorite bite of sweet potatoes.

"I don't really like sweet potatoes."

Maybe you could have shared that before this. It's hard to make a dish you don't like and do it well.

She texted back, "It's ok. I hate the soupy green bean thing even more."

We all do Sara.

So, the sweet potatoes… Do you want them in chunky bites or whipped like mashed potatoes?

We went back and forth. Maple syrup or brown sugar? Walnuts? Pineapple? Marshmallows?

In the end she decided on whipped sweet potatoes smothered in butter, bourbon, vanilla and brown sugar—with a twist. She was excited by the twist. We practiced the recipe in a small quantity and her co-workers LOVED it.

"I am so sick of sweet potatoes," Sara texted one day.
I hear you girl. This has become an obsession for both of us.
"My sister is not going to know what hit her!"
Atta girl.

As I sat in my undecorated home, counting the days until the holidays were over, Sara's upcoming Christmas dinner was the only one that mattered to me. I felt no personal connection to the spirit of the season. Every text from her was a little bit of holiday cheer.

As we finished Sara's preparations for her Midwest Christmas, I planned my own holiday dinner: homemade pumpkin curry soup, a small game hen with dressing, brussel sprouts, mashed potatoes and sweet potatoes—two ways.

On Christmas day, I threw open the doors, put on the yule log YouTube video, and cranked Ella Fitzgerald as I cooked. I hummed along contentedly as I stirred and basted. I roasted my savory sweet potatoes to perfection. Then, I added a generous pinch of fresh black pepper to my sweet potato casserole, before I covered it in marshmallows and set it in the oven to brown.

Sara had been alarmed when I told her about the pepper.

"They'll be ruined! That will taste horrible!" she worried.
I assured her that the sharp note of pepper would cut the sweet just enough to give it balance.
"OMG I'm a friggin gourmet!"
As I settled in for my Christmas dinner, I checked my phone. Nothing from Sara.
I washed up after dinner, enjoyed wine and sunset on the patio and headed to bed early.
Around midnight my phone dinged.
"They LOVED the sweet potatoes!"

"I think you're my Christmas angel."

A string of holiday emojis.
"My sister asked for the recipe."
I never heard from Sara again. I dropped my phone and cracked it soon after that and lost all my old text messages when I got my new phone. While I remember Sara with fondness, I love that our friendship was random and ephemeral. I treasure how her confidence grew over that month we cooked together. I wonder what she's cooking this

year. I hope she always remembers that it's that note of sharpness that balances the sweet and makes it sweeter.

JENNIFER LONGDON is a professional speaker, freelance writer and a member of the Arizona House of Representatives. Follow her on Twitter and Instagram @jenlongdon.

THERE'S NO SUCH THING AS A CHRISTMAS BRISKET

AMY SILVERMAN

SO, HERE'S THE THING no one really ever tells you about Christmas.

It gets harder as you get older.

This occurred to me last week, when my daughter Sophie ran sobbing to her room at the news that we were going to purchase a Christmas tree that evening.

She's terrified that Santa Claus is going to come into her bedroom.

Whoever came up with

He sees you when you're sleeping
He knows when you're awake

Is an asshole.

I looked it up. His name was Haven Gillespie and he wrote the lyrics to the 1934 smash hit "Santa Claus Is Comin' To Town." Gillespie died in 1975. According to

Wikipedia, he drank heavily for most of his life—something I plan to do, at least until New Year's.

Christmas is hard. I am old.

Sophie's old, too. For a Santa believer, anyway. She's 15 and a half. Sophie has Down syndrome, so it takes her longer to figure some things out.

Santa is one of those things. In between bouts of terror, she loves to believe—she writes Santa letters asking about Mrs. Claus, asking how their Thanksgiving was, asking if Santa knows she has Down syndrome.

This year she removed "bras" from her Christmas wish list. "That's not appropriate to ask Santa for," she told me solemnly.

She checks several times a day to see if the response to her letter has arrived.

I realize that I'm a shitty parent for not having clued her in, but really, which one of you wants to be the one to break the news to Sophie?

That's what I thought.

My wise friend Jennifer has it right.

"Christmas is really at its peak when you're three or four years old," she told me. The rest is downhill.

I think that's true—for most people. Me, I peaked late.

Growing up Jewish, I never got the chance to believe in Santa. My sister and I got blue and white stockings with a pack of Carefree gum in the toe. There was nothing magical about it. Don't feel sorry for me—I was hardly deprived—but I always longed for the opportunity to really celebrate Christmas.

I finally got my chance at 27, when I started dating my now-husband, Ray.

Ray's family was not religious. His mother put the kids in Catholic school when they were little, but it didn't stick, probably because Ray's father is a devout atheist.

But I think that man loved Christmas more than anyone. Every year on Christmas Day, he pulled out this faded old velvet smoking jacket and put it on over his undershirt and wore it all day. Ray's family never left the house on Christmas. Everything was beautifully orchestrated, carefully planned over weeks (maybe months), down to the bowl of red and green M&Ms on the plastic poinsettia tablecloth in the modest Tempe tract home the family purchased in the 1970s, shortly after moving here from Queens.

Ray's father had retired early from the New York City fire department. He loved being a fireman but the smoke inhalation got him. Ray's mom found a job doing data entry at the Mesa Police Department. They took Ray and his sister on long summer road trips to national parks till the kids were too old. So far, no one had gotten too old for Christmas.

I immediately accepted an invitation to that first Christmas at Ray's house—and never looked back. His mom puffy-painted my name on a felt stocking that she hung next to the one she'd needlepointed for Ray when he was a baby. Each year I brought her an ornament for the tree, which she would carefully store with the rest and proudly hang the following Christmas.

We'd arrive early on Christmas morning, sit down to coffee and homemade Irish soda bread (one loaf with raisins, the other without, because Ray hates raisins in his Irish soda bread) and enjoy the spectacle of the lit tree and the stacks of gifts, then take turns opening until there was a giant pile of tissue and boxes, just like in the movies!

Ray, his sister, and I would watch TV and nap while their parents bustled for hours in the small kitchen. Ray's dad always made mashed potatoes from scratch, and together they roasted a turkey, microwaved vegetables, and prepared an elaborate family recipe for stuffing that involves boiling sausage and mixing it with loaves of Wonder Bread that have been left out for days.

Ray's mom would swap the plastic tablecloth for a real one and put out her good dishes.

She made the whole thing look effortless. Every year, I would ask her, "How do you do it? How do you make it so every dish is ready at the same time?"

"Practice," she would tell me, hiding a proud smile. "Years of practice."

Then she'd slip into the kitchen to make hot tea, serving it with the cookies I'd baked and mentioning that she was hiding one of my pink iced stars to have the next morning with her coffee. As we scooped up piles of gifts to take home, Ray's dad would sigh, dejected. He hated it when Christmas was over, he'd tell us.

I totally related.

Ray and I got engaged, then married, then we had a baby, then another baby. His mom added stockings by the fireplace, and the mounds of tissue paper grew. But really, nothing about Christmas ever changed, which is exactly the way I liked it.

And then everything changed.

Just after the holidays one year, Ray's mom began complaining that her throat hurt. She never complained. By spring, the diagnosis was lung cancer. We celebrated one last Christmas in 2008, and by the next February, she was gone.

I wasn't completely surprised when, the following summer, Christmas arrived on our doorstep in the form of several Rubbermaid bins. Ray's dad had left nothing out—he included the stockings, the hooked rug tree skirt, every ornament.

Suddenly, Ray and I were the adults. Over the years, we've developed some pretty good holiday traditions—every Christmas Eve we take our daughters out to look at lights. We get home late and the girls go to sleep and Ray and I stay up and drink Bailey's and wrap gifts, shooing poor Sophie away every time she emerges, worried about Santa watching her sleep.

Christmas morning, I serve homemade Irish soda bread (one loaf with raisins, one without), and I always put out a bowl of red and green M&Ms.

It's all good. Until it's time to make Christmas dinner.

We have to have poultry because that's what goes best with the centerpiece of the meal, the stuffing—that family recipe that involves the aging of white bread and the use of pretty much every utensil in the kitchen. It's become tradition that Ray makes the stuffing, and he attacks the task with equal parts precision and abandon, which means that he's inconsolable if the bread isn't quite stale enough, and also that the kitchen walls wind up covered in onion.

Things aren't as pretty on my side of the kitchen. The first Christmas dinner we hosted, I made a traditional turkey and we didn't eat till it was past everyone's bedtime. The next year I made a turkey breast, which dried up like jerky and tasted like sawdust. Cornish game hens were a big pain in the ass (and a little creepy), and the spatchcocked turkey wouldn't stay in the largest roasting pan I could find. Parts kept popping out of the pan; that turkey looked like a naked lady with her legs splayed.

I'm not much better at sides, and I've never attempted mashed potatoes. But Ray's stuffing is always delicious, a point of pride.

My father-in-law hasn't tried it in years. A couple Christmases after my mother-in-law died, Ray's dad stopped coming over. He's got a girlfriend, now, and they always schedule a trip over the holidays. I wish Ray's dad would partake in our new traditions, if only for his granddaughters. I want to be mad at him, and then I picture my father-in-law in his velvet smoking jacket, standing in the doorway as we drive away, sad because Christmas is over.

Last year I decided that it doesn't really matter what I cook for Christmas dinner. I made my grandmother's Jewish brisket, the only main dish I can prepare with any degree of certainty of success. Everyone raved, but the truth was that it was a little gross, meaty and greasy next to the sausage stuffing. It didn't feel right. It wasn't Christmas-y. The truth is, I wasn't Christmas-y. I'm just an imposter, I thought. What's the point?

There's no such thing as Christmas brisket.

"What if we order in Chinese this year?" I asked Ray last month. "You know, ditch Christmas dinner and make things a little easier on ourselves?"

"Okay," he said. "That sounds good. But I'll still make the sausage stuffing, right?"

"And can you get some of those Cornish game hens?"

Despite Sophie's protests, Ray went out and bought a tree, and at some point the four of us will honor another tradition—and decorate it. I'll open the boxes with my mother-in-law's ornaments—delicate glass balls, the popsicle figures Ray made in grade school, the snapshot of his family dog sitting on Santa's lap, and several tiny framed pictures of our girls.

My favorite ornament is a Santa carved from wood, painted in bright colors and shaped like a star. On the side, in my mother-in-law's handwriting, it says "Amy, 1995."

Tonight I'll stop at the grocery store on my way home and buy the Wonder Bread—so there's plenty of time for it to get good and stale before Christmas. And I'll see if the butcher has Cornish game hens. I might even try to make mashed potatoes.

We can order Chinese another night.

AMY SILVERMAN is a Tempe-based journalist and the co-creator of Bar Flies. Follow her on Instagram @amysilvermanaz and find her at amy-silverman.com.

RUSSELL TO THE FRONT

JASON P. WOODBURY

THE DAY AFTER THANKSGIVING, the store owner would change the satellite radio station from the familiar '50s and '60s station, with its even blend of doo wop standards, inoffensive '60s rock, and crooners, to the Christmas station. So that's what we'd listen to for a month—loops of "Jingle Bell Rock," "Santa Baby," "Do They Know It's Christmas"—as we schlepped slick boxes of masa onto the shelves, stocked the dairy case with eggnog, and built towering monuments out of cartons of Swiss Miss. Most any Christmas song is fine enough to hear once, but that unceasing megamix, treacly and buzzing overheard, seemed to infect every corner of the grocery store. It was oppressive. Now days, people tell me they hate Christmas music and I assume they're adopting a fashionable, anti-cheer pose, but no, when I give them the benefit of the doubt, I know what they mean, thinking about how I'd hide in the walk-in cooler with the milk, seeking the industrial hum of the fan as a means to drown out another go 'round of "Frosty the Snowman," knowing he'd "be back again one day." Sooner, even.

I wasn't an especially morose 17-year-old, no matter how the jewel cases out in my Mercury Tracer suggested otherwise. But music wasn't just something "on" for me, not then, not ever. I probably paid too much attention to the overhead radio at my grocery store job, which came in handy on the occasions that the owner, the former mayor of our small Arizona cotton town, would come by and grill me on pop trivia. He was an upright, conservative fella, always on me to cut my damn hair, but he had a thing for Leonard Cohen, so I learned a lot from him. There were no folk rock quizzes when we switched to "Holiday Classics," just knowing nods. We'll get through it, we seemed to say telepathically.

The store was normally busy, but Christmas was another story altogether, and when things got busy enough, I didn't even notice the music. Pulling cartons of Liggetts out of the locked case for the ranchers—"I said soft pack, not hard pack"—rushing back to the cereal aisle to grab the right box of Kix puffed cereal for the moms with WIC cards. "Berry Berry Kix"—those weren't covered, plain stuff only. Quick clean ups over by the yogurt, a jaunt into the butcher shop to ask if more ham hocks were on the way out. Not only did the rush make the day go by faster and drown out the silver bells, but it made me feel useful, part of a community, an actual assistance to weird, dusty people in my weird, dusty town. I'd walk old ladies out to their station wagons and carefully load the brown paper sacks filled with leafy greens and rolls into their ride, and I took self-self-righteous pleasure in refusing their tips, waving my hand to signal to them the no goodness of their crumbled ones and occasional fives. It wasn't just that I wasn't allowed to accept them—a couple of my pals did, knowing they'd catch hell if a manager spotted them, but risking it anyway—I honestly took satisfaction in being helpful.

That was how I worked in days, with a glad heart. Except for the days I didn't, like when my best friend Jacob and I would make a game of avoiding the manager, making an extended show out of loading up the soda machine with generic cola and lemon lime, "dropping" a can straight into the air, tracing the distance of carbonated fizz that would jet from the can as it hit the asphalt with an electrifying crack. One night, we were tasked with disposing of dead fluorescent light tubes, and we took turns smashing them against the dumpster, coming back in with chalky glass dust on our jeans and Converse. We worked hard most of the time; we figured it justified occasionally screwing around.

The annual Christmas party was held on a Sunday, and this year, and unlike the year before, I was invited. Jacob and I were scheduled an opening shift, with just enough time to head home after work and get changed before the party at the owner's house that evening. The last couple hours of that shift, as the sun poured late afternoon light through the store windows, dragged forever. So Jake and I decided to hide out in the soda aisle, where we had a killer view of the front of the store, through a wire display holding boxes of Canada Dry and Hawaiian Punch, a spot where we could identify any managers before they spotted us slacking. "I Saw Mommy Kissing Santa Claus" ringing overhead, we talked about a trip to the Valley to make our usual rounds: Zia to see what was good on the listening stations, Bookman's for cheap used vinyl, the Werehouse to scour for

CDs we'd read reviews of in the latest issue of Alternative Press. We were killing time beautifully when the call came over the overhead paging system: "Russell to the front."

See, "Russell to the front" was code. It meant all able-bodied young men to the entrance. Someone was about to make a run for it. People were always shoplifting, and while we weren't encouraged to get physical with people ripping stuff off, we weren't *not* encouraged to do so either. With our surplus of teenage energy and boredom, we made for the front of the store, right as a young guy made a dash for the door, a clerk shouting out after him. Ray, my second favorite manager and a lifer in the grocery biz, pushed out the swinging door after the guy, Jake and I close behind in hot pursuit. To my surprise, the runner didn't bolt straight across the parking lot, to a waiting vehicle or even toward the busy street, but instead he turned the corner past the ice and soda machines and headed toward the back of the store. We were gaining on him as he passed the dumpster and vaulted, I mean just straight up bounded, over the stucco wall that separated the loading dock from the neighborhood behind the store. "Damn," Ray wheezed, trailing, but Jake and I, we hit the middle of the wall and climbed over.

"Come on, man," I shouted as we gained on him, his pace slowing as he moved down the alley. Breathing heavily, he stopped. He turned to look at us as we tried in vain to pump the breaks, our sneakers skidding in the dust. He didn't say anything as our eyes met. He was my age, maybe a couple years older, a Latino kid, his face smooth save for a wispy mustache. Breathing hard, he raised his hands in the air, and a fat pack of ribs slipped from underneath his hoodie, falling to the alleyway dirt. We stood there for half a second, Jake and I uncertain what exactly was supposed to happen next. We heard Ray calling behind us. Jake picked up the meat. I kept the kid's gaze, kind of stunned, until he turned and bolted away. He was gone by the time Ray caught up to us, Jake cradling the ribs against his red polo uniform shirt. "Hell," he exclaimed at the recovered spare ribs. We started back for the store.

A few hours later, at the Christmas party, Ray regaled the gathered crowd with the story of me and Jake, acting like "a couple of junkyard dogs." Jerry, the produce guy and a real macho asshole, came by and pounded me on the back. I think the butchers might've actually clapped for us. "Proud of you boys," the store owner said, encouraging us to get in line for posole and enchiladas.

But I couldn't shake a nagging feeling as the night went on. I kept thinking about the look on that guy's face. I kept thinking about how he let the ribs drop, dejected, and how upon getting them back into the store, Roy told us we'd have to toss them out anyway, that you couldn't sell them now. You don't steal meat to turn a profit. That's not why you risk it. You dash in and make a run for it in the hopes that maybe you'll be able to bring something delicious home. Something indulgent.

But stealing's wrong, I told myself, my heroic delusions fading. Sure, but somehow my part in the story was more wrong; those ribs, wrapped in cellophane over yellow styrofoam, were in a trashcan somewhere. They could have been feeding people at a Sunday night BBQ, one just like ours, people gathered to try and share a night under twinkling lights.

Someone turned up a radio, and more yuletide music droned on. People laughed, passed plates of food, danced a little. I smiled and tried to get back to the party, my mind drifting. I knew one thing: I'd had my fill of Christmas songs for the season.

JASON P. WOODBURY writes for the online magazine Aquarium Drunkard and is a record slinger for Zia Records in Phoenix, Tucson, and Las Vegas.

A CHRISTMAS CRIME

AMY L. YOUNG

DURING THE HOLIDAY SEASON OF 1994, I discovered two things that don't really go so well together: Christmas and crystal meth. I was living in Tempe at the time and though I was working a steady job, I was far more concerned with making a career out of drinking whiskey at dive bars, collecting books and records, and gaining the life experiences that would surely pay off when I wrote about them later. I had plenty of time to frolic and learn life lessons, after all, that big time writer money was just around the corner. I was drinking heartily, like all the dead writers I loved, but I wasn't as dedicated to drugs as I was to mind-altering things served in bottles. Not saying I didn't engage, but I wasn't pounding the pavement to keep my drug drawer filled. As a thoughtful person, however, I certainly didn't want to offend someone who wanted to share. So, when my friend Jack popped by on Christmas Eve to polish off his meth stash with our friend Jennifer and myself before flying off to see his family, it seemed rude to say no. That winter, Jen and I were hanging around with a couple of wayward characters, a dynamically dysfunctional duo who could find trouble just by waking up in the morning. This night, they were unsurprisingly nowhere to be found, so we were happy to take Jack up on his offer.

We got fully engaged in the holiday spirit by cranking up the tunes and snorting up the crank. We added some drinks to the mix and proceeded to blab at a fiery, energetic pace all night long, popping record upon record on the turntable and stuffing the CD player with discs until the daylight started to creep in, finding our pal Jack ready to call a cab for his trip. We escorted him out, had a smoke and said our holiday goodbyes... and there we were, insanely awake, sweaty, bug-eyed and covered in a coat of the smoke from multiple packs of Camel Lights: a real Christmas-morning vision. So, we did what seemed to be the next logical thing to do—we hit the Jack in the Box drive-through for a bag full of grease. Not hungry and not paying attention to the fact that we were going to my mom's to have Christmas dinner with her and the six adults with intellectual disabilities that were in her care, we ordered a couple of signature Jumbo Jacks and fries. We took the food back to my apartment and chowed with the same amount of energy that we had throughout the night. We still hadn't heard anything from our boyfriends and after speculating where we might find them—probably at a bar, it being Christmas morning and all—we decided to do what seemed like the next logical thing: more meth.

We laughed our way through some lousy TV, continuing to work our way through the meth mountain until it was time to head to my mom's place. She was happy to see us, because she was a nice person and also because at the beginning of any event, she was thinking about the end of the event. She'd be handing you a to-go container just as you were getting comfortable. She ushered us to the living room, where we were treated to the best holiday show ever by one of the gentlemen in her care, Mark Hardy. Mark loved musicals, show tunes, and any cause for celebration. And for him, it was the best when he had an audience. He put some thought into that year's fabulous ensemble—a holiday sweater, a tutu, and a Santa hat. When he turned down the TV volume, I knew what was next. He put on a CD of holiday classics and gave us the most glorious lip sync and dance show we could ask for. You didn't think about getting up when Mark was performing, he'd point and nod your ass back to couch level without missing a beat of his signature disco ballet moves. When he was finished, my mom called us in for dinner, and as we eyeballed her giant spread, our minds and bodies finally connected to alert us what they should have done as we rounded the corner to Jack in the Box: Food and meth don't mix. Our stomachs gurgled at the thought of sticking a fork into the turkey. I wanted to run out the door when my mom dropped a slice of ham onto my plate. My face must have shown my dismay because she took that opportunity to point out that it wasn't just any old ham I was frowning upon, it was a *spiral* ham. I'd been wondering how long it was going to take for her to drop that tidbit—usually it happened via phone right after the chunky hunk of pig was purchased: "I got the ham. It's a spiral ham. It's *spiral*." She emphasized the word spiral and gave a knowing look that suggested that somehow that curly-edged ham held the secrets of the universe. I don't even really like ham, I wouldn't have cared if that thing was carved into a sculpture of AbraHAM Lincoln.

Anyhow, we pushed some food around our plates, exchanged some gifts, watched a little holiday television and started talking about what we were gonna do that night. We'd been invited to a party but neither of us were big fans of the host; he was a lecherous and sneaky fellow from Australia that everyone referred to, unoriginally, as "the Kiwi." I guess the only other option would have been "the Koala," but that really would only work for someone like an Australian mob boss, cueing the appropriate irony. So even though we didn't dig him very much, we knew a bunch of our friends would be there, maybe even those elusive boyfriends, and it was a way to keep our Christmas party train in motion.

We headed back to my apartment, where we took showers, got spruced up, finished off the rest of the snortable snow and headed over to the party. At this point we were in a state of exhilaration and exhaustion; we just weren't ready to let the underlying tiredness take over. We sat around the fire pit chatting and drinking some kind of hot bourbon punch. Eventually the Kiwi made his way over to us, sliding between us to throw an arm around each of us and deliver his best—and I can't do an Aussie accent to save my life— "'Ello ladies." We both choked out a greeting and squirmed beneath his grip, hoping he would take the hint and remove his paws; he didn't. He told us about how he'd been cooking all day and that we should go inside and get a plate. The words mushed together as he rambled on and then, suddenly, two words popped out of his endless sentence like a tiny rainbow after a crappy storm: Oyster stuffing.

Big fans of bread and food from the sea, we figured "what the hell?" and made our way to the kitchen. There was a pretty good crowd of people partaking of the Kiwi's culinary treats. We gave some hugs and had some toasts as we pushed through the room on a mission. And finally, we spotted it. One hearty brick of stuffing bursting out of its glimmering foil pouch. We grabbed some plates and forks and dug in. Within one bite, it was as if a beam of light came in and parted us from the rest of the room. We looked at each other in a way that indicated that we both knew that everything that happened in the last day had led to this moment. Hell, maybe a lot of life's choices were just to take us on this path. Unsatisfying jobs, thoughtless boyfriends, all just part of the journey. That fishy, mushy bread was FUCKING MAGICAL.

We ate as much as we could without looking greedy and then did what seemed to be the next logical thing to do—we launched a plan to steal the stuffing. While Jen went and pulled her getaway car around to the alley right near the house's back door, I told the other kitchen dwellers that the Kiwi said he had some kind of surprise to unveil out by the fire pit. When the coast was clear, I sealed up that foil and took off running in a paranoia fueled by meth and by the ramifications of getting caught stealing a popular holiday dish. What would people say? Would I get a food-related nickname like Lisa Thomas, a girl from high school who in ninth grade was standing in a silent march with the rest of our marching band, waiting for our band leader to cue us back into the building, when her mom came up and announced to everyone in earshot, "Lisa Marie Thomas, you hurry up and put your tuba away, I've got cabbage and noodles on the stove at home." Four years of being greeted by "Hey, what's up cabbage and noodles?" had to have a long-term effect on her psyche. I didn't want a food-based nickname! Especially one that referred to shellfish or Christmas. We picked up the pace and ran down the alley until I saw the passenger door of Jen's little Geo Metro pop open. I hopped in and we hustled the loot back to my place. At that time, when life seemed to be all about trying endlessly to take things to more extreme levels, our little act of thievery, while illegal, was a glorious slice of the goofy innocence we were so desperately running from at all costs. Once in my apartment, we grabbed a couple of forks and stretched out in the room littered with CD cases and butt-filled ashtrays and ate the hell out of that delightful dish, laughing all the way.

AMY L. YOUNG is an editor and journalist based in Phoenix. She co-hosts a podcast and a radio show. Find her on Twitter and Instagram @missamyyoung.

TANGLED TINSEL

KATHY CANO-MURILLO

"**CAN WE PLEASE** just have a little bit of Christmas magic? I'm not picky, I'll take anything. Anything!"

That sums up my thoughts for the holiday season of 2002. Between skimpy finances, long work hours, parenting, and fulfilling art and craft orders, all of it took its toll on my emotional bandwidth. No matter what, I vowed to give my kids a memorable Christmas.

One day, my wish for holiday enchantment arrived. My mom-in-law showed up with a dozen of her steamy homemade tamales and… an artificial Christmas tree, brand new, still taped up in the box. We hadn't told her, but she knew we needed one.

My daughter Maya, in fifth grade at the time, shot her skinny arm up to volunteer as head decorator, and took 100% ownership. I didn't argue, I had other issues to tend to.

The source of our family angst?

DeAngelo's seventh-grade math.

The entire semester had been a storm of stress—slaving over complicated homework problems, parent-teacher conferences that left me with PTSD. DeAngelo's world, like most seventh graders, revolved around Halo and Super Smash Brothers.

Earlier that fall season, he agreed to join an afterschool math program as long as I would chill from the constant nagging, bribing and threatening - and trust him to complete his assignments. Every day he came home and excitedly assured me he turned in all his work. He absolutely needed to pass the class to make it to eighth grade, while on the outside I cheered him on, inside I prayed myself into a headache for him to please be telling the truth.

December rolled around. Between DeAngelo's new sense of confidence, Maya's youthful efficiency, life was sweeter than a pumpkin empanada. Then Queen Maya cleared her schedule to tend to the tree. We all stepped out of her way.

Maya sorted every holiday decoration according to size and color and displayed them on the couch. She spent two hours choosing then auditioning each ornament on one pristine plastic branch after another. As a lasting touch, she trimmed it from top to bottom with mini-twinkling lights and red velvet ribbon bows.

She finished, and we stood back and admired her hard work. A hug, a pat on the back, then I sent her out to grab the mail while I cleaned up the empty ornament boxes. A moment of peace. She returned and dropped the stack on the counter.

From the corner of my eye, I see the logo from DeAngelo's school on the top letter.

Hmmmm. I hummed curiously. Who am I kidding? Before I even ripped open the flap, I knew. I'd been played.

I inhaled and read.

"Hi Mrs. Murillo! Happy Holidays! We have a smidge of bummer news. It appears your beloved son, DeAngelo, hasn't kept up with his math homework. His future grade is grim. We know you're going to have a lot of drama in your house tonight, so here is a gift card for a free glass of wine at Applebees. And BTW—Never forget that you are an awesome mom!"

Well, that's the version I would have relayed if I were in charge at that school. But no. The real letter went like this:

"DeAngelo Murillo will be receiving a failing grade in the following courses: MATH." Next to that? A little box checked that said "Reason: failure to turn in assignments, poor test grades."

It only took a few moments for me to click into early stages of Hulk mode. Flashes of green, the fast, heavy breathing, shaking of my head in disbelief. I stared up at the invisible movie screen in the air and replayed all our math conversations from the past months. Like my dad always said, "If something is too good to be true, it probably is."

The lies, the false hope from this little boy whom I loved so much—all of it suffocated my rational thinking, and there was no brown paper bag to breathe into. I didn't even have a chance to process my anger when guess who strolls in from school?

"Hi, Mom! Wow, the tree looks great!!" DeAngelo quipped, nodding towards Maya's festive swag work.

"Hi." I replied sharply, one eyebrow popping up. "Sooooo. How's math?"

He stuttered a little bit. "Uh, fine."

"NOT FINE!' I screamed, stomped and I lunged toward him, waving the crumpled correspondence over my head. "Look at this letter that came from your school, you are failing math! You've been lying this whole time! Why?"

He dropped his book bag, slumped his shoulders and stared at the tile floor. "I don't know."

No matter what I asked, he shrugged and replied, "I don't know."

I grabbed his book and inspected the stack of blank homework assignments. One after another.

My heart beat faster.

"Do you want to flunk out of school and have to go work in the fields?" I'd just seen "La Bamba" earlier that week, you know how Ritchie Valens family started off as farm-workers in the beginning of the film? I think that's where the visual came from—anyway, I went with it.

"I don't know" he said.

"Does it feel good for you to hurt my feelings?"

"I don't know."

In the meantime, Maya and Patrick stood on the sidelines, and watched our conver-sation like a tennis ball going back and forth. Then there is the decorated tree observing the entire scene too, thinking, "Oh, fun, leave it to me to be stuck with the drama fam-ily...."

"If you say I don't know one more time, I'M GOING TO PICK UP THIS TREE AND THROW IT ACROSS THE ROOM!" I shouted as I pointed to our tinseled hol-iday guest.

DeAngelo didn't make a peep. He didn't even look up from the floor. I could have sworn I saw the tree cautiously inch away from me.

I then lowered my voice calmly. "Why. Didn't. You. Do. Your. Homework?" All I needed was a simple "Because I hate math, Mom" or even just "I'm sorry." Didn't he know the stress I'd been under this holiday season? I chewed on my inner lip to see which of the above he would choose. I would accept either and move forward with love and com-passion.

"I...I...I..." he stuttered.

"Don't say it, DeAngelo.... Please. I'm warning you..." I whispered. "Don't say it."

"I don't know."

And then the rest? Slo mo.

Mom Beast unleashed... my head tilted back and I grrrrowled. With one giant step, I reached both hands over to the brand new tree and put it in a choke hold, raised it over my head, and threw it across the length of the family room.

Calm down, it was artificial. Light on weight, heavy on visual impact!

Silence. Except for the few bulbs that shattered against the wall. Patrick and the kids stood there, speechless and in shock. This is what happens—Gangster Mom— when you push her over the edge during the holiday season.

The tree rested limply against the wall, bent branches, ornaments dangling by a thread, tangled garland. Just like the sugarplum holiday dreams of my children. That's how it stayed the rest of the season. We covered the tree with a sheet. Every time I passed it, I felt the Walk of Shame. That $50 tree had the nerve to judge me. Slow clap from its branch hands, "You are one piece of work, Missy. I had one job. You broke my soul. You broke all our souls."

Regret, totally. But throwing that tree was a physical manifestation of my frustration of feeling helpless. Sometimes life is hard on these mom streets! I eventually talked about it with other moms at a bloggers conference and one lady said her family pissed her off so much one year, she threw the Thanksgiving turkey out the front window!

Turns out, I'm not alone! Finger snaps if your kids have pushed you over the edge? Flipped your switch? Am I right?

Now my kids are 25 and 28. Truth talk— Maya hadn't decorated a tree since. Thankfully, here we are 15 years after the incident, and I'm happy to report she frilled up her first Douglas Fir at her new home in Los Angeles. She decked it out with two giant googly eyes and a few red plastic balls. I'd call that a win.

And DeAngelo? He passed his math class, and every year thereafter. He now works as an insurance agent, crunching numbers for clients! And he finally did apologize. Double win!

Now forever I live with, "Remember when Mom threw the Christmas tree?" Some call it a mommy meltdown, I call it the day I became BOSS. Scared Straight, my friends. Mom version. And you know what? I'll take that as a form of Christmas magic!

KATHY CANO-MURILLO is an author, artist, and founder of CraftyChica.com. Follow her on social media @craftychica.

SOMETHING ELSE

NIKKI DeLEON MARTIN

THE LAST TIME I CALLED MY MOTHER-IN-LAW, she would not come to the phone.

It was a November evening. My marriage to her son would have been 10 years old, if it had not ended that summer. Before the split, Cristina and I didn't miss a week without speaking. At first, I tried to give her space. But now months had passed, and still, nothing, and so I called.

My father-in-law sounded shocked to hear my voice, and after a moment, asked me to hold on. A few moments later he returned.

"Sorry, Nikki," he said, "She's already asleep." It was 6:30.

I decided not to call again. I would wait for her to call me.

Six years later, my phone rang early one Sunday. I grabbed for it, squinting through eyes encrusted with sleep to make out the screen.

CRISTINA - SUEGRA.

Cristina?

For a moment, I felt out of time, as if somehow during the night, I had moved backward through the years, and now everything I had undone in my life over the last decade was now stitched back together, whole again. But next to me, my new husband snored loudly.

"Hello?" I said, with more uncertainty than any other time in my telephone-answering experience.

On the other side of the line, I heard a cacophony of clanging pots, the familiar sounds of a woman who lived most of her waking life in the kitchen.

"*Lucy?*" Her voice sounded higher, shaky.

"No, it's Nikki."

"Who?"

"Um, Nikki?" I started to say *your nuera*, but I hadn't been her daughter-in-law in some time. I tried to think of something else to call myself. "I...uh...used to be married...to your son...for nine years?"

"Oh, Nikki!" she said, sounding so surprised I wondered if maybe I had called her, perhaps sleep-dialed her.

"Cristina, you called me."

"Oh, I meant to call—"

"Lucy?"

"Who?"

"Never mind."

"*Aye, que la Nikki,*" she said, laughing as if we had not gone six years without speaking. "*Escuchame.* I'm making tamales. Come make some for your *gringo* husband."

I wasn't sure how she knew I was married again, let alone to a *gringo*, or why she wanted to see me. Maybe she'd gone a bit mad. She often weaved in and out of the lines dividing normal from cuckoo-bananas. Like the time she found a black-satin skirt in my closet which she stole and turned into a pillow for herself.

"I miss you," she said, her voice lower. "Plus, I have cancer, but I made a cake. Come over and make tamales." Before I could respond, she added, "Not for Christmas."

There had been a time I would not have missed an opportunity to go to my mother-in-law's house, which is still my favorite place. Small and cramped, it always smelled of something delicious simmering on the stove, of tortillas on the *comal*. It was loud, filled with old Spanish standards blasting from a paint-spattered boom box.

The first time we met, I was her youngest son's new girlfriend, showing up to learn to make tamales. Cristina, which she insisted I call her, was nine inches shorter, but stood taller than her 4'9" due to a halo of expertly teased golden curls she had set each week and a pair of three-inch heels she wore daily despite having broken her ankle. There was always a dusting of flour on her clothing. She was a tiny but commanding presence, ordering her family around, barking out instructions as they began the prep work.

There had also been a time, long before I was born, when her annual tamale party had been for Christmas.

My mother-in-law had grown up as the oldest girl in a family of seven, the child of

Mexican immigrants who arrived after the Depression. As Christmas drew near, Cristina and her mother began the laborious process of making tamales. They began, just after dawn, mixing the *masa* and the *manteca* with their hands, tending to the meat simmering in the oven, and soon, constructing by hand each tamale that would be the basis of most meals during the holiday season.

In the 1950s, Cristina fell in love with and married Nate, a shy boy from the neighborhood, growing their family until, by the 1970s, she had five children of her own. That tamale-making tradition became an annual party when her brothers' wives gathered to fill Cristina's kitchen in West Phoenix, decorating a twinkling Christmas tree. Each of the women followed Cristina's expert directions for perfect tamales the way her mother taught her, the way I would learn years later—a thick slather of *masa*, a spoonful of shredded pork, and two green olives, dotting the center. They made dozens, enough to feed their families, with a few extras to spare. It was Cristina's favorite thing in life, when her family was together in one place, their stomachs full.

When I knew her, she didn't have those parties anymore. Sometime in the late '60s, she received a copy of *The Watchtower* magazine, featuring a child playing with a lion in a beautiful garden. The magazine promised peace on earth, not as a wish but a guarantee. Once she began studying with Jehovah's Witnesses, she could no longer celebrate holidays, including birthdays and Christmas tamale parties.

When I knew her, tamale-making had shrunk to include only her husband, children and their spouses. By then, there was no more twinkling Christmas tree. She rarely spoke to her brothers or their wives. Gone were the giant family parties. Gone too was the hand-mixed *masa*.

"We buy our *masa* from La Purisima now," she explained to me. "It's better there anyway."

And yet, despite all of the limitations of her faith, she still only made tamales when the calendar that hung in her kitchen turned to *diciembre*.

Once I got a hankering for her tamales in September. We'd all gone away together to Disneyland for a family vacation. Cristina and I sat on a bench together in the middle of the park. "We should make tamales when we get back," I said.

She smiled and shook her head. "Wait til December."

Our food calendar was limited in other ways. Each year we had a turkey dinner with all the fixings, never on Thanksgiving, but always the Saturday after. In late December, she made a giant, juicy ham studded with open-mouthed pineapple rings with cherry centers, always a few days after December 25.

"Another great Christmas ham that's not a Christmas ham," I would tease her.

"*Aye, que la Nikki,*" she would say, and laugh.

I could set my watch by her non-celebrations, her house filled with her children and grandchildren. It wasn't until I lost my place in her kitchen that I understood her regimented, seasonal doings, stand-ins for what she wanted to do, like a phone call she pretended was a wrong number. Some things are just too painful to lose completely.

I didn't show up to make tamales. I wanted to, but it didn't seem right. It was the kind of thing that once lost, could never be regained. But I called her a week later, and this time, instead of refusing to answer, she kept me on the phone for an hour. We talked about the summers her family worked the fields as migrant labor in Bakersfield, walking barefoot through the crops, dancing in the fields with her cousins while fireworks lit up the sky on July 4.

And the next week, she called again. We began to talk an hour each week, but never about her health.

"How are you feeling?" I would ask.

"Fine," she'd say, and then spent the next hour talking about her children and their marriages that seemed to wax and wane with love and indifference.

When I brought up her chemotherapy, she brought up the time we drove from Sacramento to San Francisco, traveling not along I-80, but through the back roads following the delta. It stormed, and Cristina worried we'd never make it. I was only half-listening; on the radio a song played, a woman wondering if the man she loved would ever be strong enough to love her. In the darkness, I began to cry silently. I turned my face away toward the passing golden lights in the windows of farmhouses and tiny motels punctuating the night. Cristina had reached up and touched my arm in the narrow space between the door and my seat, where her son couldn't see.

"I liked that night. It was long but we made it," she said on the phone, 10 years later. She cleared her throat, and blurted, "I want you to write my eulogy if I die."

It was a Tuesday in October when they decided to cease all treatment. It was only delaying the inevitable, Cristina said, and besides, it made her too sick. "I thought the worst part would be losing my hair," she said, "but the worst is I don't want to eat. I don't even want tamales this year," she said. "But come over anyway. I want to see you."

I drove to her house on the opposite side of town, my favorite place I have ever been. Seven years since I'd last seen it, it was small and cramped, still full of green plants she kept alive with her incomparable green thumb. Her golden up-do was gone, her painfully small head hidden under a knotted scarf. She was thinner than I had ever seen her, and looked strangely chic in a pair of skinny jeans and three-inch heels.

She hugged me for a long time when she saw me, and told me I was fatter but more beautiful. "People always get fat when they're happy," she said, and grasped my hand. She confessed she was happy too. "When I die, I'll close my eyes, and then I'll open them in paradise," she said, referencing the beliefs she valued so much she had let go of the things she once loved, of Christmas tamale parties, of frosted birthday cakes, of July fireworks.

"You will see paradise," I said, wanting it to be true for her.

"I just worry about my children," she said. After a moment, she added, "You're my children too."

I tried to imagine a life without her too-early phone calls, without the knowledge that even if I was gone, she was still here, getting her hair set each week, humming Elvis under her breath, and secretly buying masa from a bakery in Glendale.

"I don't care what anyone thinks," she said suddenly. "I want you to sit in the front row at my funeral, and write my eulogy. Nothing sad. Say I loved Nate and my children. And say I was a good cook."

She died a week later, in early November, too early for a non-Thanksgiving turkey, and too early to make tamales not for Christmas. I came to the funeral, and sat in the front row. But I did not write her eulogy. Her religion did not allow women to deliver eulogies, especially one who had left the church as I had.

I often think about what I could have said in that eulogy I didn't write. I think I would like to have said:

My mother-in-law was something else, and I loved her.

Once she stole a skirt from my closet and turned it into a pillow.

Her favorite room of any house was the kitchen.

She met the love of her life when she was 16, and was his wife for nearly 60 years.

She loved her children, and always knew what they should be doing but wouldn't.

She had a crush on Elvis Presley when she was a teenager that never went away.

Once, I called her and she didn't come to the phone for six years.

She had pretend holidays and once she called and pretended to have the wrong number, because sometimes, when you can't do what you want, you do what you need, and you learn to call it something else.

And before I forget, she wants to make sure I tell you that she was a very good cook.

NIKKI DeLEON MARTIN is a fiction writer, essayist, and storyteller who lives in Phoenix with two beagles and one husband.

THIS IS ALL I CAN SAY WITH THESE RULES

TRICIA PARKER

MR. EDDIE SEES MY 95-YEAR-OLD GRANDMOTHER every Saturday morning. He rolls her short platinum hair, sets her under a dryer with a Ladies' Home Journal, then teases her little blonde sausages into a coif and gives the outcome a solid spray. She sleeps motionless on her back, like a vampire, and this helmet-hair lasts an entire week. I like taking my grandmother to see Mr. Eddie, watching the other old ladies in their various stages of mobility. Their vanity is strange and sweet. I feel young there. But I cannot end up there.

My grandmother lives with my parents, which is a) the best, "right" thing, and, b) a most difficult reality for all of them. My grandmother's epic, emergency-room nose-bleeds notwithstanding, they have a pretty seamless routine. But what my mother really lives for—her passion of the manger—is Christmas, so I will be taking Grandma to Mr. Eddie's this Saturday, the Saturday before Christmas, as I do every year.

Crone, my son's girlfriend told me recently in an effort to make me feel less awful about my own gray hair, is the most respected stage of female life in the Wiccan tradition. Maiden. Mother. Crone. I am, apparently, a crone, so I can use this word.

Efficient, multi-tasking Mr. Eddie handles three or four crones at once, and I return my grandmother before lunch. A few years ago, my mom, as she often does, greeted us in the driveway. Hobbling. She does hobble a bit—a sore heel, a twingey hip, an unreliable knee—but this was mean pain.

I jumped out of the car, thinking all those selfish thoughts we think as our old people grow older and more infirm: Where does this leave *me*?

She threw her back out making Swedish meatballs. Years later, she'll deny this. She minimizes her chronic pain, nicknames it "holiday back." She is crazy busy, remember? Decking halls, writing cards (a set from her and a set from my grandmother), baking, more baking, more baking, shopping, wrapping, stuffing stockings—yes, mine and my brothers', still!, shelling a single raw almond for rice pudding....

But I know it's the tiny, hand-rolled, dipped in flour, individually fried Swedish meatballs. I blame meatballs.

* * *

"My Swedish Meatballs"
        recipe by Patsy

    6 pounds meat—4 pounds ground beef, 2 pounds ground pork
    6 eggs, slightly beaten
    ¾ can milk (whole, 9 oz)
    2 TSP salt, 2 TSP pepper
    1 tsp each ground cardamom, nutmeg
    3 TSP Worcestershire sauce
    2 cups bread crumbs
    mix well with hands
    roll into tiny balls

My mother—who has since adjusted the painstaking method that follows those ingredients—threw her back out mixing six pounds of meat *well* with her hands.

* * *

My son, home for the weekend, explains why math is not about numbers, but logic. He is studying theoretical algebra, and I kind of try to understand.

"Newton didn't do math, he did arithmetic," Zach tells me, "tedious, shitty calculus. He never proved anything; he just happened to be right. Mathematics is the study of logic, giving yourself a set of rules and trying to exhaust what can be known—get to the very edge of what you're allowed to discover and glean from these rules. To know, 'This is all I can say with these rules.'"

I tell him I want to write about the Swedish meatballs, but I don't know where to begin. Or end.

"What's the kernel of the story?" someone asks.

Zach does this cool thing—my brother does it, too —where he perks up and goes super-introspective simultaneously. "Kernel is a math term," he says, the way people say when they *know* things.

A set is a collection of things. A group is a set with rules, and the rules can result in different arrangements, the composition of the rules (he uses a nickel and a penny to demonstrate the different arrangements of the coins). He tries to explain function, group action, domain and range, binary operations, associativity, identity elements.

Kernel—a subset in the domain, which he calls Group 1. "Kernel is a subset of Group 1. Always non-empty, always has Group 1's identity element in it."

Always non-empty.

I want to understand this thing, this kernel of my son's passion and frustration. I'm stuck on Newton. The equal and opposite reaction thing.

"Physics is just applied arithmetic, Mom." Newton. Ugh, the equal and opposite reaction thing is a gross oversimplification of equal forces on interacting objects.

"Like the domain and range example," I say pointing to a diagram he's drawn. "The inverse for every identity."

"It's nothing like that," he sighs.

* * *

In my child's mind cardamom seeds looked like grapefruit seeds. I know now that those are pods, and inside are the actual seeds, tiny, dark, and irregular. My mom opened the pods and arranged the seeds inside a tea towel, folded it over several times, and violently pounded them with a metal meat tenderizer on the counter. They were expensive and exotic, and we weren't to play with them or otherwise complicate her process and the more serious holiday kitchen rituals, the meatballs and her *julekake*, Norwegian Christmas cake, white, sweet, and round like Hawaiian bread. Knead, let rise, deflate, and shape into rounds for baking. Sometimes, she let my brothers and me deflate the dough; we stood on a chair over the thick, mustard-yellow crockery bowl, and punched the yeasty, cardamom-y, aromatic bubble down into a hissing blob.

She doesn't take the Christmas tree down until after Epiphany. Some of her carefully wrapped and catalogued ornaments are over 100 years old—fragile and gold-leafed. Others are yarn-tied pinecones or cheesy construction-paper frames around decades-old school photos of my brothers and me. She crocheted our stockings, the ones we still use, and downplayed Santa Claus. Her Hummel crèche with its blonde baby Jesus and one Black wise man is not historically accurate but must be as precious to her as salvation.

Is my life an opposite or an inverse reaction?

Is Zach's?

He used to believe—even in leprechauns! If it weren't for my daughter—the romantic to whom my mother's 500 ornaments are promised—I likely wouldn't bother at all with a tree or Christmas morning at all. I bother, but just a little—always non-empty.

There's trouble in my group. This is all I can say with these rules. Seeing my mom bent over that day presented a new wrinkle. My mom, too young to be the old crone, is taking care of the old crone. Our problem is that we are too many crones.

* * *

It's not like my mom assumed this meatball responsibility from my grandmother. Grandma always roasted a leg of pork on Christmas, baked Swedish coffee cake, not *julekake*, favored a sparse, mid-century modern aesthetic, and decorated her trees strictly in red lights and a few carefully curated ornaments—no kiddie crafts.

We are a collection of associative things reacting together. No matter the binary operation, we maintain our identity element. There's an inverse for every element, but the action always returns to its original state. When you smash the inverse, you get the identity element.

* * *

My kids love those Swedish meatballs, and I used to love them, too. I stopped eating meat long ago, but last year I absentmindedly licked gravy off my finger after fixing my grandmother's plate, and for a moment I considered giving up 10 years of my sole discipline.

They are magically delicious. Why? Is it the expensive, exotic cardamom, peeled and ground by hand? The savory combination of two kinds of meat, pork and beef? The sacrifice involved? Who hunched over harvesting this? Who hunched over slaughtering or butchering this? Who hunched over pinching pierogi after pierogi, assembling tamale after tamale, rolling tiny meatball after tiny meatball after tiny meatball?

* * *

The identity element from Group 1 always gets mapped. Even when you smash the inverse, you get the identity.

* * *

"Explain the identity element to me again."

"Remember my coins? The identity element is the rule that didn't mix them up."

But, I remember, Zach also told me that with some rules, groups can collapse on themselves. I don't understand any of it. I, in my early but supposedly venerable cronedom, already exhausting what can be known—about my group? About myself?

I thought the identity element always got mapped. Me? Christmas? An equal and opposite reaction.

* * *

Abstract algebra is how math reacts with *itself*. Maybe we're more like physics—or shitty, tedious calculus.

Zach—because he says the identity element always gets mapped—should apprentice himself to my mom as her journeyman meatball maker. He doesn't care about Wiccans or Hummel figurines or Epiphany. He is neither crone, nor mother, nor maiden. Every year he takes leftover meatballs to go. This work won't kill him. He is a young, clear-headed, unromantic mathematician who knows, theoretically, that a set plus rules makes a group.

He will count to 250.

He has a strong back.

TRICIA PARKER teaches English at a public high school in Phoenix. She's sometimes on Twitter @wasbotten.

IT'S A CYNICAL LIFE

KIM PORTER

I'M IN LINE AT SAFEWAY unloading groceries onto the conveyor belt and planning what quippy observation I'll make once Dave, the cashier, starts ringing me up. I look over my items. It's the week before Christmas 2014, and I'm buying a fruit cake (for me), egg nog (for my husband, I lie, it's also for me), and a little gingerbread-house kit (for the kids). But I also have vegetables, which is why I feel virtuous enough for Dave's line.

I have a crush on Dave. If "crush" is the right word to describe the compulsion I feel to make an aloof person rue the day they underestimated me.

Less romance more revenge.

I've been skittish around Dave for years, since that time he made a possibly snarky comment about the quantity of potato chips I was buying. I say "possibly" because he was muttering and I'm prone to shame, so I can't be 100%. But, I thought he said, "There are other food groups." So, I decided to go ahead and be offended, just in case. *How dare he? He doesn't know me. I'm cool as hell. I'll show him. I'm gonna make this asshole wish he was me.*

Disdain triggers me. If you ever want to trap me, put a cynic in a cage as bait, instruct them to withhold their approval and I'll climb straight in and remain there until I win them over or die trying. Like with my dad. Who died years ago, while I was still trying.

I don't know anything about Dave but that hasn't stopped me from imagining I do. I imagine he's single, because even though he's cute in a Woody Harrelson kind of way, he seems self-righteous. (You should see him handing out those Monopoly game-pieces like his soul is dying). I imagine he has a Kill Your TV bumper sticker, because I've noticed a sort of technology-weary quality to the way he sighs and avoids eye-contact with the cash register. I imagine he studied philosophy in college but didn't finish, which is why he always seems a little bit mad. He bags groceries like a perfectionist with too few outlets. I imagine he loathes anything sappy or manipulative, like when they were doing that charity fundraiser and management made them "whoo-hoo" over the loudspeaker. Dave's flat "whoo-hoo" was everything to me. He's judgmental, sure, but his authenticity is unimpeachable. I imagine he's great at trivia but hates the trivial, his tolerance for pop-culture having been eroded by his proximity to tabloids. I imagine Christmas makes him rant about capitalism to his housemates. I imagine he has house-mates.

I look at my groceries with an eye for what's funny? Maybe the fruitcake? People love to hate fruitcake.

Over the years I've figured out what amuses Dave: harsh truths, astute observations, and sudden literary references. Disarming Dave has been exhilarating but terrifying. It's only a matter of time before he realizes I'm not the cool-cat I pretend to be. I'm actually a tender-hearted dope who's easily undone by anything remotely sweet.

I've spent my whole life cultivating an edgy façade to conceal my gushy innards. First from my dad, who mocked sweetness like it was in his mission statement, and then later (after Dad died) from the string of aloof boyfriends who stood in as proxy.

When I slip up and get saccharin in public I'm quick to ridicule myself, beating everyone to the punch. But, it's exhausting, being always the puncher *and* the punchee.

And it's not enough just to lampoon yourself, if you want to be convincing you also have to deride the sappy thing itself. You can ruin pretty much anything by looking for the shadow it casts and asking yourself, *How is this so-called sweet thing actually an asshole?"*

I know; I've murdered every tender notion that used to make me dingy with joy. And at no time is that more evident than Christmas. Elf on a Shelf? Asshole. Black Friday? Asshole. Santa Claus? Have you seen how he treated Rudolph?

But, there is one Christmas tradition which I hold sacred and have managed to guard against ruination. "It's a Wonderful Life."

If you ever want to trap me, get a TV, stick it in a cage and put on "It's a Wonderful Life". I'll climb straight in and stay there, weeping like a punctured milk carton, until the day I die.

I love that movie.

From the very beginning when Clarence (George's guardian angel) asks if George is sick and that other angel goes, "No, worse. He's discouraged." To the very end when the whole town belts out Auld Lang Syne.

I love when kid George goes, "Mr. Gower, you're hurting my sore ear."

I love the run on the bank! When George is placating the mob, "Now, just remember this isn't as black as it appears," and the silence is broken by a siren.

I love all of Uncle Billy's inexplicable pets. The crow. The Owl. That Squirrel.

I love when George is on that bridge working up the courage to jump and suddenly there's Clarence smiling, cute as a puppy in a bow tie.

Or when Clarence grants George's wish and like that [snap] the winds change.

How Nick the bartender goes, "Out you two pixies go."

I just love how George meticulously turns his watch-pocket inside out looking for Zuzu's petals.

And how he stumble-runs down main street shouting "Merry Christmas, emporium!"

One time I befriended a woman who was visiting from Australia. Over lunch in an Ethiopian restaurant I asked her if they watch "It's a Wonderful Life" in Australia. She said she'd never heard of it. So I decided to summarize the whole movie for her. "Ok. So. It's about this guy named *George Bailey*." My voice careened out of control as I clamped down on a sob. I tried again. "He's from this town called *Bedford Falls*!" It was immediately clear to me that I wouldn't be able to tell this story without scream/crying like a lunatic, but that didn't stop me. I spent the next 20 minutes hysterically yelling the plot. She sat across from me, eyes darting like a hostage. Later, that same woman made the mistake of telling me she'd never seen "Old Yeller."

"It's a Wonderful Life" is the last sentimental thing I've managed not to murder. Which is why I rarely talk about it, just in case I'm tempted to sacrifice it to look cool.

So. Here I am at Safeway. Dave moves the bar out of the way and starts scanning my groceries. I haven't thought up anything clever, maybe some banter will arise organically. But Dave seems sad. No, worse. Discouraged. He's been disgruntled since Albertsons bought out Safeway last year. A few weeks ago, I asked him why I hadn't seen him around much, he said they'd slashed his schedule and moved him to nights.

He rings up my fruitcake. Suddenly my fruitcake seems inauthentic. My egg nog. Egg Nog is objectively disgusting. The ginger-bread kit. What kind of shitty mother buys a pre-fab ginger-bread kit? Even my vegetables seem desperate for approval.

Soon our transaction will be complete and I'll have lost this opportunity to prove, once again, I'm cool enough.

God! Why do I even care if this probable asshole thinks I'm cool?

And when will I finally be able to trace an unhealthy impulse down to its origin and not find "did my dead dad really love me?" sitting like a poison kernel at the heart of it. Not yet, apparently.

I feel dull. No, worse. Discouraged. I notice there's a long line of customers at the Wells Fargo bank in the front of the store. I turn to Dave, hitch my thumb, and to my horror, throw my favorite movie under the bus: "That's got all the earmarks of being a run on the bank."

I'm stunned by the mocking tone of my own voice. It's as if I just said, "Are you familiar with 'It's a Wonderful Life'? Isn't it just the hokiest? Shall we lampoon it together?"

I glance at Dave to see if he's impressed or embarrassed for me. He looks up from my kale to the line of bank customers. His hands still moving mechanically, scanner beeping in rhythm.

I have invited some dude I barely know to mock my last best Christmas tradition. I feel see-through and ashamed. But Dave does something I could never have anticipated.

Dave looks me in the eyes and becomes Jimmy Stewart, "No, but you're thinking of this place all wrong. As if I had the money back in the safe. The money's not here. Well, your money's in Joe's house that's right next to yours. And then the Kennedy house and a hunnerd others. You're lending them the money to build and then they're going to pay it back to you as best they can. Now, listen, now listen to me. If Potter gets ahold of this Building and Loan, there'll never be another decent house built in this town. Joe, you had one of those Potter houses didn't you? Well, have you forgotten, have you forgotten what he charged you for that broken-down shack? Don't you see what's happening? Potter isn't selling. Potter's buying. And why? Because we're panicking and he's not. That's why. Now we can get through this thing all right. We've got to stick together. We've got to have faith in each other."

And with that, he sort of trails off, chuckling, mumbling, and begins to bag my groceries. He has a little smile at the corner of his mouth and his face is kind of flushed.

We made magic and we know it.

I feel giddy. I swipe my debit card.

He looks at me as if for approval. I give it, I laugh.

This Dave is not the Dave I thought I knew. My Dave would've never known every word of that monologue nor had a perfect Jimmy Stewart in his pocket ready to whip out at the flimsiest invitation like a couple of Zuzu's petals.

That movie is gospel to me, and even I can't quote it word for word. I feel my eyes misting and I'm torn between letting myself feel it or striking a derisive pose. I risk it.

"I love that movie."

"Me too." He says, "I watch it every year."

It feels like a gust of fresh air has blown through the store, through my whole life. Like the winds have changed.

If Dave's not who I thought he was. Maybe nobody's who I think they are. Maybe I'm not who I think I am. Maybe my dad wasn't. Or maybe he was but maybe I don't have to care. Maybe I'm free to be who I want to be.

Dave hands me my receipt and thanks me by name. And I am sent out into the world to contemplate all the sweet things I could enjoy again if only I have the courage.

KIM PORTER is a writer/performer and zealous developer of other people's stories.

GOODBYE

OH HENRY

DEBORAH H. SUSSMAN

EVERY DOG OWNER WILL TELL YOU that their dog is special. But Henry the border collie wasn't just special. Henry was legendary.

Henry was the first dog I ever knew and loved. That's not why he's legendary. That's just a fact.

In my life, I had met dogs, petted dogs, even liked some dogs—well enough. But I had always preferred cats. Cats were mysterious and aloof. Dogs were so…obvious. And sometimes they drooled. And mostly your hands smelled funny after you touched their fur. Also, they could bite you; a dog had tried, once, as I was racing down to the bus stop at the bottom of the hill where my family lived, on a bitter Montreal winter day. I was 15, late for school as usual, lost in my head making up excuses for why I was late again, when a neighbor's dalmatian flew at me and took a big bite out of what would have been my arm if I hadn't been wearing a puffy down jacket. The dog's teeth tore the dark blue fabric of the jacket and took a clump of feathers with them. I was shocked, but I also suddenly had an excellent excuse for being late, and dramatic evidence.

I was almost 30 and living in Charlottesville, Virginia, when my boyfriend, who lived a thousand miles away in a small house in the cornfields of Iowa, decided to adopt a dog. David was a journalist and an obsessive; he gathered information methodically and exhaustively on every subject he undertook, in print and in life. Before settling on the idea of a border collie, he researched dog breeds and temperament, breeds and training, breeds and geographical location. For months, he entertained the idea of the perfect dog, as that idea morphed from wire-haired to long-haired, from terrier to retriever, from mid-size to larger and back again. And he did all this research pre-Google.

The perfect dog, in whatever shape or size, would be loyal, athletic, and intelligent—much like David. Whether or not David was also going for "obsessive," that's what he got.

Why he decided on a border collie exactly, I don't know. Maybe it had something to do with visiting me and imagining driving out into the rolling green hills of Virginia to the sheep farm where Henry and his siblings frolicked in the grass. Maybe it was because none of his friends had border collies. Whatever the reason, he fell in love with Henry the minute he saw him. I knew David had a soft spot. I had no idea how big it was.

Border collies are working dogs. This means they need a schedule and a job to do or they become neurotic. They are not lounge-on-the-couch-and-watch-television dogs—not unless they've already played Frisbee with you for a couple of hours and maybe hiked a mountain or two. David knew this going in—he knew that Henry's father was a champion sheepherding dog from Scotland, so Henry would be smart and motivated, and he had already settled on a kind of dog Bible for training Henry, written by a group of monks who spent their waking hours praying and training dogs.

Henry was black and white, mostly, with dapples of golden brown, and he had the face of a much older and wiser dog even as a puppy—attentive eyes, long slender nose. The tip of his tail was pale and naked, missing its fur; this troubled David, but not enough to prevent him from taking the puppy home with us to the condo I shared with my roommate. And David, who was fairly particular about his car, didn't mind when the puppy threw up all over the back seat. He was more worried about the dog than he was about his car's interior, which indicated to me how serious he was about caring for this creature. It was the first of many car rides Henry would take with us, up and down the East Coast, and back and forth between Iowa and Virginia.

When I tell you Henry was brilliant, I am not exaggerating. Some of it was the breed: Border collies are keen and inquisitive and eager to please, motivated not by food—although he certainly enjoyed a nice pig's ear—but by praise for a job well done. When Henry was still a puppy, we took him back to the sheep farm where he was born and put him in the field with a few of the farmer's sheep. He was a fraction of their size, but he immediately herded them all into a corner. It was like watching a fish swim.

Henry's training routine was thorough and consistent. David taught him to be comfortable in a crate, to fetch and return an object (a ball, a Frisbee, a dessicated corn cob), and to poop on command—the command was "Let 'er rip," and his friends would threaten to drive out to his little house in the cornfields when he wasn't there and yell,

"Let 'er rip, Henry!" through the mail slot in the front door. Henry also learned not to step into the street, any street, without first being told it was ok. He knew all the usual commands: Sit, Lie down, Up—and if you told Henry to shake, instead of giving you his paw, Henry would shake all over, the way a dog does when it's just jumped out of the water. Henry, it must be said, was better behaved than most people.

I was very proud of Henry. I loved it when my friend Alex held up his thumb and forefinger said, "He's THIS FAR from speech." I loved it when Henry greeted me at the door. I loved taking Henry for walks in the woods, and how incredibly fast and graceful he was. I loved when Henry outran a greyhound at the dog park.

I was becoming a dog person. And when David and I broke up, and he suggested that Henry might be better off with me in Virginia than couch surfing in New York City with him, I agreed. He loved Henry enough to let him go.

And when my parents asked me if I would come home to Denver to spend time with my father, who had been diagnosed with cancer, Henry came with me.

As children, my brothers and I were not allowed to have pets, unless you count goldfish, mice and gerbils, and I did NOT. When I was 12, I wore my parents down with my begging and they let me adopt a small grey kitten. But a dog was out of the question. I knew better than to even ask for one, although I *did* ask, out of curiosity and more than once, "Why not??" My mother said it was because my father had grown up in small apartments in Europe and wasn't used to dogs.

The chemo made my father tired and he often seemed distracted or sad. He was cordial with Henry, but slightly wary. Gradually Henry wore him down. He didn't leap or lick or beg, but when my father sat in his chair by the window in the living room, Henry sat next to him, with his head right about at petting height, and waited. And one day, my father patted him on the top of his dark head, gingerly at first, and said, "Hello, Henry." I like to think it brought him some comfort. Dogs are good at comforting us when people don't know what to do.

My father's death crushed me. It was so cruel, and I missed him so much. Back in Virginia, I went through the motions, but I felt lost. One winter night, I was out walking Henry around the neighborhood, trying to understand where and how my father had gone. As I walked, I would throw the Frisbee for Henry and he would bring it back and place it precisely at my feet, as usual. If I was too lost in thought, he'd pick it up and drop it right at my feet again and look me in the eyes, as if to say, "Come on, get it together." Henry had a job to do. And then, Henry brought the Frisbee back—but not to me: He dropped it a few feet to my left, and began looking intently up into nothing—as if someone was standing next to me, someone I couldn't see. And I, who do not necessarily believe in ghosts, realized suddenly and surely that I did not feel alone. I felt my father's presence. I dismissed it as a fluke, as wishful thinking born of grief—and then Henry repeated the performance: dropped the frisbee a few feet away from me and locked eyes with the air. And another time. He would only reluctantly pick the Frisbee up and give it to me instead after I asked him repeatedly—he really wanted the invisible person to play with him.

Henry came with me and my new husband to Arizona. He adjusted to the heat, and to the new mostly treeless landscape. He adjusted to the new baby in the house and to our erratic brand-new-parent schedule.

The situation improved when our baby began to eat solid food and Henry discovered that if he stayed close, delicious bits of people food would rain down from the high chair. Henry and our daughter became inseparable, like siblings from different species. He herded her gently around the house, along with our two cats, and his name was one of the first words she ever said: Henny.

Henry died at the relatively old age of 14, not suddenly but slowly, the way healthy dogs do. His death was my daughter's first, and she took it better than I did. I'd had no idea that losing a dog would feel so much like losing a person. Henry wasn't a pet. He was a member of the family. In the days after we said goodbye to Henry, the house felt strange. The rhythm of my days no longer made sense. There was no dog to feed, to walk, to worry about, to love. I realized that as much as I'd thought we were training Henry all those years, he'd been training us, gently and well.

I've had other dogs since Henry. I share my home with one now, a rescue dog named Chai who is, as near as we can tell, a chuggle—part chihuahua, part pug, part beagle. She is the size, shape, and color of a mostly baked loaf of bread, and I love her beyond reason. It's a love tinged with the knowledge that I will have to say goodbye to her, too, eventually, and usher her over what our vet's office refers to as the rainbow bridge—into a better place, where I imagine she will find Henry, sitting with my father and patiently waiting for news of us.

DEBORAH H. SUSSMAN is a writer and editor in Tempe.

THE DUSTY TRAVELER

PAPAY SOLOMON

MY YOUNG DUSTY FEET have walked many many miles to where I am currently. They have traveled through a great wealth of rocky paths, filled with broken bottles, that have caused my heart to bleed on several occasions. Yet these dusty feet have also ventured across warm comforting sand leading to horizons illuminated by the brightness of the morning sun.

The story begins with me frantically shooting out of bed, in the middle of the night, like a bullet that was dispatched out of a gun held by a child. As I struggled to get a little grip on reality, I heard my mother's modulated voice rush to my eardrums from what seemed like afar, but she was right next to me.

"Are you okay?"

She asked with an accent straight from the streets of Liberia, as she quickly turned towards me to confirm that all was well. I slowly nodded my head while I simultaneously rubbed the sleep out of my eyes. Then, as I opened my eyes, I noticed that my mother was wide awake sitting on the right side of the bed while my older sister, who was 15 at the time, lay to the left side engaged in what seemed like a peaceful sleep.

My mother must have been up for at least an hour before I rocketed out of bed, because everything in the room indicated that she was in the middle of an operation. She had our kerosene lamp turned on. The little bit of clothes, important documents, and photos we managed to save throughout the years were covered with large sheets of plastic. She also had the pots and pans that were used for cooking and eating placed in different areas of the room, including on our bed, to collect droplets that fell freely from the ceiling. All of a sudden, it dawned on me. It had been raining the whole time my sister and I slept and my mother was up trying to prevent the little we had from getting drenched.

My mother, sister, and I lived and stored everything we owned in a room which was eight by eight feet wide. On the left side of us existed two rooms of the same size, while three lined up on the right. One and a half feet against our door stood another unit of six rooms with doors facing us. Every single room was occupied by a different family and, combined, created a huge structure with one roof. The frame of this structure was made out of lumber. The roof and walls, however, were made out of waterproof cloth which we referred to as tarpaulin. Gold was easier to attain than privacy. The walls were thin to an extent where you could hear a neighbor whisper from the farthest end. There was no such thing as running water, and air conditioning was a myth. A simple decision to get drinking water or water to bathe required a journey of a few miles by feet. The small room that I referred to as home was not responsible for providing me an escape from the busyness and intrusiveness of the world. It barely protected me from harsh weather and danger— that became even more evident every time the sky decided to cry a thousand tears.

This was not a foreign experience. Every time it rained, which it did for almost half the year, our poorly constructed roof leaked massively. As the result, on one vibrant morning, after we were done eating a meal that was going to last us until the end of the day, my mother suggested a brief meeting as she washed her hands with a portion of drinking water.

"My children, you listen. You know that it's been raining a lot lately, right?"

"Uh huh!" my sister and I responded sharply.

"Well, here is the plan: Whenever you notice that it's going to rain, make sure your hurry up and let me know so I can cover all our important clothes and documents with the big plastic we have in the room. I don't want the rain to destroy everything we have. You hear me?"

From that day forth, whenever any of us had even the slightest feeling that it was going to rain, we ran to our mother and meticulously covered everything that was of value with the now memorable plastic sheets. This was the best and most affordable strategy we could come up with, and we made it work for the most part. For this particular night however, Mother Nature was playing a game that we did not see coming.

This was just life for a regular 13-year-old boy living in a refugee camp located in the middle of a remote area in Guinea. I stood twigly and slight. My elongated face, generously anointed with homemade palm nut oil, made my forehead gleam in every direction, bringing attention to the clearly defined bones that appeared on my face. Like an abstract expressionistic painting, my teeth unevenly laid on top and beside one another patiently waiting to crawl out of my mouth whenever I attempted to smile. My head was obviously much bigger than the body that it sat on, but this was the norm. At that point in my life, in the year 2007, it was easily noticeable that I had accumulated about eight years of life experience as a refugee.

As the year grew older, the hunger pains became stronger. My mother, who was once healthy and in control became worried and frail. It had already been almost a year since I had attended school, and my sister had been out much longer. In the camp, the maximum level of free education a child was permitted to acquire was the sixth grade, and after graduation, the parents or guardians were responsible to sponsor anything higher. For my family and many others, that only meant that education was no longer an option. Luckily for me, I had something else that was eager to become the captain of my attention. It was art. As I dedicated most of my time drawing and doodling on line paper that I borrowed from my messy old notebooks, my abilities matured gradually. My sister, on the other hand, invested most of her time associating with people who the community frowned upon and as the result, a baby was introduced to our family when she was 16. Although babies are a blessing, this was farfetched for what reality was for us.

Finally, during the early months of 2008, it was announced to my family that we were scheduled to resettle to America in a matter of a few months. As I heard those words penetrate through my ears, tears gracefully rolled down my bony cheeks as I imagined how different my life was going to become. It was a dream that was on the verge of becoming a reality. Going to America basically meant going to heaven without having to die. It meant that all the hardship, hunger, and abuse we had endured till that moment was about to vanish in thin air. My family and I had waited for almost five years to hear such words uttered, and it was nothing less than a blessing. Before we could put our fingers on it, the news had circulated the entire camp quicker than a bonfire and overnight, we became local celebrities.

On the fourth day of August, 2008, after an entire week of traveling in a car to Conakry, the capital city of Guinea, and a plane flight that lasted for almost two days, we arrived to our final destination, Phoenix Arizona, at the middle of the night. Upon exiting the airport to meet our pickup, with my entire family dressed in freeze defense jackets, we were instantly welcomed by a gust of wind that was hotter than the pits of hell. It was a completely different world. I was amazed by everything I laid my eyes upon. I had never seen so many White people in my life! In just over a week and some days, I started to notice how much our lives were starting to change. With the assistance from various organizations like the Catholic Charities and Welcome to America, we now had air conditioning and a perfectly lit two-bedroom space that was furnished with walls that could not be sliced open with a razor blade. We had enough food to eat and water to drink. To top it all up, we even had a stove and a refrigerator.

A few months later, my mother attained a job that paid minimum wage. My sister and I enrolled into high school and shortly after, the assistance dried up. It was then that I started to notice how America was not the heaven that I once thought it was. Compared to the majority of other families, we were at the bare bottom of the food chain. Over a decade later, I have arrived at the realization that only I can truly rescue myself. I have survived for way too long. It is now rightfully time to transform myself from just a survivor, to one who thrives.

PAPAY SOLOMON is a Phoenix-based painter whose current work focuses on depicting visual narratives of young African émigrés. Follow him on Instagram @papaysolomon.

OF BARNEY AND BRETT KAVANAUGH

KATIE CAMPBELL

I WENT HOME RECENTLY to say goodbye to my grandma.

And that's bad enough already—saying goodbye to someone you love.

But it was worse, although worse really isn't the right word for it, because the very first thing she wanted to tell me was how she'd been assaulted as a teenager.

Luckily for our family, she was all there right up until the very end. My same kind of kooky, kind of sassy, always out-there grandma. But this wasn't that.

She had the news on, and someone was speculating about whether Brett Kavanaugh would get the votes he needed to become Justice Brett Kavanaugh. And she just launched into this story.

In the week or so before my visit, she'd been following the news about Christine Blasey Ford, watching her testify in D.C. and listening to the endless commentary about did he or didn't he.

And at some point in the middle of all of that, she suddenly remembered.

She suddenly remembered that some guy, some boat guy working on the ferry that takes you to the Statue of Liberty, grabbed her. She didn't say much more about what happened after that, but she talked a lot about how embarrassed she was. How embarrassed she was for what he did. It was her senior trip. She was getting ready to graduate high school. But she didn't even walk at her graduation. She said she couldn't bring herself to go back to her school after that, as if everyone knew and blamed her.

She had to have her brother take her books back to the school for her. And looking back, she realized he must've known something was wrong, but you just didn't talk about that stuff back then.

The embarrassment was so overwhelming that she just kind of forgot about it. Or more accurately, she blocked it entirely from memory, always sensing this looming shadow in the back of her mind but just choosing not to acknowledge it. That is until it was right there on the TV screen being questioned by a bunch of politicians.

She told my mom first. My mom was her rock, not just in her last weeks but for most of her life.

My mom is everyone's rock. She's one of four, but she spent the most time with my grandma, a) because she lived the closest and b) because she was the most responsible, the most caring, the most selfless, the most patient.

And so she was also the first to hear this story. I wasn't there for that telling, but I can imagine how she must have felt.

I was stunned to say the least, but more so because I was so angry inside and she wasn't.

I specifically remember her saying she wasn't having nightmares, and I remember that because it was my first thought like oh my god this is haunting my grandma in her last weeks on earth fuck that guy. But that wasn't the case at all.

She said she felt relieved to finally talk about it, after burying it in her memory for decades. Decades.

It took a complete stranger's courage to shake that memory loose and to reassure my grandma that she was allowed to now not only remember that moment but to talk about it.

Decades later.

Every generation wants their children to have more than they did. I assume anyway. I don't have kids. I just want to raise my cats in peace.

There was always this unspoken promise that my life would somehow be better. It went without saying that I was going to college, that I was going to see the world and that I was going to be safe.

And I think my grandma really took solace in the fact that women are now not just talking about sexual harassment and assault but publicly calling out their attackers and leaving them to feel that embarrassment that haunted her for decades. That even if Brett Kavanaugh was Justice Brett Kavanaugh, he, too, was going to feel that heat rise into his pasty cheeks.

For the next week I was with my grandma, she did this Kavanaugh impression over and over.

"I like beer," she would say in the closest she could come to a deep, caveman-esque voice, making these exaggerated motions with her hands.

It wasn't SNL-worthy, but I thought it was pretty damn funny.

She was funny. And she was warm. Sometimes fiery, willing to stand up for herself.

I went back and forth a lot about whether this is the story I wanted to tell you because these stories inevitably define the people in them. Victim.

That's just not who my grandma was.

She was an avid cyclist, reader, and smoker, the latter of which led to the cancer that took her life.

When I was little, she spoiled me rotten with Dollar Store toys and let me do the dishes even though I mostly just played with the water.

I slept over a lot when my mom worked late, and she'd sleep in the guest room with me, listening to me prattle on and on for hours until I finally closed my eyes.

She wasn't a very good cook, pretty bad cook actually. But she always had ice cream in the house, and she let me dip ginger snaps in her coffee. I blame my sweet tooth and the extra padding around my hips on her.

I only took one thing of hers with me when I came back to Phoenix. A photo from my third birthday.

My grandpa is holding me, my grandma is holding my cousin, and in the middle, there is my hero. Barney the purple dinosaur. And my face says it all—my life peaked that day, folks. I am smiling so big that my head is kind of jutting forward to emphasize how big I'm smiling, and my arms are wrapped around Barney's giant snout. If you look just carefully enough, you can see my dad's eye peeking out of Barney's nostril. But if I noticed he wasn't at the party, I didn't care, because Barney was there and that was really all that mattered.

I smile almost as big every time I look at that picture. It wasn't just me; pure joy radiates from it. Grandpa is smiling, my cousin is smiling, although I convince myself I detect the slightest hint of jealousy, and Grandma is mid-laugh, head slightly tilted like she's getting a glamour shot taken.

It all looks so perfect. It was perfect.

I haven't framed it yet because it almost hurts to see how perfect it was.

Brett Kavanaugh and that guy from the ferry didn't exist that day.

It felt strangely empowering to talk about that shadow that lurks behind so many of us. It is so energizing to know you aren't alone, but also so deeply, thoroughly painful.

My grandma didn't want sympathy. She wanted to know that things would change. Maybe not for her daughter, but certainly for her daughter's daughter. For me.

And in so many ways, that unspoken promise has been kept. I have had more in my life that she ever could have dreamed—hello, Barney was in my house

But that shadow that hid in the depths of her memory follows me, too. The difference is I never figured out how to tell her.

KATIE CAMPBELL is a journalist in Phoenix. Find her on Twitter and Instagram @_KECampbell.

20 WEEKS

JAMES A. AHLERS

WE ROLL UP TO THE EMERGENCY ROOM ENTRANCE at Scottsdale Shea Hospital, the smell of vomit spilling out the open windows of our Honda Pilot. My wife, Tiffany, darts around to the backseat passenger door, hoists up our little boy, and carefully bundles him in his Avengers blanket, to ward off the vomit and the crisp night air.

A shifty-eyed man in jeans and a t-shirt teeters in the doorway, blocking our path as he pokes stupidly at his iPhone. He pauses, scans over our wreck of a vehicle and my distressed wife, vomity kid and all... then grunts, "Are you Uber?"

Tiffany and I lock eyes, incredulous. "No," she says, and walks inside. I pull away to park, and the man returns to his poking. "He must have come from the Phoenix Open," my wife laughs, as we meet in the lobby. "Idiot," I snarl.

* * *

I'm anxious. A scratchy throat a week ago has suddenly become a massive strep infection. What if the infection has spread to his blood? And his joints? Now he's dehydrated, and he can't hold down water, much less antibiotics. How could we miss the signs for a week? My God, we're the worst parents ever.

I wring my hands at the bedside, while Tiffany, strong and beautiful, projects calm. Our brave boy betrays no fear as he asks questions about the IV the nurses are about to insert. "Will it hurt when you put it in?" he asks. "There will be a poke," they say kindly. "We just need to find your blue lines."

He never squirms or flinches. But I flinch. And I think about past nights in the hospital.

* * *

I think of our baby girl, Isabel Ann, born late the night of August 3, 2009.

Much of that night is a blur now. I remember Tiffany and I taking turns holding her until morning, falling asleep intermittently. I remember feeling guilty that I lacked the strength to stay awake through the night, losing precious minutes with her. I remember a lovely nurse named "Taffy," who, unironically, couldn't have been more sweet.

And I remember another nurse who pissed me off. She appointed herself director of what was meant to be a tasteful family photo shoot, and it quickly turned awkward. "Let's turn her head this way. Great. Now, Mom, hold her up like this. Smile, Dad." I drew the line abruptly when she put Isabel's hands together and egged us on to take pictures of her "praying."

I remember packing up, willing ourselves up from our cold metal seats, and walking arm in arm, our feet leaden on the bright, clinical tile of the birth ward hallway, sobbing gently as we forever left behind our daughter's body.

* * *

Tiffany had felt in her bones that something was off with the pregnancy. But it was just a feeling. Until the 18-week check-up, one Friday afternoon in July. "The amniotic fluid is low," the nurse observed casually. She would confer with the ob-gyn and get back to us. We agonized through the weekend.

Monday brought crushing news. The low amniotic fluid signaled a serious condition called renal agenesis. Without amniotic fluid, the baby can't develop kidneys. Without kidneys, the baby can't develop lungs. Without lungs, the baby can't breathe.

The second ob-gyn we consulted, a detached man with a Wilford Brimley-esque moustache, confirmed that our daughter had a condition that was, as he put it, "incompatible with life."

I suppose it was a nice enough way of saying "fatal."

* * *

The third ob-gyn and third ultrasound specialist—this one a radiologist—were warm, compassionate, and definitive: The baby would likely die inside the womb in a matter of weeks. If by some miracle she lived to be born, she would die as soon as she tried to take a breath. We confronted a decision I wouldn't wish on my worst enemy: end the pregnancy now, or continue it with the faintest of hope and at great risk to Tiffany's health. We sat on the couch together and cried for days. We clung tightly to our then 18-month-old son Henry, taking comfort in watching him play, smile, and sleep, while mourning that we would never see his sister do any of those things.

Our Catholic parents, seeing our anguish and feeling their own pain at the thought of losing a grandchild, asked, "Can't you just wait? Miracles happen." But I lost my religion long ago, right around the time of my eighth-grade confirmation. And my wife, though more spiritually inclined, could not deny that feeling in her bones, now confirmed by four doctors and three ultrasounds.

In our darkest moment, Tiffany and I were completely in sync. We knew that no miracle was coming to relieve our burden. We had to decide, and we needed someone with moral authority to tell us that, whatever we chose, we were still good people.

We sought out Father Gil, the Episcopal priest who had married us three years before, at Trinity Cathedral, just up the road from here. He had married us with genuine love and happiness, despite the fact that, one, he had only just met us the day of our wedding, and, two, we were not Episcopalian.

Though we hadn't seen him since, he was incredibly gracious and wise. He listened patiently, tugging pensively at his goatee, as we told him how we were struggling with the weight of our decision.

We would not take the "easy" way, we said. The doctors had suggested a "D&E," or "dilate and evacuate," crudely known as a "vacuum abortion." We wanted our almost fully formed baby girl to be born, even if she never took a live breath. Father Gil consoled us and assured us that we were soulful and caring in the face of a bad situation, one that no loving God would want for us.

We decided to induce. And a few days later, Father Gil joined our mothers and my wife's sister by our side at John C. Lincoln Memorial Hospital, where our daughter was stillborn.

On August 5th, 2009, we buried her.

* * *

The last thing Tiffany and I wanted to do was answer questions about all of this. So we sent a blast email. On August 7th, I wrote:

"Dear Family and Friends,

"As most of you know, we were looking forward to the birth of our second child.

"Unfortunately, we are writing to give you the sad news that our baby girl had a developmental defect that was incompatible with life, and she has passed away. Isabel Ann Ahlers was born and died on August 3, 2009.

"We thank you all for your prayers, well wishes and support."

My family, friends and co-workers were compassionate, though sometimes annoying. One said, "Sometimes biology just knows." In other words, shit happens. Others said "God called his little angel home." In other words, God meant for this shit to happen. Neither is very comforting.

A pregnant co-worker at my law firm backed several feet away from me in the elevator, as if she might catch death. Others asked questions that I didn't feel like answering: "Why are you back at work already?" Or, "When are you going to turn in that project?"

One co-worker did exactly the right thing. He walked into my office, opened his arms and said,

"Come here." He gave me a brief man hug, then left. I don't think I ever thanked him properly. If you're out there, Craig, thanks.

* * *

A year after Isabel's death, we returned to the maternity ward of John C. Lincoln, this time for the birth of our son Liam. All seemed well until, suddenly, the doctor announced he was coming sideways and they had to do an emergency C-section. I watched helplessly as the ob-gyn strained and strained to get him out, the look of concern on her face deepening as precious seconds and oxygen ticked away. "What's happening?" Tiffany pleaded. "I don't know!" I blurted unhelpfully, turning white as a sheet as I thought, "Oh no, not again...."

* * *

I'm happy to report that Liam is a strong, healthy 5-year-old now, fully recovered from a traumatic birth and his recent visit to the emergency room.

* * *

There is no rule book for dealing with the death of a child. How to tell people about the death, or not. How to react when your living child falls ill, and some part of you can't help but fear the worst.

For a while I struggled with how to answer the question, "How many kids do you have?" Sometimes I would say, "Three... but we lost our daughter." Let me tell you, that is one hell of a conversation stopper at a cocktail party.

* * *

I still struggle at what to tell our boys about their sister when we visit her. She is buried in the same cemetery as Tiffany's dad, the grandfather they have never met.

As you know, I'm not religious. So I can't bring myself to say that Grandpa and Isabel are laughing and playing together in Heaven. But my desire to comfort, and be comforted, rebels against my damned rationality. So I can't bring myself to say they are just rotting in the ground, either.

We tell them simply that Grandpa and Isabel look after one other, and that they are always with us. "She would have been six now," we say. Henry, now eight, says, "I wish I had a sister who wasn't dead."

He and little brother Liam protect and care for Isabel in the only way they can, angrily shooing away the ants that dare to tread on her grave marker. They place the flowers and wipe away the dust, more clearly revealing the etchings. A butterfly of stone flutters by the words that Tiffany and I chose to remember her by: "Nothing beautiful in this world is ever lost."

* * *

The sentiment reminds me of the words from Walt Whitman that I read at her burial, and that I return to now and again, in search of some solace:

I bequeath myself to the dirt to grow from the grass I love, If you want me again look for me under your bootsoles.

You will hardly know who I am or what I mean, But I shall be good health to you nevertheless, And filter and fibre your blood.

Failing to fetch me at first keep encouraged, Missing me one place search another, I stop somewhere waiting for you.

JAMES A. AHLERS is a recovering Catholic, Midwesterner, bureaucrat and journalist, and relapsed lawyer. He writes much the way he plays soccer: clumsily but with joy.

HAROLD

ROBBIE SHERWOOD

THROUGHOUT THE 1960S, '70S AND '80S, Round Valley High School, in the tiny White Mountain town of Eagar, Arizona, was a football factory. By the time I got there, the Round Valley Elks had enjoyed more than 70 winning seasons in a row, won two recent state championships and had set the state record for consecutive victories with 34.

We were coached by a squat, sadistic, no-neck little pile of muscle and gut named Tot Workman. Despite standing all of 5-foot-5, Workman exuded a loud, intimidating and supreme confidence in his authority and ability to motivate young men to do—with as much intensity as humanly possible—whatever he told them. A devout Mormon, Workman's voice was nevertheless perpetually hoarse from screaming at us. These tirades included the occasional epithet, which would then produce more anger at us for having made him break one of the tenets of the faith. We would succeed, he told us, "if I have to sacrifice every drop of blood in YOUR bodies." He meant it. The idea that coaches shouldn't haul their players around by their facemasks, or hit them, had not caught on in our town.

I'm not trying to brag, but I believe I had several felonies committed on me in high school. We all did! It was the '80s.

This was Workman's system. He had the full support of the town and his players for this reason: We won. In the late summer of 1982, I became a new cog in this system: A then 5-foot-7, 130-pound linebacker.

Harold was an older and much more prominent cog in this system. Standing 6-feet-4, around 240 pounds, Harold was a senior and returning starter on the offensive and defensive line. He wasn't muscular, just big, with an even bigger mean-streak. He was the latest in a long line of aggressive, hulking, steak-fed rancher's boys to anchor Coach Workman's mauling, half-crazed style of line play. Harold idolized Coach Workman and, one suspected, would kill for him. At least that's what we sincerely believed when we were freshmen.

Harold managed this role while seeming barely literate. But he was mighty quick on the uptake when it came to spotting weaknesses in others and attacking.

To his credit, Harold's bullying could sometimes show bursts of ingenuity and absurd humor that could even be admired...but only if directed at others. Harold's habit of backhanding unwitting underclassmen in the testicles as they walked through the hall-ways—punctuated with "Take a bow!"—was always hilarious...to witness.

About two weeks before the start of school, we kicked off the football season with a hellish series of two-a-day practices. Sophomores and upperclassmen knew what to expect. Freshmen like me did not. We had barely strapped on our helmets and lined up for stretching when things started going wrong for us. Before we would ever even touch a football, Workman first assigned our captain—Harold—to show us how to do proper Round Valley Elks jumping jacks. And we were fucking them up. Unlike other teams, we Elks did not audibly count out our jumping jacks. Instead, we arrayed ourselves in five lines, five yards apart, and then, silently, executed exactly 10 jumping jacks. This show of quiet discipline made for an oddly disconcerting and intimidating sight before games. While our opponents were whooping and getting "fired up," the only sound coming from our team of black-clad football robots was made by our palms slapping our thigh pads. However, at this moment, we were weeks away from our first game. And we were discovering that it's surprisingly difficult to count to 10 when you're terrified. Every time we would come down on 10, a point at which we were supposed to stop and stare ahead silently, the arms of at least one freshman would rise and freeze in an aborted 11th jumping jack. After each mistake, Workman would blow his whistle, and the entire team—freshman, JV and varsity—would have to take off on a 100-yard series of belly flops and then redeploy for another try. As one could imagine, when everyone is punished for the transgressions of a few—and those few are invariably the youngest and weakest in the group—those few become about as popular as a fart in a diving bell. After we got in line for our third round of 10, Harold had dropped the silent part of the drill and was now flipping out and threatening to kill us. He unleashed a stream of graphic invective, punctuated by an observation I will never forget: "You look like hammered horse cum!"

It was completely involuntary, but I laughed out loud. I wasn't alone. We had just never heard that phrase before. Hammered horse cum? How would he even know about this? I grew up on a farm, too, but what the hell was going on over at Harold's place? The snickering threw Workman into a rage of his own. Twenty 100-yard sprints later, vomiting air and feeling near death, we finally accomplished 10 suitably silent jumping jacks and moved on with practice.

After two-a-days, varsity and freshman teams didn't practice together any more, thank God. But we did lift weights at the same time during a for-credit P.E. class. One snowy late-fall day, I stepped out of the gym shower and found myself face-to-face with Harold in the crowded locker room. He was smiling. This was disconcerting, not just because Harold was seemingly being friendly, but also because he was naked and sweaty.

Quickly adopting the universal body language for minding my own business, I lowered my eyes and reached for my towel hanging nearby on a row of hooks. But Harold moved faster and snatched it before I could.

"Can I borrow your towel real quick?" Harold said, all friendly-like, as if he were asking for a stick of gum.

Before I could protest, Harold slid my towel between his meaty thighs and began to vigorously and deeply floss his ass and balls. Back and forth, back and forth, like he was trying to saw himself in half from the bottom up. The audience was delighted. I just stood there, dripping, until he finished. Then he tossed the towel back to me and politely said, "Thanks!" I said nothing. If I had opened my mouth, I'm sure that my new ass-towel would have come with a fresh ass-kicking. It was about four degrees outside, but I still went to class with wet clothes plastered to my body. The towel went into the trash.

Was Harold waiting for me, or was this just a crime of opportunity? I can't be sure. I wasn't the only person he picked on, or even the most. It was probably just my turn.

That spring I had managed to earn a varsity letter in track. Don't be too impressed. Track had no junior varsity, so if you went out you lettered. But to get a coveted RV Letterman's Jacket, I first had to be initiated into the Athletic Club. Harold, as Sergeant of Arms, organized Hell Week, where initiates were enslaved and hazed. At any time, we were subject to vicious swats from a wooden paddle. Harold controlled the paddle, relishing the role a bit too much for our taste. For whatever reason—luck, mostly—I had managed to avoid getting a swat for most of the week. Then, like a dumbass, I mentioned this to some of my so-called friends. They promptly told Harold that I was *bragging* about not getting any swats.

That afternoon, as I and other slaves were washing a senior letterman's car, Harold called me out. I had no choice but to comply. He placed me, police-style, up against the car and swung for the fences. I was wearing fashionably tight polyester sugar-booty shorts, which were wet. The sting felt like it would be fatal. The second time Harold brought the paddle down, I remember, quite literally, wishing him dead.

So, you could say I had mixed feelings when a few weeks later we heard that Harold was sick. Really sick. Inoperable brain tumor sick. Being diagnosed with cancer before you graduate high school should come with instant absolution of all sins. But with me it wasn't so instant. I remember feeling very little real sympathy. I didn't really want him to die, but I harbored thoughts that Harold somehow had this coming.

A few months later it was again time for football. I was now a sophomore, and I showed up for two-a-days heavier, faster, stronger, and definitely able to count to 10. We lined up for our first set of jumping jacks and, sure enough, some little freshman screwed up and did 11. Coach Workman blew his whistle and sent us to the fence for belly flops. As we trudged our way back, I could see that another person had joined the huddle of coaches as they waited for our return. He was tall, bald and had a cane. It was Harold. Instead of doing another set of jumping jacks, Workman ordered the team over to take a knee.

"I want you to meet the toughest person I know," Workman said. I don't remember everything Harold said, but I remember the way he looked at us—with longing. He was no longer my nightmare; he was just a scared kid. He told us to cherish the time we have together as a team. Enjoy the pain because, believe it or not, we would miss it. I can't honestly say I forgave Harold right that second for being such an asshole, but I had started the process.

"I'd give anything to put on a helmet and pads again, to be out here with you guys," he said. "It'll be over before you know it." And before I would ever see him again, for Harold, it was.

ROBBIE SHERWOOD left political reporting behind but remains a nosy smartass with puns of steel. Currently spokesman for the Arizona House Democrats. Follow him on Twitter @RobbieSherwood.

TÍO LEO

MELISSA DUNMORE

EVERY NOVEMBER 2ND I light a candle, say a prayer, and pour myself a drink.

November 2nd is All Souls Day in Catholic tradition. It is also my Tío Leo's birthday. Each of us is destined to become more soul than body. Some of us arrive ahead of schedule.

Leonel Jesus Barreto was born in Puerto Rico in 1959, a year before his parents emigrated to the States. We buried him on October 19th, 2003 on his older sister's birthday and a week before my fourteenth. He was the eldest boy of seven children, four of whom perished before the age of seven. Together with my mom and aunt, they grew up like the Three Musketeers, all settling down with their children within mere miles of each other. Born with platinum blonde hair that was white until he was 10 years old, it grew gradually darker settling finally into a soft brown, evolving along a gradient from white to chestnut.

Never much one for school, at 16, he left home and worked his way up in the real world without a high school diploma. He became the youngest manager of one of the busiest and most profitable car dealerships in Brooklyn. There wasn't a thing about cars the man didn't know. And he was a wiz with numbers, doing math in his head like a mathematician. His charisma was everlasting and could win over even the choosiest consumer. His salesmanship was legendary. People still talk about it. In true New York fashion people say, "He could sell glasses to a blind man."

To see pictures of him is to see a stand-up-guy. He was snazzy, soulful, well dressed in a cafe con leche colored suit with longish hair that was joined by a downy brown beard. Round glasses adorned his face. My favorite picture of him is one where he had just come in our front door and he's boasting this dazzling smile. That was the way he'd announce his presence, smile first. That would be the picture we would use at his funeral. We all wanted to remember him smiling.

My mom tells the story of the first time he and I met. I was a few hours old and he simply tucked me inside his jacket, said goodbye, and tried to make a getaway. Oh, how he loved to tease. Finally, there was another Scorpio in our family of Libras and Aries. And I, the only girl in a bunch of boys, became an instant treasure to him. You see, he always wanted a daughter. "Muñeca" was his nickname for me, and from that day forward he prized me as a living doll. He was my mother's older brother and his paternal *cariño* permeated our relationship. It filled me up from my first moments, and I always felt it, warming me from within like a cup of coffee.

Aunts and uncles are like second parents in Puerto Rican families. Cousins are practically siblings. We were all raised together and were equally at home in each other's houses. We shared our parents much the same as we shared clothing, toys, and Capri Sun juice boxes. We shared lives. They were my immediate family. They were my everyday. My aunt was dear to me as well, however Tío was the one adult who would join in on our shenanigans rather than scold. Some days, Tío Leo would take us to school, piling us all in his Ford Explorer—which was really swanky in the '90s—just because he enjoyed having us all together.

The thing I remember most about him are his hugs. He would wrap us up in these bone crusher hugs, holding us so tightly to his torso we felt as though our ribs would shatter. Locked inside that embrace it was all cologne, and pain. I never understood why he had to hug so hard. It used to upset me because he held on so tightly and for so long. Our mother would sometimes have to come over and get him to relinquish us after which we'd rub our sore arms and bemoan his roughness.

My favorite memory of him is from my kindergarten dance recital. The auditorium was dark and I was focusing so hard on not messing up my dance steps. I looked out over the audience and made out a figure walking along the side wall. My eyes fixated on the shrouded image of Tío holding the biggest bouquet of flowers I had ever seen. He smiled at me and motioned for me to keep dancing. In my joy, I had stopped in the middle of the routine. Every time I perform, I wish he was in the audience beaming up at me like he was that night.

My least favorite memory of him was about 10 years later when I was playing in my childhood best friend James' driveway, and my eyes fell upon the ghostly visage of a shabby looking man. I was terrified and my blood ran cold. His skin had this pallor to it

I'd never seen before. But I recognized the face. I'd know that face anywhere. The floating skull smiled at me and motioned for me to come over. The sight of him scared me, but I was happy to see him nonetheless. I walked over to him and he hugged me, same as always, all cologne, and pain, and for once I was sad when he let go.

He and his wife had divorced and after living with us for a few months when I was in the fifth grade, the family lost track of him. Through a body pressed against abuela's door attached to an ear tuned like a radio dial to hushed conversations, I learned he had a severe drinking problem. My ear understood truths that my heart rejected. That pallor I encountered was jaundice. His liver was failing as were his kidneys. He would later have a series of seizures that would cause brain damage. This combination resulted in his death, many years too soon.

There was a darkness in him none of us ever comprehended. Burying three of his brothers as a child had left him with wounds that never healed. And as the only living son, his father, abuelo, was harder on him than on his sisters. Their relationship was fraught with disapproval, disappointment, and eventually, disdain. It was as though all the discipline and expectations that would've been equally spread amongst four sons were all heaped onto him.

And at some point, he decided Death was what he wanted and drinking was his one-way ticket home to the paradise of his Scriptures.

His funeral was excruciating. It was the first time I'd had to bury someone I loved. And none of us ever thought he'd be the first to go. We were furious with him for dying. For committing to a course of action that devastated our family. I learned it was possible to love someone so much and, at the same time, hate them for their choices. I felt not only my own pain but my family's. Worst of all was abuela's. She threw herself onto his casket and shrieked the most heartbreaking words. After burying four of her children decades ago, she thought she'd never live this pain again. She beseeched *La Virgen* to show her how to live in a world without her only remaining adult son. The one she hoped she'd never live to bury.

After he died and we moved away from New York to Phoenix, I often thought about how life might have been different if he'd only lived. I always imagined him dancing at my wedding, being the life of the party, the antithesis of dead. He would have helped me pass my driving test. Any and all car troubles would've been adopted as his personal responsibility. Whenever I found myself in a pickle I'd imagine how he'd talk himself out of a similar situation. And in the darkest of times, I wished he'd appear, tuck me in his coat again, and take me with him.

He had a way about him that people can't forget, least of all his three sons, Matthew, Michael, and Christopher. Watching them grow into themselves, with stubble on their faces, is like seeing him alive again. Pictures of him holding them as children cling to the walls of their childhood home looking on in silent commemoration of their bond. The bathroom cabinet where his *Pierre Cardin* cologne stands upright has become a shrine. In the tick tock of the watch he used to wear, he is there. The glint of gold from the medallion that hangs around his eldest son's neck is like the twinkle that used to dance in his eye. He lives on in his father's softness and in his mother's memory. In the hearts of his sisters and their connected past. In the pulse alighting the cells beating beneath the indelible ink on the skin of his kin, he lives. And sorrowful, though true, in the lesson his death taught us, to not let the demons within shut out the angels without, he lives. If his spirit has any unfinished business, it is that all of us learn from his life and hold on, perhaps a little too tightly, to those we love.

This November 2nd, I'll light a candle, say a prayer, and pour myself a drink.

Initially, when I began doing this, it struck me as a morbid inclination. To toast a drink to the man who lost his life to alcoholism. But that is the task of the living. To merge morbidity with meaning. The annual toast is done in reverence. And always with top shelf stuff. I toast the man born with so much soul, his birthday couldn't have been on any other day.

MELISSA DUNMORE is a Phoenix-based creative from NYC and guardian of diasporic Puerto Rican narratives. Contact her at melissa.dunmore@gmail.com or @melissadphx on Instagram.

THAT'S WHERE THE FUN IS

MAREN SHOWKEIR

"WHAT IS YOUR DEAL?" I said to my husband. "Why won't you try the drugs?"

I was sitting on our orange leather couch, earnestly using every argument I could think of to persuade my husband to do drugs.

Trust me when I say this should *not* have been a hard sell.

Jamie and I had been married for almost nine years. From the beginning of our relationship, he had openly—and frequently—waxed nostalgic about his college years at Miami University in Ohio. He characterized those years in the mid-'70s as "transcendental," thanks to meditation and "better living through chemistry." As a college football player, he'd stay relatively clean during the season. But off season? He'd try just about anything that promised to alter his mental state. He had a treasure trove of hilarious tales about hallucinating his way through the weekends.

No wonder it took him five years to graduate.

Jamie never was embarrassed or ashamed when he talked to me about his fun with drugs. In fact, a wistful tone would creep into his voice. A sentimental gleam beamed from his eyes, a reflection of the torch he carried for this sexy, bad-girl mistress—the one he loved passionately even though he knew maintaining the relationship would lead to a bad end.

The thing is, more than four decades later, he was looking at a bad end, and I didn't understand his stubborn refusal to try the drugs. "What is the deal?" I asked him. "You can't enjoy drugs if they're actually legal?"

What I'm reluctant to tell you—mostly because I don't want you looking at me with pity—is that this conversation took place several months after Jamie had been diagnosed with ALS. We got the official word on June 5, 2014, a few weeks before the ice-bucket challenge went viral on social media.

When the neurologist rolled away from us on his little doctor's stool, his hands up in a gesture of surrender—we already knew. "We've ruled out everything else," Dr. Ortega said, looking sheepish and apologetic. Just six months before, he had ruled *out* ALS as a cause for the pain and weakness in Jamie's left shoulder.

We went home that afternoon and turned on the TV. Jamie found a James Taylor concert on PBS. We sang along. "*So close your eyes. You can close your eyes, it's all right.*" And we cried. And cried.

And then we talked, because Jamie and I had always had that going for us. Conversation is what brought us together. It kept us together. It was what made us good together.

And death had never been a topic we backed away from. Both of us had lost loved ones, including our parents. He'd been with his mother when she died, and several years later, I was with mine. We often talked about how grateful we were to be present for what was, in different yet similar ways, an experience that was beautiful and sweet.

We didn't view death as an enemy or a foe to be conquered. We saw it as natural—the circle of life. We were curious about the mystery that lies beyond, but we weren't in a hurry to solve the puzzle. We didn't understand people's desperate efforts to avoid the inevitable because we didn't fear death, only the decrepitude and dependence that might precede it. We agreed that dying in our sleep, when we were really old and all used up, was the way to go.

But Jamie's diagnosis forced a conversational shift from the theoretical to a harsh reality. Jamie's future would be all about decrepitude and dependence.

Even so, as we cried and conversed on the orange leather couch that night, Jamie was adamant. He would *live* until he died.

"I am not going to stop being me," he'd said. "When I lose my ability to move, and maybe my ability to talk, I want people to remember I'm still in there."

He asked me, kind of demanded, actually, to make sure he died at home. "Of course," I'd promised. Without hesitation. Without thinking it through.

We'd both known people who had died of ALS, and I'd read "Tuesdays with Morrie." But other people's stories can never prepare you for the reality of this disease. Its conclusion is inescapable, but its path is completely unpredictable.

When Jamie was diagnosed in June, his left shoulder was weak, and he walked with a slight limp. By July, he was clutching a cane. In August, as we traveled the country visiting loved ones, he was introduced to a walker. When that became too exhausting, we pushed him in a wheelchair.

By September, he upgraded to a motorized mobility vehicle. And in October, he was unable to drive our newly purchased mobility van. By November, it was difficult for him to hold a book or lift a fork to his mouth.

And by December, his arms and fingers were so weak he could no longer flip a good bird. That really pissed him off.

"What good am I if I can't even flip people off?" he asked.

"But you can still talk," I pointed out. "You can still say, 'Fuck you.'"

"Oh yeah," he said, his expression brightening. "Good point."

By January, I was feeding him. Soon after, our home opened up to a rotation of care-givers who helped him to use the toilet, to bathe, and to dress. His rapid dependence left us exhausted. Overwhelmed. Breathless. It also ushered in a series of hard decisions we thought we'd have more time to make.

We said no to searching for miracle cures or unproven treatments that promised longevity; yes to a research study that might help others with ALS.

Jamie said no to a feeding tube; we said yes to meals brought in by caring friends.

We finally, reluctantly, said no to sleeping together; and yes to a high-tech hospital bed that would allow us both a little more sleep.

"No way" to a tracheotomy. Yes, to a BiPap machine.

By March of 2015, Jamie couldn't laugh out loud. But he could talk. Not loudly, and only between sips of air on the Bipap machine, but he could talk. Talking was our relationship lifeblood. We continued the rich conversations about death, and life, and the mundane, usually over coffee, in the quiet morning hours before the day-shift caregiver arrived.

The disease was efficient, doing exactly what it was designed to do: wreak havoc on his once athletic body. Eventually, Jamie no longer could make subtle movements with his limbs, the kinds of tiny shiftings humans do thousands of times a day to be comfort-able.

You're probably doing them now. Don't take it for granted.

As the aches and pains in his body became pronounced, and as it became more dif-ficult for him to breathe, he became agitated and anxious. This made him kind of hard to deal with, if you want to know the truth. Hence, our conversation about drugs.

The doctor had said that low doses of oxycodone and anti-anxiety meds would not, as Jamie feared, leave him in a drooling stupor. They would help him be more comfort-able in his body and relieve the panic produced by what the brain registers as "air hunger" when it's getting less oxygen.

But Jamie, who had enthusiastically embraced the altered mental states that illegal drugs delivered, stubbornly refused prescribed drugs designed to ease his anxiety and pain. "What is your deal?" I asked again. "Are you afraid of becoming an addict?"

He could still roll his eyes.

"Life is not always comfortable," he told me. "Why should death be?"

He referenced a lyric from "Blinded by the Light": *Mama always told me not to look into the eyes of the sun, but Mama, that's where the fun is.*

"Looking into the eyes of the sun is being able to look at things in their most honest and austere form," Jamie said. "That's where the excitement and the learning is. I've spent most of my life trying to embrace the pain that comes with learning. Why would I expect to die any other way? Why would I *want* to?"

After a moment, I asked, "Are you confusing pain with suffering? Because the former is inevitable, the latter optional. If drugs can relieve your mind and body, isn't it possible you'd be more present to the many gifts and graces we are receiving? Might you would be more receptive to the lessons that living/dying has to teach us?"

Maybe so, he finally agreed. He began taking the drugs.

April, May, June and July went by in a blur. Living/dying is hard, and Jamie wasn't always at his best. And no matter how much I loved him, neither was I. Decrepitude and dependence take their toll.

In my lowest, darkest moments, I found myself pondering that promise I'd made to let him die at home. Was there a way to ethically wriggle free? Wouldn't a hospice facility be easier on everyone?

On August 15, 2015, the night before Jamie's 63rd birthday, we revisited a conversation we'd had exactly one year before. He had wondered aloud if he'd make to 63.

"Of course, you will," I'd exclaimed. "You'll make it." And he did.

On Aug. 16, the day he was born and the 10th anniversary of the day we met, I slipped in a "Happy Birthday" CD mix I'd compiled the year we were married. It was a birthday tradition. He smiled when he heard the music.

I went back into the bedroom to get dressed—we were expecting a few visitors that day—but Richard, his caregiver, quickly came to get me. "Jamie's asking for you," he said.

I sat on the side of the hospital bed in our living room: "What's going on?"

"I feel like I'm dying," he whispered.

"Well…you are," I said. "But not today! It's your birthday."

He grinned as best he could and said, "I love you."

When the hospice nurse arrived a few hours later, she uttered a soft, "Oh."

After so many months of witnessing Jamie's living and dying, I know it sounds ridiculous to say it felt sudden. But it did.

I climbed up on the hospital bed and wrapped myself around him. He was still breathing, but barely.

"Do you want to remove his respiratory assist?" the nurse asked. I did, but I didn't want him to be anxious or in pain.

As she administered a last dose of morphine, she spoke clearly in his ear. "Jamie, I'm giving you something to make it easier."

So close your eyes. You can close your eyes. It's all right.

I was holding Jamie so close as he entered his next altered state.

It was beautiful. And sweet.

MAREN SHOWKEIR is an author, editor and Arizona native who dreads mercury retrograde. Find her at marenshowkeir.com and contact her at mshowkeir@gmail.com.

NEW KID

STINA SIEG

THE DAY I TURNED 23 on a Wednesday in April, it was still cold in Silver City, New Mexico. I had only moved two months before, and there was no one there to call. I drove to Walmart, bought the happiest, cheapest cake I could find, and brought it home to my little trailer. I remember sitting at my dinette set, lighting the candles shaped like a comical "2" and "3", and making some wish, now lost to history. I ate one chocolatey slice topped with billows of what tasted like sweet shaving cream and went to bed.

Exactly one year later, in the same small town, I told people I'd be celebrating my birthday at the brewpub. No pressure, but feel free to stop on by. About two dozen people did, bringing cakes and cards and some long, comfy socks I still wear now. They wrote in my diary about what their lives were like at 24, and we shared hugs and vulnerable conversations—the things I'd been craving that birthday before, but also my whole life.

I didn't take one scrap of it for granted. I remember driving home stunned.

The night was tangible proof that I had made friends, a bunch of them, friends who cared enough to do whatever voodoo it takes to make a homemade ice cream cake. I had made friends before, one I still talk to all the time, but I had no idea I could forge connections beyond the fabricated reality of high school or college, when you're thrown together with enough people that befriending a few felt inevitable to me.

This was different. This was life on the outside, life without guarantees. And the fact that I now knew I was someone whom people wanted to befriend made me feel like I could hack it. It also instantly made me afraid to leave that town, for fear that maybe this was only possible in the scrappy, creative magic of New Mexico—and New Mexico really is magic. So I tucked that party away inside myself, knowing that no matter what happened next, no matter where I moved or whom I met, that at least I had that one night when I felt truly loveable.

In the years since, I've lived in several other towns and states. Sometimes I've felt intertwined with the community. Other times, I've felt like a bit player. Birthdays seem to illustrate how it's all going. I spent 25 on my own, eating a Navajo taco and slice of cake at a nearly empty restaurant outside of Canyon De Chelly. For 26, I had a massive house party in Moab, Utah, and one of my friends wore a pink shirt with the words "I Love Stina" across her chest.

I never know which way the pendulum will swing. When it swings toward love, I am humbled and amazed, not because I think I don't deserve it, but because making friends is by no means a guarantee. It's alchemy. It's a gift. It's proof I'm in the right place. And when it feels really meant to be, it also feels easy.

Here in Phoenix, I've felt things click into place with so many good-hearted people. *Bill, Jen, Jose.*

I have never enjoyed playing Ms. Pac-Man more than when I'm playing with Ashley, even though he beats me nearly every time. *Kathryn, Tuesday, Jude.*

There's something so comforting about drinking a La Croix in Amy's kitchen. *Tracy, Kathy, Brian.*

I am grateful Jane and I took that road trip before either of us knew she was going to die soon.

I'm tucking all that, all of you, into my heart because I'm about to blow up my life again. After nearly six years in Phoenix, I'm leaving, going to Colorado to work for a big radio station that needs someone to cover small towns. At my outpost in Grand Junction, I'll be surrounded by mountains, desert, and rivers. But not by a lot of people.

If need be, I'm prepared to have another birthday alone, though I'll get the cake somewhere classier this time. I'm sure I can find an organic bundt cake in my new town that I can top with a burning "3" and "6."

Or maybe that won't be it. When I went to Colorado for my interview, the station gave me two days on my own to explore Grand Junction. It's the kind of town that has public art along its main street—which is actually called Main Street—and has two independent bookstores, a college, and an Irish pub where everyone dresses up as Harry Potter characters for Halloween. I've been there before, and it felt like a nice, friendly, blank canvas, but I had no sense of how I'd fit into it.

On my last night, I wandered over to a small town nearby, to the grand opening of a bike path. As I sipped on craft beer and listened to bluegrass in a park, I saw a flash of a face that looked familiar. The guy turned around and smiled, and said he was Scott, the Scott who used to live with my roommate in Utah before I moved in, a decade back, 100 miles away. As he was telling me about how he'd just moved here with his pregnant wife, we somehow organically met more people, some whose names I'd actually heard before. I listened to a friend's ex-girlfriend tell me all about her delightful dog, and then her friend and I got into a long discussion about her son with Down syndrome and how they'd logged hundreds of miles together on a tandem bike. Then she introduced me to another friend, a Jamaican mountain biker man with an impressive Instagram account and a flirtatious smile.

I kept drinking and talking, trying to stay present but never really forgetting how extraordinary this felt, this domino effect of human connection.

My awe floated me into the next morning, right before I flew home, when I had breakfast with a smiley woman who'd been my buddy years ago, back when I worked at a paper in another Colorado town, a place I'd never really felt at home. We hadn't kept in touch much. Maybe it was my fault. But sitting there with my eggs Benedict and her little blond daughters chirping away, it didn't feel like a whole world had risen and fallen since we'd last seen each other. We were friends, still friends, and it felt easy and right.

When we parted ways, her little girls sang out, "Goodbye, Miss Stina!" nearly in unison. And I smiled, working hard not to cry.

STINA SIEG reports across the Western Slope for Colorado Public Radio. But part of her heart is forever with Phoenix and her former station, KJZZ.

ACKNOWLEDGMENTS

THIS BOOK YOU'RE HOLDING, the show that produced the essays in the book you're holding, and, indeed, pretty much the entire downtown Phoenix music and cultural scene would not be possible were it not for Charlie Levy. He won't stand on stage to tell his own story (not yet, anyway, we're holding out hope) but that's okay because he's all over this place in all the most important ways. Thank you, Charlie, from the bottom of our hearts.

Thanks, too, to the team behind our underground home, Valley Bar, and our occasional pit stops, Crescent Ballroom and The Van Buren. Thank you to Kyle Dehn for making us look pretty, to Grasher Johnson for making us sound good, to David Moroney for keeping us running and to Jessica Hill for getting us started in the first place.

Thank you to Cindy Dach and your amazing staff at Changing Hands/First Draft Book Bar/The Newton, for our second home.

We are inspired by our compatriots in the Phoenix storytelling scene – too many to mention here, which is a testament to the power of this community. Thank you to Bar Flies' godmother, Tania Katan, whose Lit Lounge inspires us in so many ways.

Thank you to Jake Friedman for designing this beautiful book, and to Kyle Dehn for the cover. Paloma Ibañez greased all the moving parts.

Music is a huge part of Bar Flies and we are grateful to our resident DJ, Deborah Sussman, as well as the others who've provided playlists over the years.

None of this would be possible without our husbands, parents, kids, friends and others who've supported Bar Flies by holding down the merch table, taking photographs, spreading the word and more.

Thank you, finally and most importantly, to our readers. Not just the ones represented in this book, but to every single person who's stood on the Bar Flies stage. We've laughed, we've cried, we've loved all of your stories. We can't wait to hear what you have to say next.

AMY SILVERMAN & KATIE BRAVO